MW00966110

s

The Law and Practice of Legal Process Outsourcing

The Law and Practice of Legal Process Outsourcing

CCH
a Wolters Kluwer business

CCH INDIA

(Wolters Kluwer (India) Pvt Ltd)
501-A, Devika Tower,
6, Nehru Place, New Delhi
Phone: 91 11 46530000
Fax: 91 11 46530399

Customer Support
Phone: 91 11 46530341
email: support@cchindia.co.in
www.cchindia.co.in

About CCH India

WOLTERS KLUWER (INDIA) PVT LTD

CCH India (a Wolters Kluwer business) is part of the Wolters Kluwer Group, a leading global information service provider for professionals. CCH publications cover a wide range of topics such as tax, accounting, financial planning, legal, human resources and training. CCH products are a comprehensive range from annual books, loose-leaf subscription products, on-line products, solution finders, work-flow solutions software, newsletters and journals.

For more information on our products and services, log on to the CCH India website at **www.cchindia.co.in**

Disclaimer

No person should rely on the contents of this publication without first obtaining advice from a qualified professional person. This publication is sold on the terms and understanding that: (1) the authors, consultants and editors are not responsible for the results of any actions taken on the basis of information in this publication, nor for any error in or omission from this publication; and (2) the publisher is not engaged in rendering legal, accounting, professional or other advice or services. The publisher, and the authors, consultants and editors, expressly disclaim all and any liability and responsibility to any person, whether a purchaser or reader of this publication or not, in respect of anything, and of the consequences of anything, done or omitted to be done by any such person in reliance, whether wholly or partially, upon the whole or any part of the contents in this publication. Without limiting the generality of the above, no author, consultant or editor shall have any responsibility for any act or omission of any other author, consultant or editor.

First Print, 2009

ISBN-13: 978-90-411-3160-7

Published by Wolters Kluwer (India) Pvt Ltd, New Delhi

Printed and bound at Sanat Printers, Haryana

Preface

Legal Process Outsourcing is passing through infancy but delivery made by service providers India so far has led to many companies being attracted to this land of the 'snake charmers'.

Codified procedures and formal protocols are still not so much clear, and in the process of developing.

To engage a fleet of committed lawyers in India does involve infrastructure costs on the outsourcing companies comprising office space, computers, and in some cases U.S.-trained lawyers working in both India and the United States to supervise the work of Indian staff or client development teams to market services to U.S. companies.

Established LPOs give to the Indian lawyers a new dimension in the profession tapped by technology supported work environment and work culture.

LPO companies are gearing up to addresse clients concerns about quality and security although there are still no industry standards to deal with errors and malpractice. Same is the position on questions involving adherence to rules or ethics across different jurisdictions.

The present maiden edition on a subject, so fertile and embryonic, is a humble effort to attempt to explore the domain of outsourcing in the legal and paralegal zone, have a preview of the current standards of practice and scope of the expanding industry, as envisaged by the peers in this field and provide the readers with an threshold insight.

10 November 2008
Delhi

Shashi Shekhar Pandey

Acknowledgement

Legal process outsourcing is an emerging field in the KPO outsourcing Industry. This industry which is expected to be the next big thing after BPO is waiting for the response, and being a law graduate I was always eager to know more about this industry. The drive to know more about LPO motivates me to do research on this topic and then I was inspired by one of the senior advocate to write on this topic. However to complete a work of this magnitude requires a network of support, and I am very much indebted to many people, I am most especially grateful to my parents Dr. H.L. Pandey and my mother Sita Pandey for their guidance support and courage. I would like to thanks to all my colleague and associates who helped me in my work. I am again thankful to my seniors Mr. H.S. Kohli and D.S. Kohli for their kind support and inspiration.

Contents

Contents

Chapter 1   History of Outsourcing

Overview

Outsourcing is   said to have emerged a few thousand years ago. When people started living together in villages, as opposed to smaller family groups, they also started producing food and goods. Initially, these items were traded within their home communities first, and over time the practice expanded to include trading with other villages, regions, and countries. Since people weren't able to produce all the items alone, they starred exchanging it with one another. In effect it can be said that each member or group was outsourcing some activities to others. They needed to survive for themselves, you could consider this trading as being an early form of outsourcing.

¶ 1-010 Outsourcing in the 19th and Early 20th Centuries

If we look to the business practices in the 19th and early 20th century, companies did not use outsourcing as a business practice. They were vertically integrated organisations, taking care of their own production, mining and manufacturing from raw materials and then ship those finished products at their own retail outlets.

¶ 1-020 Industrial Revolution

The Industrial Revolution changed the way companies did business. During this period, company owners started to outsource some services, as opposed to keeping them in house. Independent architecture, engineering and insurance companies started opening their doors to serve multiple clients. With the development in industrial sector companies hired the expertise they needed to work in-house, including legal, insurance, and accounting professionals. If the company had the resources, the organisation also employed workers to design and construct company factories and warehouses.

The history of outsourcing shows that due to the advancement in industrial sector specialising contract became more popular particularly in the service industry. This in turn led to the first wave of outsourcing during the industrial revolution pushing the large-scale growth of services such as insurance services, architecture and engineering services, among many others. In this period the companies doing the outsourced work were more often located in the same country, in most of the cases in the same city. The political set up had changed considerably during this period. Many countries in Asia become free and outsourcing was a welcome development because infrastructure development was at its infant stage and the outsourcing benefited the developing economies by increasing employment and income levels with in all parameters.

The outsourcing history demonstrates that manufacturing was the first activity that began to move to offshore destinations in a quest for lower costs. By the passage of time manufacturing companies realized that they could outsource the production of consumer goods, such as clothing items, shoes, and toys to other lower cost labour countries. By the 1970s, many consumer electronics products were manufactured overseas. Companies looked to workers in foreign countries to work in factories due to cheap labour. Once company owners discovered that they can outsource their manufacturing work to low cost countries destination, more of them decided to outsource this portion of their business to other countries.

Today the trend of outsourcing has moved away from the earlier ones. now it's a world of Information technology data transcription and call center operations data transcription and call center operations

Studies on the history of outsourcing conclude that outsourcing is clearly not just about payrolls and call centers. The outsourcing sector increased its tentacles not only in the field of insurance, accounting, customer services, medical transcription but they have also entered in knowledge process industries and the recent example is Legal Process Outsourcing(LPO).

¶ 1-030 History of outsourcing in INDIA

The growth of outsourcing Industry in India is one of exceptional growth in a very short span of time. The idea of outsourcing has its roots in the 'competitive advantage' theory propagated by Adam Smith in his book 'The Wealth of Nations' which was published in 1776. Over the years, the meaning of the term 'outsourcing' has undergone a paradigm change when the human civilization was infant stage, outsourcing was limited to exchange of essential commodities with in the group then inter groups thereafter to villages then it come to outsourcing between different countries. But now What started off as the shifting of manufacturing to countries providing cheap labour during the Industrial Revolution, has taken on a new concept in today's scenario. In a world where IT has become the backbone of businesses worldwide, 'outsourcing' is the process through which one company hands over part of its work to another company, making it in charge for the design and implementation of the business process under strict guidelines regarding requirements and specifications from the outsourcing company. The process is advantageous for both the Offshore Outsourcing firm and the service buyer, as it enables the offshore service buyer to decrease costs & increase quality for non core areas of business by utilizing the expertise with competencies for the maximum. And now one can see the real benefit to the service organizations in India as the time of they matures, prosper of building core capabilities beyond possibilities by the Offshore Software Outsourcing companies

Since the onset of globalisation in India during the early 1990s, successive Indian governments have pursued programs of economic reform committed to liberalisation and privatization. Although the IT and Software Outsourcing industry in India has existed since the early years of 1980s, but with the mid 1990s it saw the emergence of real outsourcing work. One of the 1st services that outsourced was medical transcription, but business process outsourcing such as data processing, billing, and customer support began at the end of the era 1990.

The ITES or BPO industry is a young and budding sector in India and has been in existence for a little more than five seven years. Despite its recent arrival on the Indian scene, the industry has grown astoundingly and has now become a major part of the export-oriented IT service providing sector. The ITES/BPO market expanded its base with the entry of Indian IT companies and the ITES market of the present day is characterised by the existence of these IT giants who are able to influence their broad skill-sets and global clientele to offer a wide spectrum of services. The range of services offered by Indian companies has evolved substantially from its modest beginnings. Today, Indian companies are offering a variety of outsourced services ranging from customer care, transcription, billing services and database marketing, to Web sales/marketing, accounting, tax processing, transaction, legal drafting, document analysis, document management, telesales/telemarketing, HR hiring and biotech research, etc.

Looking at the success of India's IT/software industry, the central government identified ITES/BPO as a major contributor to economic growth prioritised the attraction of FDI in this segment by establishing 'Software Technology Parks' and 'Export Enterprise Zones'. Benefits like tax-holidays generally enjoyed by the software industry were also made available to the ITES/BPO sector. The National Telecom Policy (NTP) introduced in 1999 and the deregulation of the telecom industry opened up national, long distance, and international connectivity to competition. The governments of various states also provide assistance to companies to overcome the recruitment, retention, and training challenges in order to attract investments to their region. The National Association of Software and Service Companies (NASSCOM) has created platforms for the dissemination of knowledge and research in the industry through its survey and conferences. NASSCOM acts as an 'advisor, consultant and coordinating body' for the ITES/BPO industry and liaisons between the central and State government committees and the industry. The ardent advocacy of the ITES/BPO industry has led to the inclusion of call centers in the 'Business Auxiliary Services' segment, thereby ensuring exemption from service tax under the Finance Bill of 2003.

These measures have led to a steady inflow of investments by large foreign companies such as Reuters, for establishing large captive ITES/BPO facilities across India.

The availability of technically trained and skilled manpower in India is making companies across the world look at the country as a profitable base to shift their high-end support services. The availability of skilled and trained manpower and India's ability to keep in step with the latest technological advances in the industry is prompting foreign studios to consider India as a base to shift other high-end animation work like storyboarding and developing original content for animated films ad TV series. Legal outsourcing is the next segment that holds great promise, mainly due to the due to the high skilled work force availability in India and its large English speaking population this sector is getting momentum day by day due to the quality work performed by the highly skilled and methodologically trained employees. Legal process outsourcing future in India is seen as bright and a promising career option for bright young lads.

Chapter 2   Genesis of Legal Process Outsourcing

Introduction

¶2-010 What is outsourcing?

Outsourcing involves the transfer of the management and/or day-to-day execution of an entire business function to an external service provider outsourcing and offshoring are used interchangeably in public discourse despite important technical differences. Outsourcing involves contracting with a supplier, which may or may not involve some degree of offshoring. Offshoring is the transfer of an organisational function to another country, regardless of whether the work is outsourced or stays within the same corporation/company.

¶2-020 What is Business Process Outsourcing (BPO)?

BPO is a sort of business relation between the buyer of a service and its supplier in which the supplier is told what to do and how to do. The skill and labour is required to be put by supplier and is asked to produce the end result for which the buyer would pay appropriate fee. The method of bringing about the desired outcomes is left to the supplier. Thus there is delegation of 'control over the process' which implies that the supplier becomes the 'owner of the business processes'. The responsibility of day-to-day back office operations is transferred to an outsourcing partner who is expected to get the job done at a cheaper price without affecting the quality. This methodology ease the workload of the company or firm which enables the company to focus more efficiently on the core business. In fact less cost, standard quality and productivity are the three reasons as to why the concept has attracted the corporate world. It is to be noted that under this phenomenon only those services are off shored that can be carried out regardless of geographical location (for instance call centers and back office work, credit card companies and, bad debt retrieval by insurance, patent drafting and filing of new inventions etc). The services that require physical presence or interaction cannot be off shored (*eg*, emergency medical services, management, sale executives, hotels, etc.) Recently outsourcing has become a way of life in business world. There are certain factors that seem to have dragged the phenomenon out of its dormancy leading to its volcanic eruption to engulf the entire world. The most important ideological factor behind BPO revolution is the concept of globalisation and free market economy which in recent past has gained universal acceptance and in which consumer is in driver's seat.

Consumers want lower prices and free choice. No governments can force them to buy only homemade products. The theory of free market economy favours access to the best goods and services at the most competitive prices. Another reason for rise of this phenomenon is the compulsive impact of TINOA (There is no other alternative) factor. The logic and the pressure of the market says that either you do it (outsourcing) or lose your competitive edge and go out of business. Any wise businessman running a company knows that if his competitor begins using low-cost labor offshore, whether it is manufacturing or talent, he will have to do the same to remain competitive. The sector witnessed considerable growth during 2003–04, various multinational companies including Indian as well as foreign both stepped up hiring the services of BPO. The domestic BPO market, catalyzed by demand from the telecommunications and BFSI segments, matched the growth of BPO exports. The market experienced maturity and consolidation, a result of numerous mergers and acquisitions taking place within the sector. There were around 500 companies operating within the Indian BPO space, including captive units (of both MNCs and Indian companies) and third-party services providers. The key enabler for this has been cheaper bandwidth leading to low telecom costs for leased lines and availability of educated English speaking workforce in India.

The Indian BPO industry is in its infant stage and remains on a growth path in the coming years, emerging as one of the key investment markets in the country.

NASSCOM is a Chamber of Commerce that represents this body and lobbies for it, as well as creates a platform for members to take up common issues. NASSCOM services both the Indian Software and the Indian BPO industry.

Market size of BPO industry

The industry has been growing rapidly. It grew at a rate of 36% over 2005. For the financial year 2006 the projections is of US$7.6 billion worth of services provided by this industry. The base in terms of headcount being roughly 350,000 people directly employed in this Industry. The global BPO Industry is estimated to be worth 100-150 billion dollars, of this the offshore BPO is estimated to be some US$12.4 billion. India thus has some 6-7% share of the total Industry, but a commanding 62% share of the offshore component. The U.S $7.6 billion also represents some 20% of the IT and BPO Industry which is in total expected to have revenues worth US$37 billion for 2006. The headcount at 350,000 is some 40% of the approximate one million workers estimated to be directly employees in the IT and BPO Sector.

From a PricewaterhouseCoopers survey

Global BPO Market by Industry

Industry	Percentage (%)
Information Technology	44
Financial Services	16
Communication (Telecom)	13

Consumer Goods/Services	17
Manufacturing	9

BPO Market worldwide

Country	Percentage (%)
United States	56
Europe	28
Asia-Pacific (incl. Japan)	9
Rest of the World	7

Size of Global Outsourcing Market

Year	Size (USD Bn)
2000	117
2005	234
2008 (est.)	Above 325

Size and Growth of BPO in India

Year	Size (US$ Bn)	Growth Rate (%)
2003	2.9	58
2004	3.8	44.3
2005	5.6	43.4

Currently the Indian BPO Industry employs in excess of 245,100 people and another 94,500 jobs are expected to be added during the current financial year (2007-2008)

Table 5: per Employee cos in call centert

Country	Cost (USD/yr)
USA	18,000
Australia	16,000
Philippines	9,000
India	7,000

It is also referred as Information Technology Enabled Services or ITES, and high end work with specialisation is referred to as Knowledge Process Outsourcing or KPO. The need for capacity, pooled with intellect and workforce flexibility has led the Knowledge Process Outsourcing (KPO) market to grow rapidly in the past two to three years to around $3bn spending in 2006. Success in this sector has also led to the more recent, but rapidly growing trend of Legal Process Outsourcing (LPO).

¶ 2-030 Legal Process Outsourcing

LPO refers to the offshoring of different elements in the legal process by law-firms, corporations and house councils (mainly in the US and UK) to offshore centers (like India, China and the Philippines, etc). On the more conservative side, a report released in January 2006 by a research and outsourcing company, estimated lower statistics and projected more moderate growth. The current number of employees providing legal services to the US from India is only 1,200, and it will grow by 5,000 in December 2010, and 17,000 by December 2015. It projects that revenue of approximately $56 million is estimated in year 2005, and expected to be increase to $300 million by 2010, and $960 million till 2015.

The series of statistics represent the hazy picture about the growth of the emerging industry and leaves the truth most likely located somewhere in the middle. Despite the inequality in numbers, the overarching trend of projected growth demonstrates legal process outsourcing has become an established sector and will continue to grow in the future.

What is being outsourced in LPO? (nature of work)

Legal outsourcing refers to the practice of a law firm obtaining legal support services from an outside law firm or legal support services company. When the outsourced entity is based in another country the practice is sometimes called Offshoring.

While discussing outsourcing in legal field, ethics is the often asked query along with 'What is being outsourced?' The answer ranges from simple legal coding to exceptionally technical patent applications. The wide range of activities has implications for LPO in terms of the level of training required, efficiency and value of the processes, liability and security concerns, and may raise issues regarding specific legal restrictions.

Legally, anyone who is not a registered lawyer in the U.S. cannot give legal advice nor do anything that would constitute 'practicing law'. This has typically restricted LPO firms from supplying 'core' functions such as legal opinions, judgments, or crucial communications with clients. LPO firms, however, do perform a variety of non-core, manpower intensive functions such as legal transcription, document conversion, legal data entry, legal coding and indexing.

Within 'non-core' functions, there still exists a great range of processes LPO firms may offer. As a starting point, these basic LPO services can be categorized as "low-value" work. These categories can be divided into various types of services:

- Document Review in the context of litigation, investigations or antitrust (Second Request).

- Organization and analysis of both hard and soft data (software aswell as dbase system).

- Contract review and summarizing, including the population of contracts databases

- Legal Research services include research methodology and domain expertise required to provide practice legal research.

- Examples of research

    (i) Multi-jurisdictional surveys of state and local case laws, statutes, ordinances and regulations.

    (ii) Identification and summarization of relevant case law.

    (iii) Statutory and case law analysis in the context of litigation support (assistance in brief writing).

    (iv) Citation checking for briefs and other litigation related documents.

- Document drafting like standard contracts, agreements, letters to the clients, patent applications, etc.

Drafting includes employee contracts, non-disclosure agreements, licensing agreements, supplier agreements, lease agreements, vendor agreements, and distributor agreements. Many of these agreements follow a standard template, enabling foreign lawyers to produce a draft that can later be reviewed and modified by a U.S. attorney. Foreign lawyers can also proofread and double check documents to make sure they comply with the guidelines of the client.

- Legal Billing activities like preparation of invoices, collation of time sheets, etc.

- Intellectual Property research--substantive and administrative-: This category represents one of the riskiest and fastest growing sectors in LPO. A patent application usually includes the following: prior art searching, drafting background, drafting specifications, drafting claims, drafting summary, preparing drawings, final review and modifications for filing. Only the final review must legally be performed by an attorney registered with the United States Patent and Trademark Office (USPTO). Depending on clients' preference, LPO firms can have varying degrees of responsibility for preparing drafts of patent applications. The patent industry is in such high demand because it requires time-consuming repetitive research. Many law firms cannot process the growing number of applications at prices their clients are willing to pay and are forced to change their strategy.

- Paralegal services.

- Administrative and secretarial activities like following up with clients, etc.

Chapter 3   Global Jurisdictions

Overview of Legal Systems

The three major legal systems of the world today consist of

- Civil Law

- Common Law

- Religious Law

However, due to the disparity in the custom of countries they often develops variations on each system or incorporates many other features as per according to the prevailing customs and traditions in their society.

¶ 3-010 Civil Law

Civil law is the most widespread system of law in the world. It is also sometimes known as *Continental European Law*. The central source of law that is recognised as authoritative are codifications in a constitution or statute passed by legislature, to amend a code. Civil law systems mainly derive from the Roman Empire, and more particularly, the Corpus Juris Civil is issued by the Emperor Justinian ca. 529AD. This was an extensive reform of the law in the Byzantine Empire, bringing it together into codified documents. Civil law was also partly influenced by religious laws such as Canon law and Islamic law. Civil law today, in theory, is interpreted rather than developed or made by judges. Only legislative enactments (rather than judicial precedents) are considered legally binding. However, in reality courts do pay attention to previous decisions, especially from higher courts.

Scholars of comparative law and economists promoting the legal origins theory usually subdivide civil law into four distinct groups:

- French civil law: in France, the Benelux countries, Italy, Spain and former colonies of those countries;

- German civil law: in Germany, Austria, Croatia, Switzerland, Greece, Portugal, Turkey, Japan, South Korea and the Republic of China;

- Scandinavian civil law: in Denmark, Norway and Sweden. Finland and Iceland inherited the system from their neighbours.

- Chinese law is a mixture of civil law and socialist law.

¶ 3-020 Common law

Since 1188, English law has been described as a common law rather than a civil law system (i.e. there has been no major codification of the law, and judicial precedents are binding as opposed to persuasive). This may have been due to the Norman conquest of England, which introduced a number of legal concepts and institutions from Norman law into the English system. In the early centuries of English common law, the justices and judges were responsible for adapting the Writ system to meet everyday needs, applying a mixture of precedent and common sense to build up a body of internally consistent law, eg the Law Merchant began in the Pie-Powder Courts (a corruption of the French 'pieds-poudrés' or "dusty feet", meaning ad hoc marketplace courts). Obviously, the Biblical influences throughout precedent can be seen throughout the centuries. As Parliament developed in strength, and subject to the doctrine of separation of powers, legislation gradually overtook judicial law making so that, today, judges are only able to innovate in certain very narrowly defined areas. Time before 1189 was defined in 1276 as being time immemorial.

Precedent

One of the major problems in the early centuries was to produce a system that was certain in its operation and predictable in its outcomes. Too many judges were either partial or incompetent, acquiring their positions only by virtue of their rank in society. Thus, a standardised procedure slowly emerged, based on a system termed stare decisis. Thus, the ratio decidendi of each case will bind future cases on the same generic set of facts both horizontally and vertically. The highest appellate court in the UK is the House of Lords (the judicial members of which are termed *Law Lords* or, specifically if not commonly Lords of Appeal in Ordinary) and its decisions are binding on every other court in the hierarchy which are obliged to apply its rulings as the law of the land. The Court of Appeal binds the lower courts, and so on.

Various legal system based on common law are:

- Law of the United Kingdom

- Northern Irish law

- Scots law

- Welsh law

- Law of the British Virgin Islands, Australian law

- Canadian law

- Indian law

- Law of New Zealand

- Law of the United States

- Anglo-Saxon law

- Common law

- Equity

- English case law

United Kingdom and United States of America are the major countries outsourcing legal work in other countries. Both UK and USA have adopted their legal system on the premises of common law.

The law of the United States was originally largely derived from the common law system of English law, which was in force at the time of the

Revolutionary War. However, the supreme law of the land is the United States Constitution and, under the Constitution's Supremacy Clause, laws enacted by Congress and treaties to which the US is a party. These form the basis for federal laws under the federal constitution in the United States, circumscribing the boundaries of the jurisdiction of federal law and the laws in the fifty United States and in the territories.

Indian legal structure is also based on common law system and this is one of the major reasons why India preferred as the outsourcing destination.

¶ 3-030 Religious law

Religious law refers to the thought of a religious system where a secret document is considered as the highest law and being used as a supreme legal source, though the methodology used varies from one and other. The main kinds of religious law are Sharia in Islam, Halakha in Judaism, and Canon law in some Christian groups. Many of them are intended purely as individual moral guidance, whereas in other cases they are intended and may be used as the basis for a country's legal system. The latter was particularly common during the Middle Ages. Religious law is manly prevalent in orthodox countries and they adhered the verses, teachings as well as guidelines mentioned in this documents so firmly that a little deviation from those guidelines is serious concern.

Chapter 4

Globalisation and Legal Practice

Introduction

Globalisation in its literal sense is the process of transformation of local or regional phenomena into global ones. It can be described as a process by which the people of the world are unified into a single society and function together. This process is a combination of economic, technological, socio-cultural and political forces.

Globalisation must not be viewed from the restrictive sense as it connotes the process of making global, being present worldwide. It has brought the diverse issue of commerce, production, consumption, trade and information technology etc. under one roof. The increasing dependence of the world economies over each other and the emerging trade and commerce between developed and underdeveloped nations has its effect on each and every sector on both developed and developing economies.

Globalisation can also be seen from different perspective as the growing interdependence and enhancing interaction which leads to the proper and apt use of resources with the help of each other expertise in their respective fields.

Globalisation helps the national economies to broaden their boundaries and go beyond their national horizon into world market for goods capital and special services. The concept of Globalisation has brought about a growing tendency towards the universal homogenisation of ideas, cultures, values and even the lifestyles.

Globalisation is the most imperative force shaping the modern world. In the coming days, it is apparent that world will be seen as smaller as it can be, because interdependence prevails at large. The law of each State provides the base not only for the economic interdependence and the foundation of human rights but it will also permeate as an emerging base to globalisation. With the globalization of legal practice, there will be an increasing pressure to permit cross border practice preserving the core rules of the legal profession of native country and to allow attorneys licensed in one state to practice in another state.

Globalisation has brought sea changes in the global business arena and the BPOs then KPO and at last the LPOs are the direct offshoot of it. The KPO industry along with LPO made a paradigm shift to the global economy. LPOs have come into being in India and elsewhere in the world primarily to cater to the clients of US and UK and other developed nations not only to provide quality service but also to reduce the legal costs in legal process outsourcing. Between the period of 2000 to 2007, a good number of LPOs have opened their businesses in India and in the light of intensifying legal costs and in order to find a feasible solution to it we need to scrutinise the issue in detail.

Globalisation and the internet are a bonus not only to the banking, finance and others sectors of economy but also to the booming BPO industry and has given way to the legal process outsourcing which is still at its infant stage. With the opening up of free market economy and the revolution created by the concept of outsourcing, legal transcription and many other legal services (like legal documentation, litigation support, legal research, etc) can now be outsourced/off shored and proficiency can be availed from experts and professional of the respective field who might be sited anywhere on the globe. This allows for not only great reduction of expenses but also has other benefits like savings in time and high levels of accuracy in transcription. This indeed reduces stress and a person can get ample time to focus on core issues.

¶ 4-010 Impact of globalisation on the legal profession in India

India is numbered as worlds second largest legal profession with more than 700,000 lawyers. The principal service providers are individual lawyers, and group of skilled lawyers working together by constituting firms. These firms are involved in various types of litigation under country's adversarial litigation system. The legal profession is considered as a 'noble profession' despite services rendered often resulted in harassment of clients, these are the various factors which resulted in formulation of stringent and restrictive regulatory machinery. These regulations have been justified on the grounds of public policy and 'dignity of profession'. These principles are reinforced by judiciary, which can be reflected in words of Justice Krishna Iyer, when he noted. Law is not a trade, not briefs, not merchandise, and so the heaven of commercial competition should not vulgarise the legal profession. However, over the years courts have recognised 'Legal Service' as a 'service' rendered to the consumers and have held that lawyers are accountable to the clients in the cases of deficiency of services. In the case of *Srinath* v. *Union of India* (AIR 1996 Mad 427) Madras High Court held that, in view of section 3 of Consumer Protection Act, 1986. Consumer Redressal Forums have jurisdiction to deal with claims against advocates. Section 2(U) of Competition Act, 2002 defines the term 'service' along the lines of Consumer Protection Act, 1986. Thus, it may be concluded that legal services are becoming subject of trade related laws where consumerism and market forces should be given adequate space.

¶ 4-020 Expanding Dynamics

The increasing dependence of the world economies over each other and the emerging trade and commerce between developed and underdeveloped nations has its effect on each and every sector on both developed and developing economies. The implication of the same on the legal service sector has been both quantitative and qualitative. The past decade has been mini-revolution in legal service sector with the greatest legal impact on corporate legal arena activities in intellectual property rights, project financing, corporate taxation, agreements drafting, cyber law, environmental protection, competition law, infrastructure contract, corporate governance and investment law were almost unknown before

1980-90's. There were very few firms which were dealing in such fields. It is apparent that need of professional service is going to be terrific in the legal service sector. In last few years law firms, in house firms and individual lawyer's expertise in providing legal services in corporate sector has increased by several times. These new law firms mainly engaged in drafting and expertise on loan instrument, script infrastructural contracts, power contract, drafting of financial related agreements, contracts, analysis on transnational investment, joint venture and technology transfer contracts. This is sensitizing shift in the nature of emerging legal sectors towards settling disputes through ADRS rather than opting for adversarial litigation mode of dispute resolution. Globalisation has thus stretched the demand of legal services domestically as well as externally. Today legal services is an inevitable fact and simultaneously significant for progressive development of legal profession in India in this era of globalisation.

¶ 4-030 International Protocols

Globalisation has been facilitated by advances in technology which have reduced the costs of trade, and trade negotiation rounds, originally under the auspices of the General Agreement on Tariffs and Trade (GATT), which led to a series of agreements to remove restrictions on free trade.

Since World War II, barriers to international trade have been considerably lowered through international agreements - GATT. Particular initiatives carried out as a result of GATT and the World Trade Organization (WTO), for which GATT is the foundation, have included:

(i) Promotion of free trade:

   (a) Reduction or elimination of tariffs; creation of free trade zones with small or no tariffs

(ii) Restriction of free trade:

   (a) Harmonisation of intellectual property laws across the majority of states, with more restrictions.

(b) Supranational recognition of intellectual property restrictions (e.g. patents granted by China would be recognised in the United States)

World Trade Organization (WTO) is the successor of the General Agreement of Tariffs and Trade (GATT), which ruled the world between 1960 and 1993. Both co-existed between 1994 and 1995, when WTO came into existence, Services for the first time brought under multilateral trading system under the Uruguay Round Agreements launching WTO. Earlier the GATT System confined only to goods trade. The inclusion of services under the WTO in 1995 is an indication of growing share of services in national economics world over. It is an indication that trade in services is set to play on all important role in the economic development of countries in future. The 'developed' west economics are specialising in knowledge based service and this GATS entered the WTO agenda in 1995. It is among the WTO's most important and the first and only set of multilateral rules concerning international trade in services. It was negotiated by the governments themselves and set the framework agreement containing general rules and disciplines and the national schedules, which list basic commitments on behalf of individual countries. As with the GATT, GATS serves to create a Most Favoured Nation (MFN) status for members of the WTO through specific commitments that allow non-discriminatory treatment to be given to foreign suppliers from overseas. Members have complete freedom to select which services to commit and while granting access a country may however limit the degree to which foreign services provider can operate in the market. Thus, it is possible for a country like India to limit the number of foreign legal practitioners who may be licensed to practice here. But it goes much further than that. A whole range of non-tariff barriers exist which countries may either commit to remove, dilute or otherwise restrict in their operation so as to create a more friendly trading environment within which services can be provided across national barriers. GATS achieves its objectives following basic GATT principles using. Most Favoured National treatment under Articles II and XVII respectively while aiming to reform markets and yet allow special and differential treatment for developing countries. The two exception to GATS are—

(i)   services provided to the public in the exercise of governmental authorities and,

(ii) in the air transport structure, traffic, rights.

The upshot of globalisation and changing dimension in the legal practice curriculum force the restructuring of legal practice process in every state. The General Agreement on Trade in Services (GATS), a treaty approved by World Trade Organization (WTO), has shaped prospect in developing countries, and also become a peril to global legal scenario.

There are four different modes of providing services under GATS which are defined in paragraph 2 of Article I.

(a)   Cross border trade - delivery of a service from the territory of one country into the territory of other country,

(b)   Commercial presence - services provided by a service supplier of one country in the territory of any other country,

(c)   Consumption abroad - covers supply of a service of one country to the service consumer of any other country, and

(d)   Presence of natural persons - covers services provided by a service supplier of one country through the presence of natural persons in the territory of any other country.

The GATS schedules refer to each of these modes and all commitments are made accordingly.

¶ 4-040 GATS and legal services

There are 12 sectors classified by GATS one of them is business services. Business Services is further divided into six types of services, which include professional services. The professional service sector further divided into eleven services, which include Legal Services.

Indian government has not made any commitment in the legal services sector at present. This may be contrasted with commitments made by forty four countries in the legal service sector even same developing countries have made commitments. Such commitments are made in order to benefit all i.e. to countries as well as to consumers. As these commitments will bring trade in the legal services which will play vital role benefiting consumers countrywide.

¶ 4-050 Legal services and the consumer

The emerging legal service sector is equally beneficial to all consumers of legal services, without discrimination. In the age of consumerism and competition law, consumers right to free and fair competition is paramount and cannot be denied by any other consideration. Trade in legal services focuses on benefits accruing to consumers from legal service sector, particularly the quality of service available with respect to particular fields. In the case of In Re, *Sanjiv Datta, Secretary, Ministry of Information and Broadcasting*, the Supreme Court observed that some of the members of the profession have been adopting prospectively casual approach to the practice of the profession. They do not only amount to contempt of court but to the positive dis-service to the litigants. In our country, more often consumers are at the mercy of advocates and the system and they resort to any other service provider in absence of choice.

Secondly, the services available to consumers of India are only domestic legal service providers. Corporate legal activities are recent phenomenon in India and solution of some complicated legal issues can only be granted by professional international law firms hence allowing them shall be beneficial for satisfaction of consumers in India many countries across the globe resort to Legal Process Outsourcing (LPO) and gain best of the legal services and solutions at competitive prices. Existing regulations deprive consumers to derive benefit, which ultimately effects development.

Chapter 5   LPO and Cyber Laws

Regulatory norms in Indian cyberspace

The advent of the internet and the World Wide Web made it possible for people to communicate and transact over cyber space. It was a revolutionary step for humanity and brings out a ground breaking change in society. The widespread use and availability of the internet has enabled individuals and small businesses to contract freelancers from all over the world to get projects done at a lower cost due to lower wages and property prices. Systems such as Mechanical Turk have added the element of scalability, allowing businesses to outsource information tasks across the internet to thousands of workers. This trend runs in parallel with the tendency towards outsourcing in larger corporations, and may serve to strengthen small business' capacity to compete with their larger competitors capable of setting up offshore locations, or of arriving at major contracts with offshore companies.

However, at the same time it also created a considerable need for the regulation and governance of these activities, a requirement that lead to the creation and implementation of cyber laws across the globe. India became the 12th nation in the world to adopt a cyber law regime during 2000.

The country's cyber laws are contained in the Information Technology Act, 2000(IT Act). The Act came into effect following the clearance of the

Information Technology Bill 2000 in May 2000 by both the houses of the Parliament. The Bill received the assent of the President of India in August 2000 (IT Act, 2000). The IT Act, 2000 aims to provide the legal infrastructure for e-commerce in India. At this juncture, it is relevant to understand what the I T Act, 2000 offers and its various perspective.

¶ 5-010 Data protection under the Information Technology Act, 2000

- Section 2(1)(o) of IT Act, 2000 defines "Data": A representation of information, knowledge, facts, concepts or instructions which are being prepared or have been prepared in a formalised manner, and is intended to be processed, is being processed or has been processed in a computer system or computer network, and may be in any form or stored internally in the memory of the computer;

- Computer database[Section 43, Expl. (ii)]: A representation of information, knowledge, facts, concepts or instructions in text, image, audio, video that are being prepared or have been prepared in a formalised manner or have been produced by a computer, computer system or computer network and are intended for use in a computer, computer system or computer network.

Various other chapters deals with cyber laws are summarised as:

Chapter-II of the Act specifically stipulates that any subscriber may authenticate an electronic record by affixing his digital signature. It further states that any person can verify an electronic record by use of a public key of the subscriber.

Chapter-III of the Act details about Electronic Governance and provides inter alia amongst others that where any law provides that information or any other matter shall be in writing or in the typewritten or printed form, then, notwithstanding anything contained in such law, such requirement shall be deemed to have been satisfied if such information or matter is rendered or made available in an electronic form; and accessible so as to be usable for a subsequent reference The said chapter also details the legal recognition of Digital Signatures.

Chapter-IV of the said Act gives a scheme for Regulation of Certifying Authorities. The Act envisages a Controller of Certifying Authorities who shall perform the function of exercising supervision over the activities of the Certifying Authorities as also laying down standards and conditions governing the Certifying Authorities as also specifying the various forms and content of Digital Signature Certificates. The Act recognizes the need for recognizing foreign Certifying Authorities and it further details the various provisions for the issue of license to issue Digital Signature Certificates.

Chapter-VII of the Act details about the scheme of things relating to Digital Signature Certificates. The duties of subscribers are also enshrined in the said Act.

Chapter-IX of the said Act talks about penalties and adjudication for various offences. The penalties for damage to computer, computer systems etc. has been fixed as damages by way of compensation not exceeding Rs. 10,000,000 to affected persons. The Act talks of appointment of any officers not below the rank of a Director to the Government of India or an equivalent officer of state government as an Adjudicating Officer who shall adjudicate whether any person has made a contravention of any of the provisions of the said Act or rules framed there under. The said Adjudicating Officer has been given the powers of a Civil Court.

Chapter-X of the Act talks of the establishment of the Cyber Regulations Appellate Tribunal, which shall be an appellate body where appeals against the orders passed by the Adjudicating Officers, shall be preferred.

Chapter-XI of the Act talks about various offences and the said offences shall be investigated only by a Police Officer not below the rank of the Deputy Superintendent of Police. These offences include tampering with computer source documents, publishing of information, which is obscene in electronic form, and hacking.

The Act also provides for the constitution of the Cyber Regulations Advisory Committee, which shall advice the government as regards any rules, or for any other purpose connected with the said Act. The said

Act also proposes to amend the Indian Penal Code, 1860, the Indian Evidence Act, 1872, The Bankers' Books Evidence Act, 1891, The Reserve Bank of India Act, 1934 to make them in tune with the provisions of the IT Act, 2000.

¶ 5-020 Revolutionary and contemporary code

The IT Act, 2000 is an attempt to change outdated laws and provides ways to deal with cyber crimes. Formulation of such laws is an urgent need of work culture in corporate section, so they can easily able to overcome on the issues of data protection and confidentiality. The Act offers the much-needed legal framework so that information is not denied legal effect, validity or enforceability, solely on the ground that it is in the form of electronic records.

In view of the growth in transactions and communications carried out through electronic records, the Act seeks to empower government departments to accept filing, creating and retention of official documents in the digital format. The Act has also proposed a legal framework for the authentication and origin of electronic records/communications through digital signature.

- From the perspective of e-commerce in India, the IT Act, 2000 and its provisions contain many positive aspects. Firstly, the implications of these provisions for the e-businesses would be that email would now be a valid and legal form of communication in our country that can be duly produced and approved in a court of law.

- Digital signatures have been given legal validity and sanction in the Act.

- Companies shall now be able to carry out electronic commerce using the legal infrastructure provided by the Act.

- The Act throws open the doors for the entry of corporate companies in the business of being certifying authorities for issuing Digital Signatures Certificates.

- The Act now allows government to issue notification on the web thus heralding e-governance.

- The IT Act also addresses the important issues of security, which are so significant to the success of electronic transactions. The Act has given a legal definition to the concept of secure digital signatures that would be required to have been passed through a system of a security procedure, as stipulated by the Government at a later date.

- The Act enables the companies to file any form, application or any other document with any office, authority, body or agency owned or controlled by the appropriate Government in electronic form by means of such electronic form as may be prescribed by the appropriate Government.

- Under the IT Act, 2000, it shall now be possible for corporates to have a statutory remedy in case if anyone breaks into their computer systems or network and causes damages or copies data. The remedy provided by the Act is in the form of monetary damages, not exceeding Rs 1 crore.

¶ 5-030 Other computer related offences under the Indian Penal Code (IPC)

Special Laws

Sending threatening messages by email	Sec 503 IPC
Sending defamatory messages by email	Sec 499 and 500 IPC
Forgery of electronic records	Sec463,470, 471IPC
Bogus websites, cyber frauds	Sec 420 IPC
Web-Jacking	Sec 383 IPC

- The crime was obviously committed using "Unauthorized Access" to the "Electronic Account Space" of the customers. It is therefore firmly within the domain of "Cyber Crimes".

- ITA, 2000 is versatile enough to accommodate the aspects of crime not covered by ITA,2000 but covered by other statutes since any IPC offence committed with the use of "Electronic Documents" can be considered as a crime with the use of a "Written Documents". "Cheating", "Conspiracy", "Breach of Trust" etc are therefore applicable in the above case in addition to section in ITA, 2000.

- Under ITA, 2000 the offence is recognized both under section 66 and section 43. Accordingly, the persons involved are liable for imprisonment and fine as well as a liability to pay damage to the victims to the maximum extent of Rs 1 crore per victim for which the "Adjudication Process" can be invoked.

- The BPO is liable for lack of security that enabled the commission of the fraud as well as because of the vicarious responsibility for the ex-employee's involvement. The process of getting the PIN number was during the tenure of the persons as "Employees" and hence the organization is responsible for the crime.

- Some of the persons who have assisted others in the commission of the crime even though they may not be directly involved as beneficiaries will also be liable under section 43 of ITA,2000.

- Under section 79 and section 85 of ITA,2000, vicarious responsibilities are indicated both for the BPO and the Bank on the grounds of "Lack of Due Diligence".

- At the same time, if the crime is investigated in India under ITA-2000, then the fact that the Bank was not using digital signatures for authenticating the customer instructions is a matter which would amount to gross negligence on the part of the Bank. (However, in this particular case since the victims appear to be US Citizens and the Bank itself is US based, the crime may come under the jurisdiction of the US courts and not Indian Courts).

Cyber Security Parameters

International Organization for Standardization (ISO) is a consortium of national standards institutes from 157 countries with a Central

Secretariat in Geneva Switzerland that coordinates the system. The ISO is the world's largest developer of standards.

ISO-15443: "Information technology - Security techniques - A framework for IT security assurance",

ISO-17799: "Information technology - Security techniques - Code of practice for information security management",

ISO-20000: "Information technology - Service management", and

ISO-27001: "Information technology - Security techniques - Information security management systems" are of particular interest to information security professionals.

The USA National Institute of Standards and Technology (NIST) is a non-regulatory federal agency within the US Department of Commerce. The NIST Computer Security Division develops standards, metrics, tests and validation programs as well as publishes standards and guidelines to increase secure IT planning, implementation, management and operation. NIST is also the custodian of the USA Federal Information Processing Standard Publications (FIPS)].

The Internet Society is a professional membership society with more than 100 organization and over 20,000 individual members in over 180 countries. It provides leadership in addressing issues that confront the future of the Internet, and is the organization home for the groups responsible for Internet infrastructure standards, including the Internet Engineering Task Force (IETF) and the Internet Architecture Board (IAB). The ISOC hosts the Requests for Comments (RFCs) which includes the Official Internet Protocol Standards and the RFC-2196 Site Security Handbook.

The Information Security Forum is a global non-profit organization of several hundred leading organizations in financial services, manufacturing, telecommunications, consumer goods, government, and other areas. It provides research into best practice and practice advice summarized in its biannual Standard of Good Practice, incorporating detail specifications across many areas.

¶ 5-040 Brief analysis of international contractual code and Indian law

- International contracts and International code as "Proper Law of the Contract".

- When the parties in the Contract make an express choice of law, Indian Courts have always recognized such choice of proper law.

- Under Indian Law, parties are free to stipulate their terms of contract and lay down the law by which the Contract is to be governed. Courts in India have held that the intention of parties would decide the law of which country would govern the Contract and which Court would have jurisdiction. Sections 13, 15 and 44A of the Indian Civil Procedure Code and section 41 of the Indian Evidence Act, govern the conclusiveness and enforcement of foreign judgments in India.

- The parties may also choose a foreign venue for arbitration. A Foreign arbitral award would be recognised in India if the country of venue has signed either the New York or Geneva conventions and has been notified as having reciprocal relations with India in the matter of enforcement of foreign awards. A foreign arbitral award would generally be more easily enforced in India than a foreign court judgment.

- India has ratified the World Trade Organisation (WTO) Agreement, which came into force on 1st January 1995 and has also become a party to the agreement on Trade Related Intellectual Property Rights. It has made several amendments to its laws concerning Intellectual Property to suit the international standards.

Chapter 6   Outsourcing Agreements

Access Related Outsourcing

In a recent study it was found that many organisation those looking for outsourcing contracts and agreements with foreign clients erroneously believe that the terms and conditions are about the same as onshore contracts with in-country service providers outsourcing contract drafted for in country providers will not work as templates for global outsourcing without significant modification.

The greatest risks for global outsourcing come from some emerging countries that are early entrants into outsourcing, or those that have limited governmental support, inefficient legal enforcement, undeveloped infrastructure, inadequate or non-existent intellectual property protection or immature understanding of foreign laws.

The most important areas to protect through an international outsourcing agreement are security and privacy, legal compliance, attorney-client privilege, fees and payment terms, proprietary rights, auditing rights and liability issues in case of errors. The legal systems of some countries might claim jurisdiction over any agreement regardless of which system the agreement specifies, and that other legal systems hardly any concern for intellectual property rights.

Outsourcing is the contracting out of a company's non-core, non-revenue producing activities to specialists. The structure of outsourcing contracts differ from others in the manner That outsourcing is a strategic management tool that involves the restructuring of an organization around what it does best its core competencies.

¶ 6-010 Types of outsourcing

Basically there are two types of outsourcing:

1. Traditional outsourcing

2. Greenfield outsourcing

Information Technology (IT) outsourcing and Business Process Outsourcing (BPO) comes under traditional outsourcing. BPO includes outsourcing related to accounting, human resources, benefits, payroll, and finance functions and activities. Knowledge Process Outsourcing (KPO) includes outsourcing related to legal, paralegal, and other highly skilled activities such as medical transcription, engineering research etc.

A high-quality outsourcing agreement is one which provides a comprehensive road map of the duties and obligations of both the parties - outsourcer and service provider. It reduces complications when a dispute arise. However, many a times people neglect to pay attention while drafting an outsourcing agreement. These are those issues which appear to be very minor but creates trouble when disputes arises.

Before finalising an outsourcing agreement, the terms and conditions should be thoroughly discussed and negotiated to avoid any confusion at a later stage. It is advised to consult the lawyers from all applicable jurisdiction before finalising any outsourcing agreement.

Before signing an Outsourcing Agreement the following issues must be properly addressed:

- Duties and obligations of outsourcer

- Duties and obligations of service provider

- Security and confidentiality

- Fees and payment terms

- Legal compliance

- Applicable law to outsourcing agreement

- Proprietary rights

- Auditing rights

- Term of the agreement

- Events of defaults and addressing

- Dispute Resolution Mechanism

- Time limits

- Appointment of arbitrators

- Location of arbitration

- Number of arbitrators

- Interim measures/Provisional Remedies

- Privacy agreement

- Confidentiality agreement

- Non-compete agreement

- Rules applicable

- Appeal and enforcement

- Issues related to indemnification

- Be aware of local peculiarities

- Survival terms after the termination of the outsourcing agreement

Every outsourcing agreement should be modified as applicable under different circumstances. Same code does not apply on every system. Offshore outsourcing is a legal minefield and many companies are not aware of the complication it causes. Of the 20 areas in a standard contract 16 need to be changed if the outsourcing provider is abroad.

¶ 6-020 Outsourcing agreements in corporate sector

There are various forms of outsourcing agreements recognised in corporate sector, some of them listed as:

- Business Process Outsourcing Agreements.

- **Real Estate Services:** An international real estate services outsourcing agreement.

- **Mortgage Bank:** A US large mortgage bank outsourced various customer facing and back office business processes to an Indian service provider

- **Multinational Insurance:** A group of major insurance and financial services companies formed a global outsourcing arrangement with a supplier.

- **Financial Institution:** A US financial institute outsourcing agreement with an Indian party.

- **Internal Accounting:** Outsourcing accounting, tax, and financial functions for a variety of companies.

- **Claims Processing:** Outsourcing agreement for the submission and processing of provider claims and the ongoing operation and support of such system.

- **Back Office Operations:** Outsourcing agreement for all the data processing systems and back-office operations.

- **Benefits Processing:** Outsourcing employee benefits, such as pension plans and ERISA compliance.

- **Human Resources Management:** Outsourcing human resources management functions, including hiring, benefits processing, payroll processing, and employee counseling.

- **Call Center Services:** Outsourcing call center operations including answering consumer inquiries, and assisting buyers in the use of products.

- **Ticketing Fulfillment Operation:** Representation of a web-based start-up providing travel and travel-related services in outsourcing its ticketing fulfillment and customer support operations.

- **Electric Power Utility:** Procurement and logistics outsourcing arrangements.

- Telecommunications Provider: Outsourcing agreement between a US company's data processing systems, including financial, customer usage and billing functions including financial, customer usage and billing function.

- Legal drafting and legal research: Outsourcing agreement between a US Company and an Indian provider

- Internet Banking Operation: Outsourcing of core bank operations, including the receipt and processing of customer applications and transactions.

Chapter 7 — Working Mechanics of LPO

Fidelity and Risk Management

The very first task in order to start LPO is to prepare a team of efficient attorneys. These attorneys can be taken from various law schools in India and abroad. Analysis of legal document requires high level of aptitude and intelligence which can be fulfilled by intellectuals brains only.

- Attorneys from the best law schools in India.

- A team with a proven track record.

- A dedicated quality department responsible for developing and deploying the organization's quality policies and undertake periodic reviews of its quality processes.

- Experienced attorneys other experts (in respective field).

- Equipment for clear and efficient communication example document-scanning.

- Well organised legal staff managing projects both domestically and in India.

- Exhaustive understanding of the US and UK legal system because most of the work are outsourced from these countries along with simultaneous training and imparting education.

- Identifiable and assessable quality control measures.

- High-level aptitude in management skills and operational experience.

- Best-in-industry e-discovery technology, tools and processes, with the ability to streamline the e-discovery process from inception (*i.e.*, harvesting and processing) to first level document review.

- The ability and keenness to stay apprised of e-discovery case developments and nuances.

- Close collaboration with clients (company/law firm) and case-specific legal training.

- High-level security of data processing and confidentiality measures.

¶ 7-010 Security and privacy norms

Clients are always apprehensive about the security while outsourcing their critical and confidential information to third parties. In order to build up the confidence one need world class privacy norms but also complying with security and privacy regulations to remain the preferred option for worldwide clients while offshore outsourcing providing appropriate safeguard to all kinds of information, including papers, databases, tapes, CD-ROMs and any other methods and media used to convey data, knowledge and ideas.

- The security policy covers the following areas.

- Acceptable Use/Access: set of rules which demarcate how organization's IT resources should be used by employees and other related staff to perform their professional activities. By using identity cards for our employees for proper authentication of use of infrastructure.

- **Network Connections:** policies governing the authentication, authorization and availability of network connections, such as: remote access, extranet connections and local switched LAN.

- **Data Access Control:** classification of different types of data according to their sensitivity and exposure (to attacks and viruses) throughout the IT infrastructure. This includes access through password only.

- **Protecting Physical and Logical Assets:** The hardware and associated software components which make up the IT infrastructure are sufficiently secured against unauthorized access. This include, network elements and their configurations, servers and their O/S and application set and user end-points.

- **Personnel Security:** potential threat that may arise from the employees to our offshore clients by taking up the following security measures:

  (i) Background checks such as reference checks, police checks, etc.;

  (ii) Non-disclosure and confidentiality agreements;and

  (iii) Camera surveillance.

¶ 7-020 Tell-tale indicators for interacting with foreign clients

- Market presence of your organisation

- How you introduce your organisation

- Information technology services and availability of no. systems as well as the workforce in organisation

- Understanding cultural differences

- Establishing credibility in market

- Due diligence

- Addressing IPR and data protection issues

- Endorsement of values

- Exhibit experience

- Clear terms of agreement and emphasis on indemnifying issues

- Competence and manpower

- Promptness, confidentiality and quality control

- fee arrangements and other issues related to payments

Strategic approach towards an International Client

¶ 7-030 Prospecting an international client

One of the imperative and cumbersome process while starting with the LPO is to approach a client. selecting a client is not an easy task it requires energy and patience both as well as due diligence while selecting a client the information about the background and credibility of the of the firm is essential The background of the client can be verified by :

- LPO literature

- References

- Past experience of the firm

- Approaching the person working with the firm

- Press and media in order to check the reputation

- Printed/online directory

- Publications

- Website

- advertisements

Edification

Address the client about your organisation and details of infrastructure and the work culture.

Delivery of products

A thorough understanding of the client's business objectives in the context of political, economic and social systems in the local jurisdiction.

Interactive commerce

An understanding of how different business practices, customs and etiquette can affect the relationship between the firm and its foreign client.

Business Intelligence

- Conduct due diligence incase of new client

- Website check

- Personality analysis over phone discussions

- Verify the identity of the company with the corresponding Country's embassy/government/country records

- Confirm that the signatory is authorized to sign on behalf of the company

- Verify that the company is legal and doing real business

Track Record

Previous tasks

- Fully skilled team

- Well established infrastructure

- Admiration and rewards from the client

- Completion of task on time

¶ 7-040 IPR and Data protection issues

Data protection, confidentiality-contractually enforceable, Article 21 of Constitution, common law, fiduciary duty, breach of trust-criminal offence – both IPC and IT Act.

Agreement

Points to be addressed in the engagement letter

- Availability and access

- Responsiveness

- Working language(s)

- Status reports

- Delegation of legal work

- Communications with the foreign client's home office and local subsidiaries

- Communications with third parties

- Conflict and unfair competition issues

- Staff substitution

- Billing

- Expenses and disbursements

- Payment

- Applicable law and settlement of disputes

¶ 7-050 Important considerations

Service Level Agreement

- Quality

  - The client should be able to get out of the contract if he finds the quality below par.

- Quantity

  - volume of work to be done in an hour/day/week/month as per agreed.

- Confidentiality

  - assurance that all the information and data would be not be disclosed to any third party.

- Pay Cycle

  - how to remit professional fees

- Price Increases

  - dependence of the client-ensure that for large, long-term projects, once the vendor's personnel have acquired experience on the client projects, the vendor does not result in unreasonable price increases or replacement of key employees

¶7-060 Billing

- How frequently will fees be billed?

- How much detail does the client require on the invoice?

- Billing practices vary considerably. A foreign client who is used to itemized, detailed hourly billing might take exception to the summary form of invoice that is customary for the firm's local clients

  (i) One, the flat rate fee – the clients have to pay the fixed amount of charges for the entire month's working. Second, the packaged fee – wherein the clients pay for buying the entire package of services like patents prior art search would cost them around US$ 800 for 12 hours. Third, on hourly basis. High-end jobs would cost more than even US$ 150. The value for money has to be given by keeping prices relatively reasonable.

  (ii) Depending upon the type of services being delivered, the billing charges range from US$ 10 to 200.

¶7-070 Expenses and disbursements

- Those expenses and reimbursements which are agreed to be reimbursed can vary considerably from country to country.

- Laws and perception vary from place to place, What is traditional or considered normal in one jurisdiction might be viewed as bordering on dishonesty in another?

- It is necessary to put clauses related to expenses and reimbursements because, Unless reimbursement of expenses and disbursements is discussed and agreed in engagement letter, the firm should expect the foreign client to challenge some of these charges.

¶ 7-080 Payment

Payments provisions:

- Amounts to be paid –

  (i) Lump sum contract;

  (ii) Time based contracts;

  (iii) Success fee based contract;

  (iv) Percentage contract;

  (v) Indefinite delivery contract.

- Curriculum of payments

- Payment procedures, shall be indicated in the draft contract and agreed upon Between the parties during negotiations.

- Payments may be made at regular intervals (as under time-based contracts) or for agreed outputs (as under lump sum contracts).

- Any advance payments should normally be backed by Bank Guarantee. The limit for advance payment will be as prescribed by GFR. Normally, it should not exceed 10% of the cost of the contract.

- Payments shall be made punctually in accordance with the contract provisions.

Chapter 8   Working Models of LPO

Outsourcing Initiative in India

There is a few countries around the globe involved in Legal Process Outsourcing, however, the industry's offshoring destination originated and remains concentrated in India and other neighbouring countries. India is declared as the best outsourcing destination. This holds true for several reasons.

India maintains a large and highly skilled work force with strong English language capabilities. Secondly, Indian lawyers have the built in advantage of a similar legal system based on British common law and many have additional training in US law. LPO also holds appeal for professionals in India. Approximately, 75,000 Indian lawyers graduate each year. For many of these lawyers, legal process outsourcing is a promising, profitable, lucrative and demanding alternative to the Indian legal market. Similar to the American system, the Indian legal market is dominated by competitive law firms where advancement can be a tiresome process over a period of years.

Although LPO remains concentrated in India, the structure and onshore/offshore relationship between client, legal firms, and LPO firms varies. There are four main models LPO firms typically develop and operate under. Each model, as outlined by Evalueserve, has specific implications and ethical concerns that must be considered in regard to the level of supervision between the US attorney and foreign lawyer.

- Examining the associated costs, cost savings and tax advantages for:

(i) Domestic captive centers: This model is formed when a large corporation starts its own center in foreign country responsible for its legal and business processing issues. In early 2005 General Electric became one of the first companies to set up a captive center. They did so by to employing Indian lawyers at its center in Guragon, India. Now there are almost 30 lawyers at the center responsible for supporting the majority of legal work of the company. In this model, the ethical responsibility falls mainly on the company that is hiring the foreign lawyers, and the American lawyers responsible for supervising their work. Some issues may arise in regard to disclosure, as many companies may not want to reveal they are offshoring.

(ii) Offshore captive centers: Indian laws currently do not allow foreign law firms to practice in India. As a result, some law firms in the US/UK are working with Indian law firms to set up subsidiaries to provide legal and paralegal services for export purposes only. For example, Fox and Mandal and ALMT Legal, two Indian based law firms, are teaming up with Patent Metrix, an Irvine-California based law firm. Ethical responsibility in this model is similar to the captive center in that the US/UK law firm is substituted in replace of the company.

(iii) Third party LPO service providers: This is one of the key model being used in legal process outsourcing companies. Under this model, a law firm or in-house legal department for a company will hire a third party provider (i.e. a LPO company) with trained and skilled lawyers and non-lawyers to complete a task. Examples of the top LPO companies of 2008, according to the Black Book of Outsourcing, include Law Scribe. Clutch Group, CPA Global, Integreon, and Mindcrest. This model raises ethical accountability issues for the law firm that is using the LPO company, but also for the LPO companies itself. The complicated and new ethical issues surround the LPO firms in regard to conflict of interest and the ethical/legal responsibility of US/UK, lawyers working for the LPO firm.

- Considerations when leveraging a global labor pool:

  - Hiring and managing remote workers.

  - Controlling process, quality and training.

- What are the typical transition processes and timelines?

- Evaluating the feasibility of a domestic captive center versus an offshore center:

  - Lower costs available in the mid-west

  - Opportunity to employ local resources

  - Time zone advantage

- Determining whether India can be a good offshore destination for your business goals:

  - Cost analysis

  - Availability of a qualified labor pool

  - Rate of deterioration

- What other offshore locations are being utilized or should be considered and in what way those location is advantageous for the company which is outsourcing.

¶ 8-010 Determination of Hallmarks of a successful outsourcing initiative

Selecting services to outsource

- Identifying the characteristics of services that have been outsourced for:

  - High demand

  - Scalable

  - Lower risk

- Evaluating the type of work that is most susceptible to outsourcing:

    - Intellectual property and patent litigation

    - Document review and litigation service

    - Corporate

    - Litigation and e-discovery

    - Research

    - Database technology

- Where have the greatest efficiencies and cost savings been realized?

- Deciding what services to outsource first, Determining how to know when you're ready to expand that scope

    - Practice support services versus legal processes.

¶ 8-020 Papering the Transaction

Best practices for structuring and Negotiating Outsourcing Agreement

- Laying confidentiality and preparing non-disclosure agreements to ensure your obligations for client confidentiality and privacy are met

- Ahead of the master agreement – establishing service-level benchmarks:

    - Selecting what type of service level agreements are appropriate?

    - What current benchmarks or provisions are being used in the market?

    - Secure penalties for breach

    - Pointing specific examples of service level agreements

- Audit rights – what should the contract demand or allow for?

- Defining IP rights:

    - What is the industry standard?

    - How to Banter for specific circumstances?

- Drafting provisions that will ensure knowledge transfer and a timeframe for phasing it

- Leveraging US-India tax agreements when constructing your outsourcing contract

- What to do if a security breach occurs:

  - When to notify clients

  - Restoring client confidence

  - Determining who bears fault and steps to take thereafter

- Thinking ahead – incorporating wind down provisions

  - What happens when terminating the relationship – what is the process?

  - Different termination scenarios

¶ 8-030 Frequently asked questions while selecting services of LPO

- When establishing an LPO relationship, buyers tend to focus on the answers to three key Issues:

  - How much will it cost?

  - Quality of the delivered matter?

  - How worth to work with that particular enterprenuer?

¶ 8-040 Achieving Firm Wide Buy

In incorporating change management to successfully develop and execute legal outsourcing strategy:

- Discussing the advantages of building offshore resources as a means to achieve overall resource allocation efficiency.

- Overcoming employee feelings around a loss of control – strategies for getting users to adapt and embrace new ways of working.

- Establishing appropriate management buy-in to aid in the successful adoption of legal outsourcing.

- Instilling acceptance of change within your in-house counsel or firm to overcome resistance to legal outsourcing.

¶ 8-050 Ethical Considerations when Outsourcing Legal Services

- Examining the ethical issues regarding outsourcing legal work to India:

  - Unauthorised practice of law

  - Attorney-client privilege

  - Duty to supervise

  - Data and personnel security

  - Confidentiality

  - Client conflicts of interest

  - Document retention

  - Export control compliance (patent specific)

  - Document retention

  - Billing issues for private practitioners

- State Bar Association issued opinions in august 2006 regarding the outsourcing of legal services and the unauthorized practice of law.

- Liability questions with respect to malpractice coverage.

Preserving quality of service and work product in LPO

- Developing a risk allocation framework to control or mitigate the risks surrounding LPO.

- Controlling offshore operations remotely:

  – incorporating strategies to overcome quality control challenges

  - Cultural differences

  - Linguistic issues

  - Training

- Best practices for handling day-to-day operations:

    - Instituting and maintaining appropriate communication channels for day to day administration and quality controls.

    - Resolving problems and extreme situations while avoiding business disruption

    - Tried and tested methods and metrics to evaluate and monitor quality, and to ensure accountability

- Establishing conflict resolution procedures:

    - What you need to know about utilising commercial dispute resolutions overseas to enforce commercial rights and litigation

- Business continuity planning and disaster recovery to protect customer and company information in your partner's hands

¶ 8-060 Avoidance of potential pitfalls in litigation where work has been outsourced

Preventing service performance issues caused by third party provider employees are:

- Examining potential vendor personnel problems which could negatively impact outsourced services:

    - Unqualified hires

    - Deterioration

    - Poor performance

    - Lack of motivation

- Incorporating service performance into your outsourcing agreement to prevent vendor personnel issues:

    - Requisite skill covenants

    - Skill set requirements

    - Screening requirements

    - Anti-turnover provisions

    - Incentive bonuses

    - Removal rights

    - Security levels

    - Indemnification requirements

- Incentivising vendors to select and maintain an appropriate workforce to satisfy your organisation's goals in outsourced services:

  - Implementing discretionary work as a way to offer career development and prevent attrition

  - Infrastructure and technology requirements for successful legal outsourcing

- Advice and suggestions on the types of solutions and technology being used within legal outsourcing.

- Investigating the basic mechanics of linking two organizations that can be half way around the world:

  - WAN/LAN (Wide Area Network/Local Area Network)

  - VPN (Virtual Private Network)

- Protection measures for securing confidential information.

- Training staff on the technology platform to be used to send and receive work.

Chapter 9   Indian Economy and LPO

Foreign Exchange Management Act, 1999 (FEMA) has replaced the Foreign Exchange Regulation Act, 1973 (FERA) that regulated all foreign exchange transactions. The objectives of FEMA have been to facilitate external trade and payments and to promote orderly development and maintenance of foreign exchange market. All residents can now put foreign exchange on current account transaction through an authorized dealer. Foreign firms also qualify for this under the resident status. But for sectors like banking, NBFC, civil aviation, petroleum, real estate, venture capital funds, investing companies in infrastructure and service sector, atomic energy, defense, agriculture and plantation, print media, broadcasting and postal services, automatic approval of FDI is allowed in all other sectors. The role of Reserve Bank of India and Secretariat of Industrial Assistance has become more that of a facilitator.

¶ 9-010 Gross Domestic Product and Outsourcing

India is fifteenth in services output. It provides employment to 24% of work force, and it is growing fast, growth rate 8.0% in 1991–2000 up from approximately 55% in 1951–1980. It has the largest share in the GDP, accounting for 57% in 2007 up from 14% in 1950. Business services (information technology, information technology enabled services, business process outsourcing) are among the fastest growing sectors contributing to one third of the total output of services in 2000. The growth in the IT sector is attributed to increased specialisation, availability of a large pool of low cost, but highly skilled, educated and fluent English-speaking workers. On the supply side and on the demand side, increased demand from foreign consumers interested in India's service exports or those looking to outsource their operations. India's IT industry, despite contributing significantly to its balance of payments, accounted for only about 1% of the total GDP or 1/50th of the total services in 2001· However, the contribution of IT to GDP increased to 4.8 % in 2005-06 and is projected to increase to 8% of GDP in 2008.

¶ 9-020 Foreign investment and outsourcing

The amount of FDI to India grew significantly during the mid-1940s and reached a peak in 1961. Subsequently, as the GOI introduced the policies for foreign investments in the local manufacturing companies, many of the. foreign companies withdrew from India. Finally, foreign investments started to increase with the liberalisation policies of the government from around 1978. Foreign investments in India rose sharply from 1991 following the liberalisation policies of the government. The post 1991 foreign trade and South Asian Journal of Management investment policies have, however, substantially increased foreign investments mainly in trading, marketing, business process outsourcing, clinical services, stock markets and other marketing ventures. The trend in the amount of FDI during the period 1955 to 2002 is not something which can be appreciated. But Surprisingly, the share of investment of other smaller nations including nations from Asia, Oceania and European Union has sharply increased in recent years. The shares of investments of UK, USA, Japan, and Germany, the traditional investors in India have substantially reduced in different sectors and taken shift and their investment in various other sectors such as services, infrastructure, etc.. It was found that the countries within the Asian region have actually contributed the most to the FDI in India in the recent years as against the general perception that most of its FDI is from the highly advanced economies of the world. Figure 2 illustrates the trend in the country-wise share in the number of foreign collaborations in India during the period, 1951 to 2002.

¶ 9-030 Export including outsourcing from India

India's outsourcing industry is estimated to be worth about $52 billion. India continues to dominate global outsourcing market. Banking and financial services contribute nearly 40 percent to India's outsourcing industry.

The amount of exports, the nature of exports and the kind of outsourcing can be looked at to explain the degree of globalisation of India. The nature of exports will indicate how competitive the Indian industry has been and whether the global economy depends on India just as Indian economy depends on the global economy.

A large portion of foreign investment has come to India for outsourcing purposes. Cheap and - skilled labor, intense competition, saturated markets and thin margins have compelled countries to outsource their supplies/services from countries like India. The major areas of outsourcing from India have been information technology, software. Pharmaceuticals, textile, auto components, and other backend services. An estimated $5 billion worth of low value engineering goods, auto components, pharmaceutical products and textiles products have been outsourced from India over the past four years. However, none of the outsourced items are unique to India, and hence, are not sustainable over a long period of time as other low economies can offer these products and services.

¶ 9-040 Tax incentives for exporters

The New Export-Import Policy provides substantial tax incentives for investments in Export Oriented Units (EOU's) and industries sited in the Special Economic Zones (SEZ's). Secretariats are giving instant approvals for Industrial setting up to 100% Export Oriented Units (EOU). Incentives and facilities available under the EOU scheme include concessional rent for lease of industrial plots, preferential power allocation and supply, exemption from import duty for capital goods and raw materials for power sector industries as well as for trading companies primarily engaged in export activity.

There are seven major Special Eeconomic Zones (SEZ's) and 27 other SEZ's or free trade zones located in different parts of the country. These zones are designed to make available internationally competitive infrastructure facilities and duty-free and low cost environment. Various monetary and non-monetary incentives are granted which include import duty exemption, complete tax holiday, decentralized "single window clearance," etc.

Indian Government Proposal

- Foreign Direct Investment (FDI) for 100 per cent of the equity in BPO companies-options to foreign companies to engage independent service provider, branch office, set up JV or wholly owned subsidiary, acquire exiting company.

- Foreign Investment Regulations Software development and BPO services is now under the automatic route and no foreign investment approvals are required to set up a wholly owned subsidiary; only certain filings need to be made after receipt and issue of share capital. However, acquisition of shares in an existing Indian company may still require a prior foreign investment approval.

- Most foreign corporations set up their subsidiaries as private limited companies with liability limited by share capital.

  - Promotions of STPs which provide ready-to-plug IT and telecom infrastructure

  - Indian tax laws have recently included provisions relating to transfer pricing, requiring pricing of transactions between associated enterprises to be at arms length

  - Allows repatriation of profits, calculated in accordance with approved accounting rules.

  - National Venture Fund for the Software and IT Industry with a corpus of Rs. 100 crore

  - The tax incentives offered to the investors by the Government of India are a boon for firms involved in IT outsourcing to India. The incentives that facilitate economic growth and development are:

    (i) Infrastructure: A 10 years tax holiday to ventures engaged in developing and/or maintaining and operating an infrastructure facility.

(ii)   Power: 10 years tax holiday to undertakings, which generate and/or distribute power.

(iii) Telecom: 5 years tax holiday for companies providing telecom services including Internet services and broadband services. Also 30% deduction from profits for the next 5 years in any 10 continuous years out of first 10 years is also offered.

(iv)   Industrial Parks and Special Economic Zones

- 10 years tax holiday is applicable to ventures that develop and/or operate or maintain in notified IT parks and special economic zones.

Tax Rebates

- 5. Other Industries:

- 5-year tax holiday is available for new industrial units to be set up in backward states and districts.

- 6. Incentives for Exports:

- No Tax is deducted on exporters profits for unit set up on EPZs, STPs, EHTPs, FTZ and SEZs.

- 7. Other Incentives:

  Tax concessions are allowed for FTI and a weighted deduction of 150% for scientific research and development expenditure have been offered. 10 years tax holiday is available for R and D companies engaged in scientific and industrial research.

¶ 9-050 Outsourcing and American economy

Contrary to common perception, information technology outsourcing benefits the US economy by increasing the number of US jobs, improving real wages for American workers, and pushing the US economy to perform at a higher level, according to a new study.

"Global sourcing continues to be a net positive for American workers and the US economy," said Harris N. Miller, president of Information Technology Association of America, the leading trade association for the IT industry.

The study, conducted by Global Insight, found that worldwide sourcing of IT services and software generated an additional 257,042 net new US jobs in 2005, a number that is expected to rise to 337,625 by 2010. With low inflation and high productivity, global sourcing also increased real hourly wages in the US by $0.06 in 2005.

The report added that worldwide sourcing contributed $68.7 billion in real US GDP.

The benefits of free trade clearly provide a boost to the US economy, Global Insight chief economist Nariman Behravesh said.

Despite the short term job loss associated with offshore outsourcing, it is expected that the practice will ultimately push U.S. workers into a higher level "skill paradigm." It's important for governments and companies to implement training programs for those displaced by outsourcing, he added obviously, outsourcing phenomenon in USA is nothing new. US companies and governments have been outsourcing domestically for decades such services as payroll, data base management, and janitorial services. The new bend has been the recent increase in foreign outsourcing, or offshoring in various fields in which legal sector is capturing the major chunk which is now an eye opener for many in this field. Foreign outsourcing has been made increasingly cost-effective because of the personal computer, which has digitized much of our work along with high-speed and uninterrupted transmission of that information through broadband and the Internet.

US economy is certainly going to be benefited by the foreign outsourcing in the short as well as the long run. Like more conventional forms of trade, foreign outsourcing allows US companies to drastically cut the cost of certain information technology services. As a result, US companies become more competitive in what they do best, their "core competencies." standard quality and more affordable services become available for consumers and taxpayers. Outsourcing allows companies to operate on an around-the-clock 24/7 production cycle, further adding to productivity. It is even making possible work that simply wouldn't exist otherwise, such as chasing down delinquent accounts receivable that were thought to be beyond collection. It could help control spiraling costs in such sectors as healthcare and education.

Foreign outsourcings of services stimulate the US economy, raising productivity and creating new opportunities. According to a 2003 study by Diana Farrell at the McKinsey Global Institute, outsourcing delivers large and measurable benefits to the US economy. It reduces costs for information technology (IT) and other services by as much as 60 percent, keeping US companies competitive in global markets, benefiting workers and shareholders alike. It stokes demand abroad for the export of US-supplied computers, telecommunications hardware, software, and legal, financial, and marketing services. It returns profits from US-owned affiliates abroad, and it allows US companies to re-deploy workers in more productive jobs here at home. In fact, McKinsey calculates that every $1 spent on foreign outsourcing creates $1.12 to $1.14 of additional economic activity in the U.S. economy. Global outsourcing contributed $5.1 billion to US exports in 2005 and is expected to grow to $9.7 billion by 2010. Foreign outsourcing could deliver the same scale of productivity gains to the IT services industry as it has to the hardware industry.

Chapter 10   LPO/Foreign Firms

Have they intruded forbidden Indian legal system?

India is in the process of globalising its economy. The legal profession in India has experienced a seachange, emerging as highly competitive and ready to move along with other developing or developed economies. The interest of foreign law firms to open shop in India therefore is not unpredictable, since India offers a full range of legal services, of comparable quality, at literally a fraction of the price that would otherwise have to be paid. The rather conservative and if one may use the word, "protectionist" stand of the Bar Council of India on the matter has, however, prohibited foreign law firms from operating in India. A number of the more established ones, perhaps unable to resist the immense potential of the Indian legal markets, and in anticipation of the "globalisation of legal services" under the aegis of the WTO, are slowly (and quite discreetly) establishing their presence in India.

Legal profession in India is not seen as a very bright career option because of the prevailing disparity in this field the professionals who are already established are taking a large chunk of the quality work, Hence, lawyers in the top bracket are becoming increasingly wealthy even by international standards and vast majority are struggling to make both ends meet despite being otherwise competent. Entry of foreign law firms is bound to increase the disparity.

Lawyers are officers of the court and empowering them at the grass root level will undoubtedly strengthen the judiciary. Before allowing entry of foreign law firms in Indian legal field, the Bar Council must ensure inclusive growth of lawyers and its wide-ranging effects on other parameters. The concept of equitable distribution of briefs and social security amongst junior members of the bar merit consideration.

Today in India there are around 10,000 lawyers who are actually established in this field and same number of junior even more then that junior lawyers are assisting them, but the story doesn't end here, there are still thousand in number in this profession who are struggling for their daily needs. One cannot ignore this fact and our government is very well aware about it, so at this juncture is it viable to allow the foreign law firms to enter India and permit them to practice?

The issue has been hanging fire since the mid-1990s, when foreign law firms were allowed to set up liaison offices in India but couldn't do business here. Amid allegations that they were violating this rule it is quite hard to put guard on that. It is true that If foreign law firms are allowed to operate from India, it would not be possible to monitor whether they advice clients on Indian laws or foreign laws. They are likely to operate in full swing even on an advisory capacity with or without Indian partners. Moreover, in terms of sections 2(j) and 5 of Foreign Exchange Management Act, 1999, payment for availing of legal services falls within current account transactions and can be freely effected in convertible foreign exchange.

In this age we cannot put a check on the foreign law firms to operate from India. Internet facility has rolled the whole globe in such drastic way that one person sitting in any part of the world can easily communicate his counterpart with in a second, that being so it is really futile to put restrain on outsiders to have access to our law fraternity.

Foreign law firms are already making their place in the Indian market — either through arrangements for referral, talent-sharing and joint marketing efforts, or in the form of Legal Process Outsourcing (LPO), Many of them already started offshoring their work in India and its going to be the next big thing in outsourcing industry. Foreign law firms do not just handle in-bound and out-bound investments and write securities offering documents. To provide their services, they extensively recruit lawyers trained only in Indian law — not just fresh recruits from campus, but also partners with equity stakes in Indian firms.

Much of the perplexity with regard to the entry of foreign law firms is caused by the propaganda that created by the immature professionals. The mass is ill-informed about the consequences of their arrival. When one looks at the impact of the arrival of foreign firms in other sectors such as accounting, real state, telecommunication, one can only conclude that with the opening up of the sector, the earnings of Indian professionals have gone up along with the quality of service to the customer.

Despite powerful opposition to their entry, foreign law firms have tie-ups and associate offices in India with whom they are working. Some foreign law firms boast of an active 'India practice' despite not having set up shop here. Their Indian team is either based in London or in other Asian cities from where they conduct transaction work, Conversely, and for the same reason, a number of Indian law firms have offices abroad. These firms are practicing in other forms also, due to their increasing work pressure they are outsourcing their non-core function to India and get it done by the Indian recrutties who are trained particularly for that purpose. This form of legal practice is welcomed by Indian legal professional because its not going to effect their bread. conversely its flowering as a good career option for youngsters.

¶ 10-010 Role of Indian Advocates Act, 1961

Under section 7(1) of the Indian Advocates Act, 1961, one of the paramount duties of the Bar Council of India is "to recognise on a reciprocal basis foreign qualifications in law obtained outside India for the purpose of admission as an advocate under this Act". When it comes to legal education, India recognises the bachelor's degree in law of many jurisdictions for pursing a master's degree in an Indian university — a jurisdiction being the power or extent of a court within the limits of which a lawyer can practice.

India being a signatory to the General Agreement on Trade in Services (GATS) which is an organ of the World Trade Organisation (WTO) is under an obligation to open up the service sector to Member Nations.

"Services" would include any service in any sector except services supplied in the exercise of governmental authorities as defined in GATS.

"A service supplied in the exercise of governmental authorities" is also defined to mean any service that is supplied neither on a commercial basis nor in competition with one or more service suppliers.

Legal "practice" is not defined in the Advocates Act but a reading of sections 30 and 33 indicates that practice is limited to appearance before any court, tribunal or authority. It does not include legal advice, documentation, alternative methods of resolving disputes and such other services. section 24(i)(a) of the Act provides that a person shall be qualified to be admitted as an Advocate on the State Roll if he is a citizen of India provided that subject to this Act a national of any other country may be admitted as an Advocate on the State Roll if the citizens of India duly qualified are permitted to practice law in that other country.

Section 47 of the Act provides that where a country specified by the Central Govt. in this behalf by a notification in the Official Gazette prevents the citizens of India from practicing the profession of law subjects them to unfair discrimination in that country, no subject of any such country shall be entitled to practice that profession of law in India.

The basic principles set out by IBA on the question of validity of FLC's are fairness, uniform and non-discriminatory treatment, clarity and transparency, professional responsibility, reality and flexibility. The guidelines laid down by the IBA are as follows:

"Legal consultant means a person qualified to practice law in a country (home country) and who desires to be licensed to practice law as a legal consultant without being examined by a body or an authority to regulate the legal profession in a country (host country) other than a home country, such a person has to apply to the host authority for a license by following the procedure for obtaining a license subject to the reasonable conditions imposed by the host authority on the issue of licenses. This license requires renewal. A legal consultant has to submit an undertaking alongwith his application not to accept, hold, transfer, deal with a client found or assigned unless the legal consultant does so in a manner authorized by the host authority to agree and abide by the code of ethics applicable to host jurisdiction besides to abide by all the rules and regulations of both the home and host jurisdiction.

It is open to the host authority to impose the requirement of reciprocity and to impose reasonable restrictions on the practice of FLC's in the host country, that the FLC's may not appear as an attorney or plead in any court or tribunal in the host country and the FLC's may not prepare any documents or instruments whose preparation or performance of other services, is specifically reserved by the host authority for performance by its local members.

As far as the legal process outsourcing is concerned. The above mentioned regulation are not going to effect them in either way. The employee of these organisation are not servant or doing any service for any organization or rendering full time service. They are recognized as legal consultant, hence, they don't lose their identity of being a lawyer and are not required to submit their license to the Bar. Their remuneration were given as fees they charged for consultation.

In order to excel on global level, foreign law firms should be allowed to operate on a par with the Indian law firms. They should be allowed to operate on a level-playing field not because of our obligations under the WTO but on the grounds of reciprocity and international comity.

They should be allowed so that they bring with them a fresh brand of professionalism, competence, efficiency and expertise that the legal profession here has failed to develop indigenously.

Incompetence at all levels will be exposed and clients will have more to choose from, both in terms of quality and service. Their arrival should come as rude and welcome shock to most of their counterparts in India who have for generations run law firms like personal fiefdoms bereft of professionalism and vision.

In one of the statement given by CJI while delivering the keynote address on 'Judicial Reforms in India' organised by the Indo-EU Business Forum. CJI said that ""I don't think the Bar Council of India can continue to resist (the proposal to allow foreign law firms to operate in India), I cannot give you a time-frame but this (the proposal) is being handled at the senior level and it will be done," Law minister H R Bhardwaj had recently said that the legal fraternity in India should view the possibility of the entry of foreign law firms as an opportunity to grow and enjoy the 'fruits of litigation' by setting up partnership firms.

Asked if UK law firms can be allowed to do transactional work with the objective of facilitating foreign investment in India, Justice Balakrishnan said, "It should be decided by the BCI. I am sure it will come soon. Discussion between the BCI and its British counterpart has started. It may happen shortly and it will be helpful".

There are more likelihood that foreign law firms will soon be able to hang their shingles in India. This is, of course, very big news indeed.

1. It will allow foreign technology-focused law firms access to the country with probably the most important IT market in the world over the next decade or two, barring the USA. For many firms, this will allow them to serve their own existing clients in a country where they have previously been prohibited from doing so.

2. It will allow firms to outsource price-pressured commoditized and mid-level services to their own offices in India, rather than referring the work to other local firms, so keeping a tighter grip on quality and client service and improving communication and collaboration efficiencies.

3. It will create a new source of skilled and experienced talent for the premier firms in Europe and North America, who are finding it increasingly difficult to find enough junior talent of the requisite quality, to meet client demands. This may very well cause a downward pressure on associate salaries in the medium term.

All is not in place yet. The Advocates Act, 1961, which prohibits non-Indian lawyers from practicing in the country, is still very much in place. But it would appear that it may be amended to allow these changes more quickly than the 2010, that our sources in India had previously indicated to us was the most likely timeframe.

Legal process outsourcing is seen as a viable option for foreign law firms to get their job done on their own laws as well as on Indian laws. They do not need to go through the cumbersome process of getting their self registered in Indian bars or any other law which ever comes in their way, there are number of foreign law firms who have started the process or they are active in this field for years. Globalisation has now changed the perception and the economies are now coming closer to each other, hence its difficult to keep any sector away from recent developments and finding new avenues and certainly the legal system is the major concern.

Chapter 11 Hail Recession!

Summary

Recession, is not an acceptable phenomenon even an imagination of this word brings chills in spine in corporate sector but for quality legal outsourcing providers, it will mean more business, not less.it is a fact that at least one section of industry isn't unhappy about the meltdown. The recession in the US is good news for the $200-250 million Legal Process Outsourcing (LPO) industry in India.

The U.S. economy is undergoing a tough phase, and it is going to either get worse or stay this way for the rest of 2008, and perhaps much longer. The question on everyone's mind in the legal process outsourcing industry, and in the outsourcing industry in general, is whether this will have a positive or negative impact on 2009 for LPO and for other outsourcing players The whole world watches as the titans clash in the primaries of the US elections. Most of us who have been following the elections know well enough that this year, the primaries would be the most significant part of the election process. The Democrats are in control of the US Congress, a Democratic victory in the presidential elections seems imminent, and the Outsourcing industry is in for a radical overhaul.

The US economy is in recession and protectionist tendencies riding high. Barack Obama and Hillary Clinton have expressed concerns over American jobs being outsourced. The issue of Jobs outsourcing and job losses is highest on the priority list. At the Democratic primary presidential debate at the Howard University on June 28, 2007, Senator Clinton indicated that there was a need to end tax-breaks for outsourcing jobs. Senator Obama was critical of the effects of globalization on the worker communities that lost their jobs because of the outsourcing phenomenon.

However, after nourishing he globalisation phenomenon for years, United States government cannot give away or escape from initiating process of increasing liberalization in developing countries to build markets and investments. On rational terms it can be done by indirect method by providing system of incentives and disincentives to retain jobs for American workers in corporates and firms; this can include tax incentives and government investments to companies for companies to create jobs in the US.

The LPO industry will profit from the downturn in the US markets. Apart from looking to cut spending and downsizing in the departments that are not the core competencies of the business, organizations are looking to cut the rocketing costs in the legal departments and due to this fact India has seen a five-fold growth in the last six months. This is prompting them to hire at a time when other sectors are either freezing recruitments or are firing.

The increased import tariffs on services industry are unlikely to impede the offshoring of legal services, mainly due to the substantial cost-advantage enjoyed in Asia.

In this recession, when the people as well as companies are suffering losses everyone is looking for a culprit, and the litigation battle is just beginning.. Litigation activity related to the recession is bound to increase, and the resulting litigations will be, not surprisingly, discovery heavy. Combine this increase in litigation with the need to preserve cash, and litigants will look to India as a discovery solution. It's happening already, as most of the top LPO providers have seen a marked increase in litigation business in the last six months.

While outsourcing of litigation work from the US and Europe has tremendously increased, what is interesting is new forms of businesses like risk management, corporate compliance and know-your-customer (KYC) guidance work from a number of global corporates that have come up.

Barack Obama's elevation to the US Presidency will not take away any joy from the outsourcing industry. An extract from the Hindu November 5, 2008 P. Chidambaram stated "A comment here and a comment there (on outsourcing of services to India) should not bother us... once Obama is in office, he will realise that it is an interconnected world and countries have to work together", he told reporters.

"The US as the world's largest economy and India as the world's largest free market democracy have to work together," he said, adding Indo-US relations would continue to improve under the new administration.

Commenting on Obama's election as President, Chidambaram said, "It is a transformational change in the US and many ghosts have been exorcised by this election."

"I think this (election of Obama) is a tribute to the US democracy that a young, forward-looking ... black has been elected," he added.

Nasscom is aware of the political change and in no mood to take chance, Hence,

A high-profile Nasscom delegation will be travelling to the US in March 2009 to lobby officials of the Obama administration, influencers (Senators et al) and key thinktanks to ensure that no nasty surprises greet Indian tech majors on the outsourcing issue.

While it is uncertain at this stage as to who exactly from Nasscom and its membership would travel to the US with this purpose in mind, Most likely the organisation may press into delegation some of its most prominent names for this job. Nasscom President Som Mittal, in any case, is a certainty.

On its part, though, Nasscom is reluctant to describe the March 2009 trip as a lobbying mission and sees it more of an "ongoing exercise to put things in their proper perspective". "We embarked on a similar thing recently in Japan when we interacted with policymakers and key officials," Nasscom president Som Mittal told TOI on Monday. Incidentally, Nasscom had been keeping the lines of communication open with the aides of all the candidates in the fray for the US Presidency for quite some time so that the India viewpoint was understood and kept in mind during the decision making process.

With the US alone accounting for over 60% of India's software exports, it must be understood that Nasscom does not have much room for manoeuvre on this score. Despite attempts to grow other markets, the US would continue to be India's largest market for many years to come.

Nasscom has been trying to develop greater links with Japan, Germany, France and Scandinavian countries. It is also trying to identify and resolve the issues that are coming in the way of doing greater business with these countries. The UK is India's second biggest market for software exports

¶ 11-010 Impact of recession

It is true that the Indian economy is likely to lose between 1 to 2% points in GDP growth in the next fiscal year but the service industry contributes about 52% to India's GDP growth and there are likelihood that India's overall growth may be affected. Indian companies with big business deals in the US would see their profit margins shrinking.

The Finance Minister of India, commenting on the US recession, said: "India has equally large exports to Europe, to eastern countries like China and Japan. Therefore, I don't think that a slight slowdown in US economy will immediately or drastically affect India's growth prospects.....". meaning thereby that the government is confident that India is hardly going to be effected by this meltdown and if it happens it is not going to effect drastically.

The frequent query at present is whether outsourcing has a favorable impact on vendors. The general market survey by several economists reveal that recession is going to be both good and bad for outsourcing and legal outsourcing businesses, depending on their size, market footprint, industry base and the amount that their clients spend on outsourcing as a share of the total amount spent on that function.

A positive impact on the LPO industry due to recession may be attributable to the following:

- In-house legal departments will realize the opportunity of cost saving through legal outsourcing.

- Increase in Litigation due to recession with the need for cost cut.

- Exploding market awareness of LPO with outsourcing being a desirable option.

- Due emphasis being laid on cost-saving mechanism in the US, which in turn will lead towards increased off-shore work such as secretarial, legal, para-legal and e-coding.

NASSCOM prediction that India will have a shortage of more than 4 million skilled people in information technology and its enabled services.

Hence, there maybe ample opportunities at the door in the off shoring industry at the end of 2008and the whole of 2009. Therefore the need of the hour for the Indian LPO service industry is to fight the battle by broadening its business horizon and surviving unscathed throughout this year's US recession.

Amongst all, outsourcing legal services to India is no longer viewed as a uncertain procedure but more of a business imperative. Thus only high-quality providers, with eminent workforce along with good reputation will emerge as in the arena of an Indian IT and business process outsourcing industry.

Chapter 12   LPO and Advocates Code

Indian Legal Standard

Outsourcing is steadily becoming the backbone of Indian service sectors. In the forecoming years it is going to play a major role in Indian economy. After BPO/KPO/it is time for the legal sector to mark their presence in outsourcing as LPO In the last fiscal India earned $6.8 billion by providing services in software, technology and manufacturing outsourcing. According to a study by the US-based Forester Research, the current annual value of legal outsourcing which is worth $80 million can rise up to $4 bn and can fetch 79,000 jobs in India by 2015.

"The benefit of the outsourcing companies in the US would translate into a cost saving of about 10-12 per cent. The potential of the Indian resources to absorb the increasing demand in legal outsourcing is because India enjoys the economic advantages of the wage difference and less perks and overheads," the report says.

But this Rossy figure has many challenges ahead. The most important challenge to the newly-born sector is the need for Indian lawyers to pass US Bar exams, Overcoming on the cultural difference issues and conflict of interest rules and data security.

Legal outsourcing work is different from core litigation in many ways. It comprises of variety of works, of course related to legal consignments. These work includes patent drafting, legal research, contract review and monitoring. However, experts are hoping to receive high-end sophisticated contracts, which require expertise and a strong legal base of international standards. Moreover, the Indian Advocates Act, which deals with the professional conduct of lawyers, does not support work for other countries. It is in the favour of Indian advocates that, certain branches of law, which are of a global nature, like Intellectual Property laws (patents and trademarks) can give LPOs a filip in their endeavour.

Even, in specific laws governing companies and trade in securities, which hugely differ from one country to another, may limit LPOs to paralegal and secretarial work.

"As per Bar Council Rules, a lawyer cannot take another job while he is on the roll. He would have to get his licence suspended as a pre-condition. Lawyers would not be able to take employment in legal outsourcing outfits without having to give up their right to be called 'lawyers',"

Hence, it will be difficult for LPOs to retain the interest of its employees in such a case.

¶ 12-010 Background

Indian law schools produce more than 200,000 lawyers per year, but to find Indian legal talent, you first need to understand the country's methods for grooming its students.

Individuals pursuing a career in law must gain admission to a five-year course of study at a university (in contrast to four years of college and three years of law school in the United States). Like UK students, Indian students receive a Bachelor of Laws or LL.B (as opposed to an American Juris Doctor or JD). Undergraduates with three years of coursework can also apply to a three-year law school program to obtain the same degree.

Some of the leading institutions include:

- National Law School of India University (NLSIU), Bangalore

- The National University of Juridical Sciences (NUJS), Kolkata

- National Law Institute University (NLIU), Bhopal

- Panjab University- Faculty of Law, Chandigarh

- Campus law Centre ,Delhi University.

- Faculty of Law-Chandigarh University, Chandigarh

¶ 12-020 License to practice

After obtaining Bachelor's degree from the college there's no other law examination required to be passed in order to practice in India, upon graduation, prospective lawyers interested in appearing before a particular court, such as the Supreme Court of India, must take a national exam similar to the bar. Attorneys who pass this test are designated as "Advocates on Record."

Those who choose not to take the exam can simply enroll in the bar association of the state in which they intend to practice. Once the bar council is satisfied with the credentials and references of an applicant, the council accepts them as members. It's technically possible to have multiple state memberships, but it's more common to be enrolled in the bar council of a single locality such as Haryana, Punjab, West Bengal, Karnataka, Maharashtra or Gujarat -- to name a few.

¶ 12-030 Apprenticeship

On-campus interviewing is not common or extensive for law school graduates in India. New advocates will often work as "juniors" for more experienced advocates. The duration of the apprenticeship depends on how comfortable the attorney supervisor is with the skill of the apprentice, as most apprenticeships result in full-time employment. There's no fixed time period for these apprentice positions. Typically, the apprenticeship could last anywhere from a few months to a few years. The duration depends upon the personal relationship between the senior and junior attorney, skill level and performance. Although apprentice positions are designed to provide graduates with experience, they don't offer a substantial income aside from expenses. The remuneration an apprentice earns depends on the type of apprenticeship. In large law firms, juniors can earn between 10,000 and 20,000 rupees (about $220 to $400) in a month. However, for individual apprenticeships, the amount varies from 4,000 to 10,000 rupees and in rare cases expenses such as travel and other case-related costs.

It is often become difficult for juniors lawyers to compete for their own clients to supplement their income, to gain additional experience and eventually to build their own client base. In fact, many juniors take nothing more than expense reimbursements from their senior advocates, in hopes of later resigning the apprenticeship with no obligation at the same time it is also a true fact that most of the junior lawyers in the hope of a brighter career with their seniors are badly exploited and land up with frustration and disappointments with the sour taste of profession and then find it difficult to go ahead with this career options.

These are the various factors, that encourages Indian lawyers to seek alternative career choices, such as document review in an outsourcing operation. In contrast to practicing in Indian courts, which requires long days in often stressful and uncomfortable environments, reviewing discovery for an overseas company provides excellent pay, exposure to cutting-edge technology and a regular schedule (which in India, like in the United States, is attractive to people with a family). It is also a safe option for womens in the legal field. Indian womens are equally competent and efficient. They have already shown their presence in various fields and legal field is not an exception, they find outsourcing a better option rather than practicing in courts they find it beneficial both in terms of their physical safety as well as monetary aspects option of outsourcing is less stressful in comparison to cumbersome process of courts, stressful paperwork and involvement in different briefs on a daily basis.

Under such circumstances it is wise to encourage the practice of outsourcing and deriving the policies to start up more and more legal process outsourcing companies.

¶ 12-040 Barring the Bar

The prevention clause is contained in the Indian Advocates Act of 1961. Under sections 30 and 33 of the Act, the definition of 'practice' is restricted to appearance before any court, tribunal or similar authority – which leaves aside such matters as legal advice, documentation or seeking alternative routes for dispute-resolution. These areas have become chief concerns for Legal Process Outsourcing (LPO) providers in India, but firms are keen for amendments to the Advocates Act that would lead to greater convergence between the activities of Indian lawyers and their Western counterparts.

Concern has arisen in the Indian Bar Council over the intrusion of foreign firms, mainly via Indian 'liaison offices', which the council has opposed on competitive grounds. The council's interest in the debate has swelled with the news that a case over Advocates Act interpretation involving two major Western law firms is due to be heard. The case could determine whether the Act prevents foreign practice in any fashion, or just in the context of Indian law. Taking into the account the public opinion and concerns of the interested parties, the government presented the white paper before Legislature on 24 May 2006. As a result, "The Legal Service Act, 2007" has been passed.

Outsourcing managers must be mindful of the fact that while the attorney-client privilege offers similar protections in India, communications between clients and in-house lawyers are generally not protected. Under the Bar Council of India rules, an advocate cannot be a full-time employee of any person, government, firm, corporation or concern; so in-house counsel are not recognized as advocates. Although most corporate communications are protected under confidentiality agreements, they are not privileged.

Under US law, any communication between the attorney and client is considered privileged in the sense that it can be withheld from the process of discovery in litigation. Confidential communication in matters of business doesn't allow for the same security. In the United States, in-house counsel has the same status as an attorney actively practicing law. However, since in-house counsel isn't considered an advocate in India, any advice the India company receives from its legal department won't be covered under the attorney-client privilege umbrella. That's why it is so critical to explain to the India advocates that legal practices and rules regarding this aspect are very different in the United States.

Legal Services Act, 2007

¶ 12-050 Features of

A single and fully independent Office Legal Complaints (OLC) to remove complaints handling from the legal professions and restore consumer confidence.

Alternative Business Structures (ABS) that will facilitate consumers to obtain services from one business entity that brings together lawyers and non - lawyers, increasing competitiveness and providing efficient services. It also provides External investment and new business structure which are expected to give legal providers a greater flexibility to respond to market demands within the UK and Overseas.

A new Legal Service Board (LSB) to act as a single, independent and publicly accountable regulator with the power to enforce high standards in the legal sector, replacing the maze of regulators with overlapping powers. The chair of the Board will be filled with a responsible person.

A clear set of Regulatory Objectives for the regulation of legal services though which all parts of the system will need to work together to deliver, including promoting and maintaining adherence to professional principles With the advancement of Alternative Business Structures (ABS), major changes will come in the way of legal sector worth £ 20 billion along with other professional services by 21st century. It allows both lawyers and non - lawyers to setup businesses together for the first time ever, and enabling services in development of new and consumer - friendly ways.

The UK legal service market which is already intensely heading into competition, is about to experience further competition from the business world. The law firms need to find new ways to react and adapt to their changing environment.

The provision in Legal Service Act, 2007, permitting non - lawyers to work with lawyers is a boon. The traditional lawyers who are not familiar with new branches of law like patent, product design, cyber laws and space laws etc. can find help by allowing the experts in special branches of law to determine technical issues in accordance with law.

The Legal Service Act, 2007, by permitting the external investment in legal sector can provide a way for small firms to raise capital for expansion purposes, or to find investment in new technology. As a result, numerous outsourcing companies will be able to invest in legal firms in England. Access to legal services will be enhanced for the vast majority of people which indeed lead to a significant shift in the way legal services that are provided, and will certainly have implications for many firms of high street solicitors.

The Legal Service Act, 2007, is also permitting the outsourcing of Legal services which is a boon to Indian Legal Industry. Apart from this, the Law Society of England allows the Indian Advocates to practice in England through Qualified Lawyers Transfer Test (QLTT).

Chapter 13   Legal Process Outsourcing and Security Issues

Security Issues

Information security and data protection has emerged as a major concern for banks, financial institution, outsourcing companies and other businesses that use outsourcing services.

Theft of personal data has been reported from both US-based and India-based call centers and outsourcing companies In one case, one of the alleged criminals has stated that the data he offered for sale was fake. The BCSB report stated that "Customer data is subject to the same level of security as in the UK. High risk and more complex processes are subject to higher levels of scrutiny than similar activities onshore.

India's NASSCOM has said that they take breach in security extremely seriously and will assist the police in their probe.

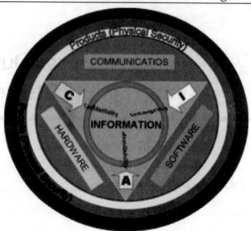

¶ 13-010 Information Security Components

This consist of, confidentiality, Integrity and availability (CIA). Information Systems are located in three main portions, hardware, software and communications with the purpose to identify and apply information security industry standards, as mechanisms of protection and prevention, at three levels or layers: physical, personal and organisational. Essentially, procedures or policies are implemented to tell people (administrators, users and operators) how to use products to ensure information security within the organisations.

Information security means protecting information and information systems from unauthorized access, use, disclosure, disruption, modification, or destruction". The terms information security, computer security and information assurance are frequently used interchangeably. These fields are interrelated and share the common goals of protecting the confidentiality, integrity and availability of information; however, there are some subtle differences between them. These differences lie primarily in the approach to the subject, the methodologies used, and the areas of concentration. Information security is concerned with the confidentiality, integrity and availability of data regardless of the form the data may take: electronic, print, or other forms.

Governments, military, corporates, financial institutions, hospitals, and private businesses amass a great deal of confidential information about their employees, customers, products, research, and financial status. Most of this information is now collected, processed and stored on electronic computers and transmitted across networks to other computers. Should confidential information about a businesses customers or finances or new product line fall into the hands of a competitor, such a breach of security could lead to lost business, law suits or even bankruptcy of the business. Protecting confidential information is a business requirement, and in many cases also an ethical and legal requirement. For the individual, information security has a significant effect on privacy, which is viewed very differently in different cultures.

The field of information security has grown and evolved significantly in recent years. As a career choice there are many ways of gaining entry into the field. It offers many areas for specialization including, Securing network and allied infrastructure, Securing Applications and database(s), Security testing, Information Systems Auditing, Business Continuity Planning and Digital Forensics Science, to name a few.

¶ 13-020 How is it defined?

For over years information security has held that confidentiality, integrity and availability (known as the CIA Triad) are the building principles of information security.

¶13-030 Confidentiality

Confidentiality is defined as preventing disclosure of information to unauthorized individuals or systems. For example, In various financial transactions like credit card transaction on the Internet, it requires the credit card number to be transmitted from the buyer to the merchant and from the merchant to a transaction processing network. The system endeavour's to enforce confidentiality by encrypting the card number during transmission, by limiting the chances and restricting its access to the locations where it might appear (in databases, log files, backups, printed receipts, and so on), If an unauthorized party obtains the card number in any way, a breach of confidentiality has occurred.

Breaches of confidentiality occur in various forms allowing someone to look over your computer screen while you have confidential data displayed on it could be a breach of confidentiality. If a laptop computer containing sensitive information about a company's employees is stolen or sold, it could result in a breach of confidentiality, taking data outside the restricted parameters cause breach of confidentiality. Giving out confidential information over the telephone or sharing it through net is a breach of confidentiality if the caller is not authorized to have the information.

¶ 13-040 Integrity

In information security, integrity denotes that data cannot be modified without authorization. (This is not the same thing as referential integrity in databases.) Integrity is violated when an employee (accidentally or with malicious intent) deletes important data files, when a computer virus infects a computer, when an employee is able to modify his own salary in a payroll database, when an unauthorized user vandalizes a web site, when someone is able to cast a very large number of votes in an online poll, and so on.

¶ 13-050 Availability

An information system will work efficiently only when information is available when it is required to satisfy the need the computer systems used to store and process the information security systems and the communication channels provided to assess it must work efficiently. Powerful systems aim to remain available at all times, preventing service disruptions due to power outages, hardware failures, virus attacks and system upgrades. Ensuring availability also involves preventing DoS attacks (denial-of-service attacks

¶ 13-060 Safety Measures

There are three identifiable types of illicit activities concerning fraud emanating from call centers:

- Crooks who pretend to be legitimate outsourcing service providers.

- Hackers who gain access to outsource companies information through illegal means

- Agents and employees who illegally misuse the information they have access to in call centres.

While items 1 and 2 are mostly subject to police action, call centres can use internal procedures to minimise risk. Such mitigation measures include but are not limited to:

- Creating a paperless environment, preventing employees from writing down and removing information by ensuring that all work processes are done on the computer, without having to record anything on forms or notes.

- Prohibiting paper, pens and digital recording devices from being brought on the working area

- Prohibiting the use of cellphones and cameras on the working area

- Preventing internet access for employees on the working area

- Limiting functionality and access of personal computers or terminals used by call center agents (for example, disabling USB ports).

- Companies may also use data loss prevention software to block attempts to download, copy, or transmit sensitive electronic data.

¶ 13-070 Risk management

The CISA Review Manual 2006 provides the following definition of risk management: Risk management is the process of identifying vulnerabilities and threats to the information resources used by an organization in achieving business objectives, and deciding what countermeasures, if any, to take in reducing risk to an acceptable level, based on the value of the information resource to the organization.

The above given definition require some clarification. First, the *process* of risk management is an continuous iterative process. It must be repeated indefinitely. The business environment is constantly changing and new threats and vulnerabilities emerge every day. Second, the choice of countermeasures (controls) or security check used to manage risks must strike a balance between productivity, cost, and efficiency of the countermeasure, and the value of the informational asset being protected.

Risk is the likelihood that something disastrous will happen that causes harm to an informational asset (or the loss of the asset). A vulnerability is a infirmity that could be used to endanger or cause harm to an informational asset. A threat is anything (man made or act of nature) that has the potential to cause harm.

The likelihood that a threat will use a vulnerability to cause harm creates a risk. When a threat does use a vulnerability to inflict harm, it has an impact. In the context of information security, the impact is a loss of availability, integrity, and confidentiality, and possibly other losses (lost income, loss of life, loss of real property). It should be pointed out that it is not possible to identify all risks, nor is it possible to eliminate all risk. The remaining risk is called *residual risk*.

A risk assessment is carried out by a team of people who have knowledge of specific areas of the business. Membership of the team may vary over time as different parts of the business are assessed. The assessment may use a subjective qualitative analysis based on informed opinion, or where reliable dollar figures and historical information is available, the analysis may use quantitative analysis.

The ISO/IEC 27002:2005 Code of practice for information security management recommends the following be examined during a risk assessment:

- security policy,

- organization of information security,

- asset management, human resources security,

- physical and environmental security,

- communications and operations management,

- access control,

- information systems acquisition,

- development and maintenance,

- information security incident management,

- business continuity management, and

- regulatory compliance.

In broad terms the risk management process consists of:

(i) Identification of assets and estimating their value. Include: people, buildings, hardware, software, data (electronic, print, other), supplies.

(ii) Conduct a threat assessment. Include: Acts of nature, acts of war, accidents, malicious acts originating from inside or outside the organization.

(iii) Conduct a vulnerability assessment, and for each vulnerability, calculate the probability that it will be exploited. Evaluate policies, procedures, standards, training, physical security, quality control, technical security.

(iv) Calculate the impact that each threat would have on each asset. Use qualitative analysis or quantitative analysis.

(v) Identify, select and implement appropriate controls. Provide a proportional response. Consider productivity, cost effectiveness, and value of the asset.

(vi) Evaluate the effectiveness of the control measures. Ensure the controls provide the required cost effective protection without discernible loss of productivity.

For any given risk, Executive Management can choose to accept the risk based upon the relative low value of the asset, the relative low frequency of occurrence, and the relative low impact on the business. Or, leadership may choose to mitigate the risk by selecting and implementing appropriate control measures to reduce the risk. In some cases, the risk can be transferred to another business by buying insurance or out-sourcing to another business. The reality of some risks may be disputed. In such cases leadership may choose to deny the risk. This is itself a potential risk.

Chapter 14   Professional Ethics

What do we mean by Ethics?

It is a system of moral principles. The branch or philosophy dealing with right and wrong and the morality of motives and ends. Various factors which build our ethical curriculum includes everything. Our experiences (or lack of); peers;day to day learning we inherit from our parents, super ego(psychological term), religious beliefs; edicts from a power we deem higher than ourselves, i.e., international law or a Supreme Consciousness; people to whom we are exposed, for better or worse; and our decision to seek out models of ethical behavior are all examples of how we shape our ethical portfolios.

Legal ethics refers to an ethical code governing the conduct of people engaged in the practice of law. In the United States, the American Bar Association has promulgated model rules that have been influential in many jurisdictions. The model rules address the *client-lawyer relationship*, duties of a lawyer as *advocate* in adversary proceedings, dealings *with persons other than clients, law firms and associations, public service, advertising,* and *maintaining the integrity of the profession.* Respect of client confidences, candor toward the tribunal, truthfulness in statements to others, and professional independence are some of the defining features of legal ethics.

As far as the question of Ethics is concerned the law of UK and USA is to be seen and scrutinized because they are major countries outsourcing their work to other countries like India, China, Philippines, and Sri lanka, hence if there is any question of Ethics, that has to be answered in the light of American and UK law.

The ethical challenges facing U.S. attorneys who use legal off shoring is not dissimilar from the challenges he or she would face in the normal practice of law. U.S.-based attorney must have an eye towards the ethical responsibility he or she owes to the client regardless of whether the legal support staff is located down the hall, across town, or in a distant foreign city. regarding the ethical norms the association of the bar of the city of New York committee on professional and judicial ethics discussed some issues in light of American laws.

Say, a New York lawyer ethically outsource legal support services overseas when the person providing those services is (a) a foreign lawyer not admitted to practice in New York or in any other US jurisdiction or (b) a layperson? If so, what ethical considerations must the New York lawyer address?

A New York lawyer may ethically outsource legal support services overseas to a non-lawyer, if the New York lawyer

(a) rigorously supervises the non-lawyer, so as to avoid aiding the non-lawyer in the unauthorized practice of law and to ensure that the non-lawyer's work contributes to the lawyer's competent representation of the client;

(b) duty to avoid aiding a non-lawyer in the unauthorized practice of law:

(c) avoids conflicts of interest when outsourcing;

(d) bills for outsourcing appropriately; and

(e) when necessary, obtains advance client consent to outsourcing.

In 2006 the New York Bar Association opined that foreign lawyers who are not certified to practice law in the United States are legally "non-lawyers."

Under DR 3-101(A), "[A] lawyer shall not aid a non-lawyer in the unauthorized practice of law." In turn, Judiciary Law § 478 makes it "unlawful for any natural person to practice or appear as an attorney-at-law ... without having first been duly and regularly licensed and admitted to practice law in the courts of record of this state and without having taken the constitutional oath." Prohibiting the unauthorized practice of law "aims to protect our citizens against the dangers of legal representation and advice given by persons not trained, examined and licensed for such work, whether they be laymen or lawyers from other jurisdictions." *Spivak v. Sachs*, 16 N.Y.2d 163, 168, 211 N.E.2d 329, 331, 263 N.Y.S.2d 953, 956 (1965).

The supervisory responsibilities of law firms and lawyers in this context are set forth, respectively, in DR 1-104(C) and (D).7 DR 1-104(C) articulates the supervisory responsibility of a law firm for the work of partners, associates, and non-lawyers who work at the firm:

(A) A law firm shall adequately supervise, as appropriate, the work of partners, associates and non-lawyers who work at the firm. The degree of supervision required is that which is reasonable under the circumstances, taking into account factors such as the experience of the person whose work is being supervised, the amount of work involved in a particular matter, and the likelihood that ethical problems might arise in the course of working on the matter.

(B) DR 1-104(D) articulates the supervisory responsibilities of a lawyer for a violation of the Disciplinary Rules by another lawyer and for the conduct of a non-lawyer "employed or retained by or associated with the lawyer":

(C)(a) A lawyer shall be responsible for a violation of the Disciplinary Rules by another lawyer or for conduct of a non-lawyer employed or retained by or associated with the lawyer that would be a violation of the Disciplinary Rules if engaged in by a lawyer if:

(i) The lawyer orders, or directs the specific conduct, or with knowledge of the specific conduct, ratifies it; or

(ii) The lawyer is a partner in the law firm in which the other lawyer practices or the non-lawyer is employed, or has supervisory authority over the other lawyer or the non-lawyer, and knows of such conduct, or in the exercise of reasonable management or supervisory authority should have known of the conduct so that reasonable remedial action could be or could have been taken at a time when its consequences could be or could have been avoided or mitigated.

(b) The duty to preserve the client's confidences and secrets when outsourcing overseas.

DR 4-101 imposes a duty on a lawyer to preserve the confidences and secrets of clients. Under DR 4-101, a "confidence" is "information protected by the attorney-client privilege under applicable law," and a "secret" is "other information gained in the professional relationship that the client has requested be held inviolate or the disclosure of which would be embarrassing or would be likely to be detrimental to the client." DR 4-101(A). DR 4-101(D) requires that a lawyer "exercise reasonable care to prevent his or her employees, associates, and others whose services are utilized by the lawyer from disclosing or using confidences or secrets of a client."

(D) The Duty to Bill Appropriately for Outsourcing Overseas:

By definition, the non-lawyer performing legal support services overseas is not performing legal services. It is thus inappropriate for the New York lawyer to include the cost of outsourcing in his or her legal fees. *See* DR 3-102. Absent a specific agreement with the client to the contrary, the lawyer should charge the client no more than the direct cost associated with outsourcing, plus a reasonable allocation of overhead expenses directly associated with providing that service. ABA Formal Opinion 93-379 (1993).

(E) The Duty to Obtain Advance Client Consent to Outsourcing Overseas:

In the case of contract or temporary lawyers, this Committee has previously opined that "the law firm has an ethical obligation in all cases (i) to make full disclosure in advance to the client of the temporary lawyer's participation in the law firm's rendering of services to the client, and (ii) to obtain the client's consent to that participation." N.Y. City Formal Opinion 1989-2; *see also* N.Y. City Formal Opinion 1988-3 ("The temporary lawyer and the Firm have a duty to disclose the temporary nature of their relationship to the client," citing DR 5-107(A)(1)); EC 2-22 ("Without the consent of the client, a lawyer should not associate in a particular matter another lawyer outside the lawyer's firm); EC 4-2 ("[I]n the absence of consent of the client after full disclosure, a lawyer should not associate another lawyer in the handling of a matter ......"). Similarly, many ethics opinions from other jurisdictions have concluded that clients should be informed in advance of the use of temporary attorneys in all situations.

In 2006 the New York Bar Association opined that foreign lawyers who are not certified to practice law in the United States are legally "non-lawyers." In this regard, Rule 5.3 of the ABA Model Rules requires lawyers have a "direct supervisory authority" over a non-lawyer employed and the lawyer must make reasonable efforts to ensure that the non-lawyer's conduct is "compatible" with the professional obligations of the lawyer. In taking these two opinions together, it would be logical to extrapolate that a U.S. attorney assumes supervisory responsibilities. However, it is still not completely clear how these rules apply to foreign lawyers who have been hired directly, or through a separate business. In the words of Mark Tuft, a legal ethics scholar:

"The difficulty lies in instituting measures that give reasonable assurance that foreign lawyers will conform to the rules of professional conduct applicable to the domestic law firm and that the conduct of foreign non-lawyer assistants will be compatible with the U.S. lawyer's professional obligations."

Foreign lawyers in principle have no legal obligation to American laws. The ethical standards they are bound by may differ from US standards at crucial points; for example, client confidentiality. Furthermore, there is a practical difficulty in providing adequate supervision over an employee working in another country.

The 2006 New York Bar Association Opinion did not state that a U.S. attorney working with foreign lawyers or non-lawyers was responsible to ensure compliance with the Disciplinary Rules of New York, but it did imply obligations of supervision. These include the responsibility for the US lawyer to ensure non-lawyers are competent to perform the tasks, uphold standards of confidentiality, and take reasonable measures to ensure they do not violate New York code.

¶ 14-010 Confidentiality

Confidentiality is a essential element of a client-lawyer relationship. ABA Model Rule 1.6 addresses the issue, and a further comment on the rule explicitly states that a lawyer must act to safeguard unauthorized information from lawyers or other people under the lawyer's supervision that may be working on the case.

¶ 14-020 Disclosure and client consent

ABA Model Rule 7.5(d) "articulates the underlying policy that a client is entitled to know who/what entity is representing the client"

¶ 14-030 Fee sharing

The issue of fee sharing is an important ethical issue to discuss as it gets to the heart of what some think will be the LPO revolution of the legal industry. Many cite the profitable pyramid structure based on billable hours of western law firms as the driving force behind LPO.

The second method of billing is to list offshoring as an expense incurred by the law firm. In this case the bill should represent the actual amount spent on the legal services with no mark up. In this scenario the cost saving is passed onto the client.

The issue of fee sharing is an important ethical issue to discuss as it gets to the heart of what some think will be the LPO revolution of the legal industry. Many cite the profitable pyramid structure based on billable hours of western law firms as the driving force behind.

¶ 14-040 Professional discipline

The concern of discipline is key to insure safeguard if there is a problem with offshoring, but it is still in haze that what ethical standards on the violation of which an outsourced lawyer will be held accountable to. Darya Pollack aptly phrases the issue regarding discipline writing:

"Are outsourced lawyers bound only by:

- the ethical rules of their home bar;

- the ethical rules of each state for which they perform services;

- the ABA Model Rules of Professional Conduct; or

- some combination of the above?"

It is not possible to apply any standard universally using the standards of a lawyer's home bar is not practicable because of the differences in ethical rules between countries regarding important issues. It would be similarly impractical to regulate on a state by state basis within the US, because outsourced lawyers are likely to practice in more than one state. The best option would be to have all outsourced lawyers bound by the ABA Model Rules of Professional Conduct, or something of its equivalent. Even this situation is a hypothetical as the Model Rules are currently only advisory and if they were to become the standard, it would require State Bar Associations to secede some of their power.

Along with the problem of ethical standard, equally important question is of its enforcement. Who would have the right to bring enforcement actions, and where would they be brought? Furthermore, who would they be brought against- who will be having the jurisdiction in case of breach, who will be held liable for compensation, who will indemnify the losses? the U.S. law firm, the LPO firm/business, or the individual lawyer performing outsourced work, Finally, what would be the consequence of an ethical violation, and how would violations be documented to prevent another outsourcing company from hiring the same lawyer?

Summarisation of ABA Ethics Committee Issues Opinion

It is stated by the American bar association that U.S. lawyers are free to outsource legal work, including to lawyers or non lawyers outside the country, if they adhere to ethics rules requiring competence, supervision, protection of confidential information, reasonable fees and not assisting unauthorized practice of law.

Those are the response of the American Bar Association Standing Committee on Ethics and Professional Responsibility queries, which describes outsourcing as a salutary trend in a global economy. Many lawyers do outsource work, using lawyers or non-lawyers as independent contractors, hiring them directly or through intermediaries and on temporary or ongoing bases, says the committee.

Outsourcing can reduce client costs and enable small firms to provide labor intensive services such as large, discovery intense litigation, even though the firms might not maintain sufficient ongoing staff to handle the work, according to a new ethics opinion issued today. Ethics Opinion 08-451 details ethics obligations of lawyers and firms that do elect to outsource legal work.

Outsourcing lawyers are under an obligation to provide quality services to their clients or their counterparts who are analyzing their work in other countries, it is the duty of the lawyers outsourcing their work that they supervise and comply with ethics rules governing lawyers. The committee notes that outsourcing lawyers may face challenges in assuring competence and in overseeing work by others, particularly when separated by thousands of miles and substantial time differences. Indeed, outsourcing lawyers should conduct reference checks and background investigations of lawyer or non lawyer service providers and any intermediaries. They may also wish to interview principal lawyers on a project, assessing their educational background, and evaluate the quality and character of any employees likely to access client information, review security systems, and even visit the premises of the service provider.

If the provider is in a foreign country, the outsourcing lawyer should determine whether the legal education system in that country is similar to that of the U.S., and whether professional regulatory systems incorporate equivalent core ethics principles and effective disciplinary enforcement systems. Some circumstances may require more rigorous supervision than others, according to the committee. The outsourcing lawyer also should determine whether the foreign legal system protects client confidentiality and provides effective remedies to the lawyer's client in case disputes arise.

Chapter 15   Future prospects of LPO Industry in India

LPO's future

NASSCOM had came out with a report on LPO, predicting that once the world wakes up to the possibilities of that industry, it will really take off. It said that paralegal and research support, contract drafting and revising and contract management, library services, patent and trademark prosecution and litigation support are all outsourceable, making the addressable market potential for legal services outsourceable from the US alone around $3-4 billion. It went on to say, though, that only 2-3 per cent of this market had been tapped at the time of the reports release ($60-80 million).

India as we all know is one of the most upcoming economies in the present times. Its growth has been immense in the past 5-7 yrs and it is expected to climb more in the coming days. Prior to the current meltdown, country's stock markets had become a regular feature at times reaching a mark of 20k which shows the impressive growth of the economy. It is well known that dollars poured in and we are doing excellent in various sectors of economy but there are still so many areas where India can mark its presence and add up to the national income in result by , making our economy strong.

One of such growing industry is the LPO or legal process outsourcing or LPOs which is expected to rise to $25 billion by 2015. It is helping in the success of law schools that will be able to absorb as many as 20,000 law graduates which pass out every year and can opt for bright career in this sector. LPO opportunities can make a paradigm shift to the legal industry by drawing law graduates into work that's not just large in volume but diverse and qualitative in nature.

According to Nasscom there are presently just 2000 Indian lawyers who are working in the various LPO's throughout the country. Forrester Research estimates that there could be a demand for as many as 79,000 LPO professionals in the next 7-8 years. Are you aware of that at law firms in Delhi, Bangalore and Mumbai, who serve the legal requirements of several MNCs which are based in the US and Europe, the work of such companies is outsourced.

Legal outsourcing to India had earlier begun at a very low pace and the quality of work was low-end which included transcription. With rising legal costs in the US and in the EU, and the quality work that they were receiving from India as well as other low wages country, are amongst a variety of other factors that are driving the legal work to India. The recent trend is that there is now offshoring work is done at every level of expertise which appeals a number of legal professionals. The major factor is that Indian legal services are reasonably priced and more proficient too. As for competency, Indian lawyers work out cheaper for the foreign firm as to get the same kind of work done in India as compared to a US law firm. Everything done from patent application drafting, data analysis, legal research, document analysis, advising clients, analyzing drafted documents, writing software licensing agreements to drafting distribution agreement is presently being outsourced to India. The kind of work that Indian lawyers do is that they make pleadings ready and provide back-up support for litigation-related research.

Currently, there are around 80 big and small law firms in India which are dedicated to serve their clients in the US, UK and other European countries. Already 150 of the top 200 US law firms outsource atleast some portion of their work. But several leading LPOs including Quislex, Law

Scribe, and Mind Crest have created such business models for high-volume high-value opportunities which they strongly believe are out there for everyone to see. Research, Transaction Support, Case Analysis are good examples of high-value work that's also coming across in large volumes to the LPO's.

¶ 15-010 Career with an LPO

For a young legal professional, a career with an LPO is attractive for several reasons:

- It is a sunrise industry which should see a boom in the next 3-5 years.

- There is a tremendous variety of work at all levels of expertise.

- High-end opportunities for graduates of top law schools with hefty pay packages and future management prospects.

- Gives an opportunity to work in a corporate structure without borders.

- A platform for those who are considering legal and paralegal careers in the UK or the US.

A person who is taking up an LPO as a profession will have to be well versed in English. Currently, 80% of all LPO work emanates from the U.S. So knowing American English, drafting and research methodology are essential. Knowing how to work on MS Office/Adobe software's is also essential. Only a tiny percentage of graduating lawyers are equipped with all the skills needed for the LPO industry. Proper training and imparting education in reference to English and American legal system will help to overcome on this problem to a great extent.

An Educated and Skilled Pool of Lawyers Makes India the Ideal LPO Location on the Globe.

Of course, for an LPO to really be both high-quality and efficient, it needs to be equipped with an educated, legally skilled workforce, capable of sovereign thinking, decision-making and analytical research. India is therefore the ideal location. There are currently over a million lawyers in

India and an average of 75,000 more graduate every year from Indian law schools, many of them prominent. The generally acknowledged list of India's top-ranked law schools is as follows:

- National Law School (NLSIU), Bangalore

- Nalsar University of Law, Hyderabad.

- Faculty of Law, Delhi University

- WB National University of Juridical Sciences (NUJS), Kolkata

- National Law Institute University (NLIU) Bhopal

- Government Law College, Mumbai

- Faculty of Law, BAH

- University College of Law, Bangalore

- Faculty of Law, AMU

- Bangalore Institute of Legal Studies

- Faculty of Law, BHU

- Faculty of Law, University of Madras

- ILS Law College, Pune

- Symbiosis College, Pune

The legal graduates India produces are versed with analytical and research skills and the ability to write and speak in English. One of the important advantage to the Indian legal system is that it is a common-law jurisdiction and the same is rooted in British legal traditions and systems. Indian legal training and Appellate and Supreme Court proceedings are conducted in English; legal opinions are written in English; lawyers in India are trained with similar rigor and methodologies as those in the US

As such, the access to legal talent in India is largely not an issue, at least for those LPOs promising high-end, challenging work. The relatively low cost of living standard in India, together with the fact that the domestic legal profession in India is relatively less remunerative (except at the senior level), also help in making India the hub of outsourced legal services, and in ensuring that LPOs have a steady supply of talented and willing workers.

Both consumers and forward-looking providers of legal services are on the threshold of taking full advantage of all India has to offer in terms of knowledge process outsourcing, as it shifts offshored services from commodity processes to higher skilled knowledge work, such as legal research, preparation of pleadings, docketing, proof-reading, document analysis, agreement drafting, transcription of recorded documents, litigation support, case studies, immigration visa processing and even law firm marketing, etc.

There is a large portion of work that can be done, or in some cases is required to be done by non-lawyers. For instance, there is a tremendous demand for engineers in the intellectual property rights for doing patent work. They are the ones who go through the patent applications. The work involves analyzing scientific and technological inventions for the purposes of crafting legal protection for the same. This work needs to be done by those with technological skills and experience.

¶ 15-020 Preference for destination India?

- Experienced Legal professionals.

- Professionals skilled in use of IT.

- Presence of IT Infrastructure and Government facilitated schemes for ITES sector, better telecommunication initiatives, power and transport facilities.

- Supports regional assignments.

- The advantage of the time zone.

- Availability of English speaking attorneys

- Familiarity with common law doctrines

- Indian attorneys with US/UK qualifications are in plenty

- Labour cost differential- It almost costs up to 80 percent less than the US firms

- The quality and speed of work done

- Most LPO outfits in India are reported to be staffed 24/7

- The Indian legal professionals are taught to analytically interpret the laws

- Regulations of the Land by generously drawing on the similar legislations of other similar legal systems and are exposed to Common English Laws.

¶ 15-030 India: A trustworthy destination

Despite a lot of high end legal work has begun to be outsourced to India, some U.S. entities are cynical about (a) data privacy and preserving confidentiality of the client's information and (b) the quality of work done by non-U.S. Lawyers

Data privacy and confidentiality are areas of supreme concern and importance to the legal outsourcing industry. Presently, India does not have codified data protection laws, but various commercial forums and associations, such as NASSCOM, are working in close association with the government to enact **data protection laws** that are on par with **international** legislation. indisputably, Indian companies realize that they need to scale up their security mechanics in order to cater to these concerns

Moreover, the work which is being done by the Indian lawyers is on a par with the deliverables of U.S. attorneys and legal professionals and in no way inferior to their counterparts in America or England. In fact, associated personnel engaged in legal outsourcing are rigorously trained. Indian legal professionals have to undergo stringent training and orientation programs and are well-versed with the relevant legal stipulations in the U.S. As a result, the quality of the deliverables is not compromised and the move makes sound fiscal and business sense to all the business entities involved.

¶ 15-040 An enthusiastic Workforce can deliver the best possible results

The greatest asset in the Indian workforce is its high level of drive or motivation. Despite notable economic progress in the past years and India's prominence on the global stage, many in this nation are still struggling to make ends meet. The prospect of being employed by an outsourcing venture that pays a regular and above-average wage therefore presents a golden opportunity to scores of Indians, who have a strong work ethic.

According to Mark Kobayashi-Hillary, author of "Outsourcing to India," Indians make for loyal and determined employees. "When a task is going well," Kobayashi-Hillary writes, "I have witnessed people working long hours through the sheer enjoyment of completing a task. When things are bad, I have seen dedicated teams work through the night without a complaint. In my opinion, this spirit of utter dedication to getting the job done does not exist in any other nation."

Ideally Situated Geographical Positioning:

The geographical location of India lends itself extremely well to a 24/7 operation. The time difference between the United States' Pacific Standard Time (PST) is about 12 hours, meaning thereby that a job submitted at 6 p.m. PST reaches India at 6 a.m. and can be completed by 6 am. PST the following day. Depending on the time of year, India is 4.5 to 5.5 hours ahead of the UK and 9.5 to 10.5 hours ahead of New York and Eastern Standard Time (EST). This difference provides similar extended hours, especially crucial on quick turnaround assignments.

Chapter 16   Employees Safety and Outsourcing Industry

Introduction

Maintaining a balance is the real fulfillment in this stressfull life. In the rat race of our present day existence, especially in the culture of long working hours in our industry, we forget to maintain a balance between work and family. The result is disturbing and devastating: high levels of stress, trauma, and even nervous breakdowns. The Government and the corporate sector should visualize at employment laws as different from the labor laws for the business process outsourcing (BPO) industry as well as for other kpo industries. There is a need for a forum to redress the grievances of employees in the BPO/KPO/LPO sector. In a public survey conducted by the IT companies it was opined by most of the participants that the outsourcing industry lacks a regulatory framework from Foreign Direct Investment (FDI) regulations to issues of security, technology transfer and employee welfare.

On the question of employee welfare the IT/outsourcing industries need to reformulate their policy which includes appraisal based promotions, work incentives, entertainment, and other life time benefits these are the various measure to overcome the attrition rate in these outsourcing industries.

¶ 16-010 Inspiring the workforce

In order to overcome the global competition, a technological edge supported by talented manpower has become fundamental for survival in the market, which is why organisations give top priority to technology advancement programmes. HR managers are now performing the role of motivators for their knowledge workers to accept new changes.

Employee Benefits Provided By Majority of the Outsourcing Companies.

A part from the legal and mandatory benefits such as provident-fund and gratuity, below is a list of other benefits... professionals IN BPO/KPO/LPO are entitled to:

1. Medi-claim Insurance Scheme: This insurance scheme is to provide adequate insurance coverage of employees for expenses related to hospitalization due to illness, disease, infirmity caused during employment, or injury or pregnancy in case of female employees or spouse of male employees in addition it is the positive aspect of these schemes that employees dependent family members are eligible to claim. Dependent family members include spouse, non-earning parents and children above three months

2. Accident Insurance Scheme: This scheme is to provide adequate insurance coverage for Hospitalization expenses arising out of injuries sustained in an accident. This covers total/partial disablement/death due to accident and due to accidents.

3. Accommodation facilities: Some of the companies provides accommodation by hiring houses in the city so the employees feels comfortable in case they transferred.

4. Amusement activities, clubs, Cafeteria, ATM, Gym and Concierge facilities: The recreation facilities include Various indoor games. Companies also have well equipped gyms, personal trainers and showers at facilities.

5. Corporate Credit Card: The main purpose of the corporate credit card is enable the timely and efficient payment of official expenses which the employees undertake for purposes such as travel related expenses like Hotel bills, Air tickets etc

6. Routine Health Care Facility (Regular medical check-ups): Some of the IT Companies provides the facility for extensive health check-up. For employees with above 40 years of age, the medical check-up can be done once a year.

7. Low Interest Loans: Many companies provide loan facility on three different occasions: Employees are provided with financial assistance in case of a medical emergency. Employees are also provided with financial assistance at the time of their wedding. And, The new recruits are provided with interest free loans to assist them in their initial settlement at the work location.

8. Educational Benefits: IT IS one of the major obligation on part of any company to enhance the knowledge level of their employees and take keen interest in their personality development because the employee reputation and value is the reputation of the company vis-a-vis. Hence, the companies should take initiative or encourage their employees in pursuing various management degrees from top business schools

9. Performance appraisal: In many outsourcing companies they have plans for, performance based incentive scheme. The parameters for calculation are process performance i.e. speed, accuracy and productivity of each process. The Pay for Performance can be as much as 25% of the salary.

10. Flexi-time: The main objective of the flextime policy is to provide opportunity to employees to work with flexible work schedules and set out conditions for availing this provision. Flexible work schedules are initiated by employees and approved by management to meet business commitments while supporting employee personal life needs. The factors on which Flexi time is allowed to an employee include: Child or Parent care, Health situation, Maternity, Formal education program

11. Flexible Salary Benefits: Its main objective is to provide flexibility to the employees to plan a tax-effective compensation structure by balancing the monthly net income, yearly benefits and income tax payable. It is applicable of all the employees of the organization. The Salary consists of Basic, DA and Conveyance Allowance. The Flexible Benefit Plan consists of: House Rent Allowance, Leave Travel Assistance, Medical Reimbursement, Special Allowance

12. Regular Get together and other cultural programs: The companies organizes cultural program as and when possible but most of the times, once in a quarter, in which all the employees are given an opportunity to display their talents in dramatics, singing, acting, dancing etc. Apart from that the organizations also conduct various sports programs such as Cricket, football, etc and regularly play matches with the teams of other organizations and colleges.

13. Paid Time Off (PTO) and Holidays. Paid time off includes vacation days as well as personal days. PTO eligibility per year depends on employees' length of service.

¶ 16-020 Attrition — A Big Challenge

Fundamental changes are observed in the work force and the workplace that promise to drastically alter the way companies relate to their employees not only Hiring but retaining good employees have become the chief concerns of nearly every company in every industry. Companies that understand what their employees need and expectation in the workplace and effort to proactively fulfill those needs will become the dominant players in their respective markets.

The company should work on establish and maintain an environment that:

- Value individual differences

- strength consistent, mutual respect and open communication of ideas

- Increases competitive advantage by leveraging the knowledge, skills, and unique talents of our employees

- Enhance career opportunities for all employees by working to develop each employee to his or her full potential

- Provide a richer, more fertile climate for creativity and innovation.

- Attracts, develops, motivate, supports, and retains a diverse workforce with the ability to compete in the global market

- Is recognized by employees, clients, and the community as a fair and rewarding place to work.

¶ 16-030 Reward promptly

Rewards should be given as soon as possible after the performance has taken place. This is why the most successful gain-sharing programs pay employees monthly, rather than quarterly or annually as in the past.

There is a well-accepted law of behavioral psychology, proper rewarding of any particular act enhances repetition that act. Hence, employer should recognize the work of their employees and motivate them.

"When a senior manager in one organization was trying to figure out a way to recognize an employee who had just done a great job, he spontaneously picked up a banana (which his wife had packed in his lunch), and handed it to the astonished employee with hearty congratulations. Now, one of the highest honors in that company has been dubbed the "Golden Banana Award"."

¶ 16-040 Creating a benchmark

There are number of ways of honoring the fittest: One of the keys to create a benchmark is symbolism. The more symbolic an item is of the accomplishment, the more likely it is to continue reminding the employee of why it was given. For instance, a T-shirt of coffee mug with a meaningful inscription will continue rewarding those who wear it, or use it, long after its initial receipt rather than reward in the form of cash. Non monetary rewards such as promotions, an encouraging pat on the back in front of other employees is much more motivating than just a cash reward.

Security in Odd Working Hours in Outsourcing Industry

Pratibha Srikanth Murthy, 24, was raped and murdered on her way to work at a Bangalore call center in the early hours of December 13, 2005.this has raised the issue regarding physical security of the outsourcing employees as far as the legal process outsourcing is concerned night shift is an exception is an exception rather then the rule, there is a trend in the outsourcing industry to work 24X7 because of the demand of the nature of work in Business process outsourcing companies. In LPO'S the nature of work is different from other outsourcing , in legal process outsourcing the employees are not required to be connected continuously with the client, hence no t required to work 24X7,resulting no night shift. Therefore employees working in LPO ARE LESS vulnerable to night attacks, loots etc. in comparison to their counterparts in other outsourcing industry.

Chapter 17   Data Protection Laws in India

Overview

Today in the age of information technology one need to know how far his communication are safe and what are the laws which govern these data communication.

In Last few years data protection is one of the heated topic around the world and India was more particularly observed and analyzed by most countries in relation to the laws made by other countries.

Certainly, the EU law plays major role when it comes to data protection laws and has even flustered the USA. According to the guidelines, EU countries will cease to part with data which are considered the subject matter of protection to any third country unless they adhere to similar laws. Though both US and the European Union focus on enhancing privacy protection of their citizens, US takes a different approach to privacy from that of the European Union. US adopted the sectoral approach that relies of mix of legislation, regulation, and self regulation. In US, data are grouped into several classes on the basis of their utility and importance. Thereafter, accordingly a different degree of protection is awarded to the different classes of data.

There are commercial interests involved in implementing the guidelines as envisaged by EU and the US appears to be avoiding a law on the subject and preferring to let it be handled through self regulation. .

A recent study has found that more than 40 countries around the world have enacted, or are preparing to enact, laws that protect the privacy and integrity of personal consumer data.

India is not however one amongst them. Some time back, NASSCOM did take some initiatives to push through a drafting exercise but it appears that the exercise has not been pursued further.

The EU guidelines are an out come of the OECD (is a group of countries who recognized data protection rules) guidelines of 1980 which has listed eight broad principles to be adhered in protecting personal information of the citizens of the country. They are,

1. Collection limitation principle

There should be confines to the collection of personal data and any such data should be obtained by lawful and fair means and, where appropriate, with the knowledge or consent of the data subject.

2. Data quality principle

Personal data should be pertinent to the purposes for which they are to be used, and, to the extent necessary for those purposes, should be precise, absolute and kept up-to-date.

3. Idea specification principle

The purposes for which personal data are collected should be specified not later than at the time of data collection and the subsequent use limited to the fulfilment of those purposes or such others as are not incompatible with those purposes and as are specified on each occasion of change of purpose.

4. Exploit limitation principle

Personal data should not be disclosed, made available or otherwise used except:

(a)   with the consent of the data subject; or

(b)   by the authority of law.

5. safety measures principle

Personal data should be protected by reasonable security safeguards against such risks as loss or unauthorized access, destruction, use, modification or disclosure of data.

6. Openness principle

There should be a general policy of openness about developments, practices and policies with respect to personal data. Means should be readily available of establishing the existence and nature of personal data, and the main purposes of their use, as well as the identity and usual residence of the data controller.

7. Individual participation principle

An individual should have the right:

(a) to obtain from a data controller, or otherwise, confirmation of whether or not the data controller has data relating to him;

(b) to have communicated to him, data relating to him within a reasonable time;

at a charge, if any, that is not excessive;

in a reasonable manner; and

in a form that is readily intelligible to him;

(c) to be given reasons if a request made under subparagraphs (a) and (b) is denied, and to be able to challenge such denial; and

(d) to challenge data relating to him and, if the challenge is successful to have the data erased, rectified, completed or amended.

8. Liability principle

A data controller should be accountable for complying with measures which give effect to the principles stated above.

The United States has approved the OECD Guidelines but appear to be hesitant in its implementation.

Since most of the European countries adopted the principles so the USA is under under an obligation to observe it.

This will create a pressure on India also since one of the essential features of the law would be to prevent the flow of data to non complying countries and such a provision when implemented may result in a loss of "Data Processing" business to some of the Indian companies.

When these laws are framed, the data protection right of an individual may have to be balanced with the requirement of the law enforcement authorities who are Scanning every move that a Native makes on the net.

We are familiar with the level of interest of law enforcement authorities in India to monitor electronic transactions as expressed in the demand of the Mumbai police that every visitor to a Cyber cafe needs to be identified through a photo-ID card and monitored.

As long as India is a country affected by terrorism of the kind we are presently facing, it will be difficult to pass any strict privacy laws in the country. Rather the POTA will ensure that information can be extracted forcibly if the authorities think it is necessary in the interest of the country.

Interception rights are already available in ITA-2000 and will also be retained by authorities in the forthcoming legislation on Communication Convergence.

In this scenario, the Government should have to be careful in enacting data protection laws. If its possible , the laws should be passed without jeopardizing the interests of the law enforcement authorities.

¶ 17-010 The Personal Data Protection Bill, 2006

Upon the footprints of the foreign laws, this bill has been introduced in the Rajya Sabha on December 8th 2006. The purpose of this bill is to provide protection of personal data and information of an individual collected for a particular purpose by one organization, and to prevent its usage by other organization for commercial or other purposes and entitle the individual to claim compensation or damages due to disclosure of personal data or information of any individual without his consent and for matters connected with the Act or incidental to the Act. Provisions contained in this Act are relating to nature of data to be obtained for the specific purpose and the quantum of data to be obtained for that purpose.

Data controllers have been proposed to be appointed to look upon the matters relating to violation of the proposed Act.

¶ 17-020 U.K Law

U.K. parliament framed its Data Protection Act (DPA) in the year 1984 which thereafter repealed by the DPA of 1998. The Act aim to provide protection and privacy of the personal data of the individuals in UK. The Act covers data which can be used to identify a living person. This includes names, birthday, anniversary dates, addresses, telephone numbers, fax numbers, e-mail addresses etc. It applies only to the data which is held or intended to be held, on computers or other equipments operating automatically in response to instructions given for that purpose or held in a relevant filing system.

As per the Act, the persons and organizations which store personal data must register with the information commissioner, which has been appointed as the government official to oversee the Act. The Act put restrictions on collection of data. Personal data can be obtained only for one or more specified and lawful purposes, and shall not be further processed in any manner incompatible with that purpose or purposes. The personal data shall be adequate, relevant, and not excessive in relation to the purpose or purposes for which they are processed.

Laws is not suffice to cover the broad range of issues and circumstances that make the new digital environment a threat to personal privacy. Furthermore, the US Government has been reluctant to impose a regulatory burden on Electronic Commerce activities that could hamper its development and has looked for an answer in self regulation.

Annexure 1   Information Technology Act, 2000

An Act to provide legal recognition for transactions carried out by means of electronic data interchange and other means of electronic communication, commonly referred to as "electronic commerce", which involve the use of alternatives to paper-based methods of communication and storage of information, to facilitate electronic filing of documents with the Government agencies and further to amend the Indian Penal Code, the Indian Evidence Act, 1872, the Bankers' Books Evidence Act, 1891 and the Reserve Bank of India Act, 1934 and for matters connected therewith or incidental thereto.

Whereas the General Assembly of the United Nations by resolution A/RES/51/162, dated the 30th January, 1997 has adopted the Model Law on Electronic Commerce adopted by the United Nations Commission on International Trade Law;and

whereas the said resolution recommends inter alia that all States give favourable consideration to the said Model Law when they enact or revise their laws, in view of the need for uniformity of the law applicable to alternatives to paper-cased methods of communication and storage of information;and

whereas it is considered necessary to give effect to the said resolution and to promote efficient delivery of Government services by means of reliable electronic records.

Word access is defined under section 2(a) in information technology act as:

- "access" with its grammatical variations and cognate expressions means gaining entry into, instructing or communicating with the logical, arithmetical, or memory function resources of a computer, computer system or computer network;

- "computer network" means the interconnection of one or more computers through—

  (i) the use of satellite, microwave, terrestrial line or other communication media; and

  (ii) terminals or a complex consisting of two or more interconnected computers whether or not the interconnection is continuously maintained;

- "computer resource" means computer, computer system, computer network, data, computer data base or software;

- "computer system" means a device or collection of devices, including input and output support devices and excluding calculators which are not programmable and capable of being used in conjunction with external files, which contain computer programmes, electronic instructions, input data and output data, that performs logic, arithmetic, data storage and retrieval, communication control and other functions;

- *Section 2(o) defines Data* "data" means a representation of information, knowledge, facts, concepts or instructions which are being prepared or have been prepared in a formalised manner, and is intended to be processed, is being processed or has been processed in a computer system or computer network, and may be in any form (including computer printouts magnetic or optical storage media, punched cards, punched tapes) or stored internally in the memory of the computer;

- *Section 2(p) defines Digital signature* "digital signature" means authentication of any electronic record by a subscriber by means of an electronic method or procedure in accordance with the provisions of section 3;

- "Digital Signature Certificate" means a Digital Signature Certificate issued under sub-section (4) of section 35;

- Section 2(r) defines "electronic form" with reference to information means any information generated, sent, received or stored in media, magnetic, optical, computer memory, micro film, computer generated micro fiche or similar device;

- "Electronic Gazette" means the Official Gazette published in the electronic form;

- Section 2(t) defines "electronic record" means data, record or data generated, image or sound stored, received or sent in an electronic form or micro film or computer generated micro fiche;

- (u) "function", in relation to a computer, includes logic, control arithmetical process, deletion, storage and retrieval and communication or telecommunication from or within a computer;

- Section 2(v) defines "information" includes data, text, images, sound, voice, codes, computer programmes, software and databases or micro film or computer generated micro fiche:

- (w) "intermediary" with respect to any particular electronic message means any person who on behalf of another person receives, stores or transmits that message or provides any service with respect to that message;

Section 2(ze) defines "secure system" means computer hardware, software, and procedure that—

(a) are reasonably secure from unauthorised access and misuse;

(b) provide a reasonable level of reliability and correct operation;

(c) are reasonably suited to performing the intended functions; and

(d) adhere to generally accepted security procedures;

(zf) "security procedure" means the security procedure prescribed under section 16 by the Central Government;

(zg) "subscriber" means a person in whose name the Digital Signature Certificate is issued;

(zh) "verify" in relation to a digital signature, electronic record or public key, with its grammatical variations and cognate expressions means to determine whether—

(a) the initial electronic record was affixed with the digital signature by the use of private key corresponding to the public key of the subscriber;

(b) the initial electronic record is retained intact or has been altered since such electronic record was so affixed with the digital signature.

3. Authentication of electronic records.

(1) Subject to the provisions of this section any subscriber may authenticate an electronic record by affixing his digital signature.

(2) The authentication of the electronic record shall be effected by the use of asymmetric crypto system and hash function which envelop and transform the initial electronic record into another electronic record.

Explanation.—For the purposes of this sub-section, "hash function" means an algorithm mapping or translation of one sequence of bits into another, generally smaller, set known'as "hash result" such that an electronic record yields the same hash result every time the algorithm is executed with the same electronic record as its input making it computationally infeasible-

(a) to derive or reconstruct the original electronic record from the hash result produced by the algorithm;

(b) that two electronic records can produce the same hash result using the algorithm.

(3) Any person by the use of a public key of the subscriber can verify the electronic record.

(4) The private key and the public key are unique to the subscriber and constitute a functioning key pair.

4. Legal recognition of electronic records.

Where any law provides that information or any other matter shall be in writing or in the typewritten or printed form, then, notwithstanding anything contained in such law, such requirement shall be deemed to have been satisfied if such information or matter is-

(a) rendered or made available in an electronic form; and

(b) accessible so as to be usable for a subsequent reference.

5. Legal recognition of digital signatures.

Where any law provides that information or any other matter shall be authenticated by affixing the signature or any document shall be signed or bear the signature of any person (hen, notwithstanding anything contained in such law, such requirement shall be deemed to have been satisfied, if such information or matter is authenticated by means of digital signature affixed in such manner as may be prescribed by the Central Government.

Explanation.—For the purposes of this section, "signed", with its grammatical variations and cognate expressions, shall, with reference to a person, mean affixing of his hand written signature or any mark on any document and the expression "signature" shall be construed accordingly.

6. Use of electronic records and digital signatures in Government and its agencies.

(1) Where any law provides for—

(a) the filing of any form. application or any other document with any office, authority, body or agency owned or controlled by the appropriate Government in a particular manner;

(b) the issue or grant of any licence, permit, sanction or approval by whatever name called in a particular manner;

(c) the receipt or payment of money in a particular manner,

then, notwithstanding anything contained in any other law for the time being in force, such requirement shall be deemed to have been satisfied if such filing, issue, grant, receipt or payment, as the case may be, is effected by means of such electronic form as may be prescribed by the appropriate Government.

(2) The appropriate Government may, for the purposes of sub-section (1), by rules, prescribe—

(a) the manner and format in which such electronic records shall be filed, created or issued;

(b) the manner or method of payment of any fee or charges for filing, creation or issue any electronic record under clause

7. Retention of electronic records.

(1) Where any law provides that documents, records or information shall be retained for any specific period, then, that requirement shall be deemed to have been satisfied if such documents, records or information are retained in the electronic form, if —

(a) the information contained therein remains accessible so as to be usable for a subsequent reference;

(b) the electronic record is retained in the format in which it was originally generated, sent or received or in a format which can be demonstrated to represent accurately the information originally generated, sent or received;

(c) the details which will facilitate the identification of the origin, destination, date and time of despatch or receipt of such electronic record are available in the electronic record:

Provided that this clause does not apply to any information which is automatically generated solely for the purpose of enabling an electronic record to be despatched or received.

(2) Nothing in this section shall apply to any law that expressly provides for the retention of documents, records or information in the form of electronic records.

8. Publication of rule, regulation, etc., in Electronic Gazette.

Where any law provides that any rule, regulation, order, bye-law, notification or any other matter shall be published in the Official Gazette, then, such requirement shall be deemed to have been satisfied if such rule, regulation, order, bye-law, notification or any other matter is published in the Official Gazette or Electronic Gazette:

Provided that where any rule, regulation, order, bye-law, notification or any other matter is published in the Official Gazette or Electronic

Gazette, the date of publication shall be deemed to be the date of the Gazette which was first published in any form.

9. Sections 6, 7 and 8 not to confer right to insist document should be accepted in electronic form.

Nothing contained in sections 6, 7 and 8 shall confer a right upon any person to insist that any Ministry or Department of the Central Government or the State Government or any authority or body established by or under any law or controlled or funded by the Central or State Government should accept, issue, create, retain and preserve any document in the form of electronic records or effect any monetary transaction in the electronic form.

10. Power to make rules by Central Government in respect of digital signature.

The Central Government may, for the purposes of this Act, by rules, prescribe —

(a) the type of digital signature;

(b) the manner and format in which the digital signature shall be affixed;

(c) the manner or procedure which facilitates identification of the person affixing the digital signature;

(d) control processes and procedures to ensure adequate integrity, security and confidentiality of electronic records or payments; and

(e) any other matter which is necessary to give legal effect to digital signatures.

11.Attribution of electronic records.

An electronic record shall be attributed to the originator —

(a) if it was sent by the originator himself;

(b) by a person who had the authority to act on behalf of the originator in respect of that electronic record; or

(c) by an information system programmed by or on behalf of the originator to operate automatically.

12. Acknowledgment of receipt.

(1) Where the originator has not agreed with the addressee that the acknowledgment of receipt of electronic record be given in a particular form or by a particular method, an acknowledgment may be given by-

(a) any communication by the addressee, automated or otherwise; or

(b) any conduct of the addressee, sufficient to indicate to the originator that the electronic record has been received.

(2) Where the originator has stipulated that the electronic record shall be binding only on receipt of an acknowledgment of such electronic record by him, then unless acknowledgment has been so received, the electronic record shall be deemed to have been never sent by the originator.

(3) Where the originator has not stipulated that the electronic record shall be binding only on receipt of such acknowledgment, and the acknowledgment has not been received by the originator within the time specified or agreed or, if no time has been specified or agreed to within a reasonable time, then the originator may give notice to the addressee stating that no acknowledgment has been received by him and specifying a reasonable time by which the acknowledgment must be received by him and if no acknowledgment is received within the aforesaid time limit he may after giving notice to the addressee, treat the electronic record as though it has never been sent.

13. Time and place of despatch and receipt of electronic record.

(1) Save as otherwise agreed to between the originator and the addressee, the dispatch of an electronic record occurs when it enters a computer resource outside the control of the originator.

(2) Save as otherwise agreed between the originator and the addressee, the time of receipt of an electronic record shall be determined as follows, namely:—

(a) if the addressee has designated a computer resource for the purpose of receiving electronic records,-

    (i)   receipt occurs at the time when the electronic, record enters the designated computer resource; or

    (ii)   if the electronic record is sent to a computer resource of the addressee that is not the designated computer resource, receipt occurs at the time when the electronic record is retrieved by the addressee;

(b) if the addressee has not designated a computer resource along with specified timings, if any, receipt occurs when the electronic record enters the computer resource of the addressee.

(3) Save as otherwise agreed to between the originator and the addressee, an electronic record is deemed to be dispatched at the place where the originator has his place of business, and is deemed to be received at the place where the addressee has his place of business.

(4) The provisions of sub-section (2) shall apply notwithstanding that the place where the computer resource is located may be different from the place where the electronic record is deemed to have been received under sub-section (3).

(5) For the purposes of this section, —

(a) if the originator or the addressee has more than one place of business, the principal place of business, shall be the place of business;

(b) if the originator or the addressee does not have a place of business, his usual place of residence shall be deemed to be the place of business;

(c) "usual place of residence", in relation to a body corporate, means the place where it is registered.

43. Penalty for damage to computer, computer system, etc.

If any person without permission of the owner or any other person who is incharge of a computer, computer system or computer network,-

(a) accesses or secures access to such computer, computer system or computer network;

(b) downloads, copies or extracts any data, computer data base or information from such computer, computer system or computer network including information or data held or stored in any removable storage medium;

(c) introduces or causes to be introduced any computer contaminant or computer virus into any computer, computer system or computer network;

(d) damages or causes to be damaged any computer, computer system or computer network, data, computer data base or any other programmes residing in such computer, computer system or computer network;

(e) disrupts or causes disruption of any computer, computer system or computer network;

(f) denies or causes the denial of access to any person authorised to access any computer, computer system or computer network by any means;

(g) provides any assistance to any person to facilitate access to a computer, computer system or computer network in contravention of the provisions of this Act, rules or regulations made thereunder;

(h) charges the services availed of by a person to the account of another person by tampering with or manipulating any computer, computer system, or computer network,

he shall be liable to pay damages by way of compensation not exceeding one crore rupees to the person so affected.

Explanation. – For the purposes of this section, –

(i) "computer contaminant" means any set of computer instructions that are designed –

(a) to modify, destroy, record, transmit data or programme residing within a computer, computer system or computer network; or

(b) by any means to usurp the normal operation of the computer, computer system, or computer network;

(ii) "computer data base" means a representation of information, knowledge, facts, concepts or instructions in text, image, audio, video that are being prepared or have been prepared in a formalised manner or have been produced by a computer, computer system or computer network and are intended for use in a computer, computer system or computer network;

(iii) "computer virus" means any computer instruction, information, data or programme that destroys, damages, degrades or adversely affects the performance of a computer resource or attaches itself to another computer resource and operates when a programme, daia or instruction is executed or some other event takes place in that computer resource;

(iv) "damage" means to destroy, alter, delete, add, modify or rearrange any computer resource by any means.

44. Penalty for failure to furnish information return, etc.

If any person who is required under this Act or any rules or regulations made thereunder to—

(a) furnish any document, return or report to the Controller or ?he Certifying Authority fails to furnish the same, he shall be liable to a penalty not exceeding one lakh and fifty thousand rupees for each such failure;

(b) file any return or furnish any information, books or other documents within the time specified therefor in the regulations fails to file return or furnish the same within the time specified therefor in the regulations, he shall be liable to a penalty not exceeding five thousand rupees for every day during which such failure continues;

(c) maintain books of account or records, fails to maintain the same, he shall be liable to a penalty not exceeding ten thousand rupees for every day during which the failure continues.

45. Residuary penalty

Whoever contravenes any rules or regulations made under this Act, for the contravention of which no penalty has been separately provided, shall be liable to pay a compensation not exceeding twenty-five thousand rupees to the person affected by such contravention or a penalty not exceeding twenty-five thousand rupees.

46. Power to adjudicate.

(1) For the purpose of adjudging under this Chapter whether any person has committed a contravention of any of the provisions of this Act or of any rule, regulation, direction or order made thereunder the Central Government shall, subject to the provisions of sub-section (3), appoint any officer not below the rank of a Director to the Government of India or an equivalent officer of a State Government to be an adjudicating officer'for holding an inquiry in the manner prescribed by the Central Government.

(2) The adjudicating officer shall, after giving the person referred to in sub-section (1) a reasonable opportunity for making representation in the matter and if, on such inquiry, he is satisfied that the person has committed the contravention, he may impose such penalty or award such compensation as he thinks fit in accordance with the provisions of that section.

(3) No person shall be appointed as an adjudicating officer unless he possesses such experience in the field of Information Technology and legal or judicial experience as may be prescribed by the Central Government.

(4) Where more than one adjudicating officers are appointed, the Central Government shall specify by order the matters and places with respect to which such officers shall exercise their jurisdiction.

(5) Every adjudicating officer shall have the powers of a civil court which are conferred oh the Cyber Appellate Tribunal under sub-section (2) of section 58, and —

(a) all proceedings before it shall be deemed to be judicial proceedings within the meaning of sections 193 and 228 of the Indian Penal Code;

(b) shall be deemed to be a civil court for the purposes of sections 345 and 346 of the Code of Criminal Procedure, 1973.

47. Factors to be taken into account by the adjudicating officer.

While adjudging the quantum of compensation under this Chapter, the adjudicating officer shall have due regard to the following factors, namely: —

(a) the amount of gain of unfair advantage, wherever quantifiable, made as a result of the default;

(b) the amount of loss caused to any person as a result of the default;

(c) the repetitive nature of the default

48. Establishment of Cyber Appellate Tribunal.

(1) The Central Government shall, by notification, establish one or more appellate tribunals to be known as the Cyber Regulations Appellate Tribunal.

(2) The Central Government shall also specify, in the notification referred to in sub-section (1), the matters and places in relation to which the Cyber Appellate Tribunal may exercise jurisdiction.

49. Composition of Cyber Appellate Tribunal.

A Cyber Appellate Tribunal shall consist of one person only (hereinafter referred to as the Residing Officer of the Cyber Appellate Tribunal) to be appointed, by notification, by the Central Government

50. Qualifications for appointment as Presiding Officer of the Cyber Appellate Tribunal.

A person shall not be qualified for appointment as the Presiding Officer of a Cyber Appellate Tribunal unless he-

(a) is, or has been or is qualified to be, a Judge of a High Court; or

(b) is or has been a member of the Indian Legal Service and is holding or has held a post in Grade I of that Service for at least three years.

51. Term of office

The Presiding Officer of a Cyber Appellate Tribunal shall hold office for a term of five years from the date on which he enters upon his office or until he attains the age of sixty-five years, whichever is earlier.

52. Salary, allowances and other terms and conditions of service of Presiding Officer.

The salary and allowances payable to, and the other terms and conditions of service including pension, gratuity and other retirement benefits of. the Presiding Officer of a Cyber Appellate Tribunal shall be such as may be prescribed:

Provided that neither the salary and allowances nor the other terms and conditions of service of the Presiding Officer shall be varied to his disadvantage after appointment.

53. Filling up of vacancies.

If, for reason other than temporary absence, any vacancy occurs in the office n the Presiding Officer of a Cyber Appellate Tribunal, then the Central Government shall appoint another person in accordance with the provisions of this Act to fill the vacancy and the proceedings may be continued before the Cyber Appellate Tribunal from the stage at which the vacancy is filled.

54. Resignation and removal.

(1) The Presiding Officer of a Cyber Appellate Tribunal may, by notice in writing under his hand addressed to the Central Government, resign his office:

Provided that the said Presiding Officer shall, unless he is permitted by the Central Government to relinquish his office sooner, continue to hold office until the expiry of three months from the date of receipt of such notice or until a person duly appointed as his successor enters upon his office or until the expiry of his term of office, whichever is the earliest.

(2) The Presiding Officer of a Cyber Appellate Tribunal shall not be removed from his office except by an order by the Central Government on the ground of proved misbehaviour or incapacity after an inquiry made by a Judge of the Supreme Court in which the Presiding Officer concerned has been informed of the charges against him and given a reasonable opportunity of being heard in respect of these charges.

(3) The Central Government may, by rules, regulate the procedure for the investigation of misbehaviour or incapacity of the aforesaid Presiding Officer.

55. Orders constituting Appellate Tribunal to be final and not to invalidate its proceedings.

No order of the Central Government appointing any person as the Presiding Officer of a Cyber Appellate Tribunal shall be called in question in any manner and no act or proceeding before a Cyber Appellate Tribunal shall be called in question in any manner on the ground merely of any defect in the constitution of a Cyber Appellate Tribunal.

56. Staff of the Cyber Appellate Tribunal.

(1) The Central Government shall provide the Cyber Appellate Tribunal with such officers and employees as that Government may think fit.

(2) The officers and employees of the Cyber Appellate Tribunal shall discharge their functions under general superintendence of the Presiding Officer.

(3) The salaries, allowances and other conditions of service of the officers and employees or' the Cyber Appellate Tribunal shall be such as may be prescribed by the Central Government.

57. Appeal to Cyber Appellate Tribunal.

(1) Save as provided in sub-section (2), any person aggrieved by an order made by Controller or an adjudicating officer under this Act may prefer an appeal to a Cyber Appellate Tribunal having jurisdiction in the matter.

(2) No appeal shall lie to the Cyber Appellate Tribunal from an order made by an adjudicating officer with the consent of the parties.

(3) Every appeal under sub-section (1) shall be filed within a period of tony-five days from the date on which a copy of the order made by the Controller or the adjudicating officer is received by the person aggrieved and it shall be in such form and be accompanied by such fee as may be prescribed:

Provided that the Cyber Appellate Tribunal may entertain an appeal after the expiry of the said period of tony-five days if it is satisfied that there was sufficient cause to not filing it within that period.

(4) On receipt of an appeal under sub-section (1), the Cyber Appellate Tribunal may, after giving the parties to the appeal, an opportunity of being heard, pass such orders thereon as it thinks fit, confirming, modifying or setting aside the order appealed against.

(5) The Cyber Appellate Tribunal shall send a copy of every order made by it to" the parties to the appeal and to the concerned Controller or adjudicating officer.

(6) The appeal filed before the Cyber Appellate Tribunal under sub-section (1) shall be dealt with by it as expeditiously as possible and endeavour shall be made by it to dispose of the appeal finally within six months from the date of receipt of the appeal.

58. Procedure and powers of the Cyber Appellate Tribunal.

(1) The Cyber Appellate Tribunal shall not be bound by the procedure laid down by the Code of civil Procedure, 1908 but shall be guided by the principles of natural justice and, subject to the other provisions of this Act and of any rules, the Cyber Appellate Tribunal shall have powers to regulate its own procedure including the place at which it shall have its sittings.

(2) The Cyber Appellate Tribunal shall have, for the purposes of discharging its functions under this Act, the same powers as are vested in a civil court under the Code of Civil Procedure, 1908, while trying a suit, in respect of the following matters, namely:-

(a) summoning and enforcing the attendance of any person and examining him on oath;

(b) requiring the discovery and production of documents or other electronic records;

(c) receiving evidence on affidavits;

(d) issuing commissions for the examination of witnesses or documents;

(e) reviewing its decisions;

(f) dismissing an application for default or deciding it ex pane;

(g) any other matter which may be prescribed.

(3) Every proceeding before the Cyber Appellate Tribunal shall be deemed to be a judicial proceeding within the meaning of sections 193 and 228, and for the purposes of section 196 of the Indian Penal Code and the Cyber Appellate Tribunal shall be deemed to be a civil court for the purposes of section 195 and Chapter XXVI of the Code of Criminal Procedure, 1973.

59. Right to legal representation.

The appellant may either appear in person or authorise one or more legal practitioners or any of its officers to present his or its case before the Cyber Appellate Tribunal.

60. Limitation.

The provisions of the Limitation Act, 1963, shall, as far as may be, *apply* to an appeal made to the Cyber Appellate Tribunal.

61. Civil court not to have jurisdiction.

No court shall have jurisdiction to entertain any suit or proceeding in respect of any matter which an adjudicating officer appointed under this

Act or the Cyber Appellate Tribunal constituted under this Act is empowered by or under this Act to determine and no injunction shall be granted by any court or other authority in respect of any action taken or to be taken in pursuance of any power conferred by or under this Act.

62. Appeal to High Court.

Any person aggrieved by any decision or order of the Cyber Appellate Tribunal may file an appeal to the High Court within sixty days from the date of communication of the decision or order of the Cyber Appellate Tribunal to him on any question of fact or law arising out of such order

Provided that the High Court may, if it is satisfied that the appellant was prevented by sufficient cause from filing the appeal within the said period, allow it to be filed within a further period not exceeding sixty days.

63. Compounding of contraventions.

(1) Any contravention under this Chapter may, either before or after the institution of adjudication proceedings, be compounded by the Controller or such other officer as may be specially authorised by him in this behalf or by the adjudicating officer, as the case may be, subject to such conditions as the Controller or such other officer or the adjudicating officer may specify:

Provided that such sum shall not, in any case, exceed the maximum amount of the penalty which may be imposed under this Act for the contravention so compounded.

(2) Nothing in sub-section (1) shall apply to a person who commits the same or similar contravention within a period of three years from the date on which the first contravention, committed by him, was compounded.

Explanation. – For the purposes of this sub-section, any second or subsequent contravention committed after the expiry of a period of three years from the date on which the contravention was previously compounded shall be deemed to be a first contravention.

(3) Where any contravention has been compounded under sub-section (1), no proceeding or further proceeding, as the case may be, shall be taken against the person guilty of such contravention in respect of the contravention so compounded.

64. Recovery of penalty

A penalty imposed under this Act, if it is not paid, shall be recovered as an arrear of land revenue and the licence or the Digital Signature Certificate, as the case may be, shall be suspended till the penalty is paid.

65. Tampering with computer source documents.

Whoever knowingly or intentionally conceals, destroys or alters or intentionally or knowingly causes another to conceal, destroy or alter any computer source code used for a computer, computer programme, computer system or computer network, when the computer source code is required to be kept or maintained by law for the time being in force, shall be punishable with imprisonment up to three years, or with fine which may extend up to two lakh rupees, or with both.

Explanation. – For the purposes of this section, "computer source code" means the listing of programmes, computer commands, design and layout and programme analysis of computer resource in any form.

66. Hacking with computer system.

(1) Whoever with the intent to cause or knowing that he is likely to cause wrongful loss or damage to the public or any person destroys or deletes or alters any information residing in a computer resource or diminishes its value or utility or affects it injuriously by any means, commits hack:

(2) Whoever commits hacking shall be punished with imprisonment up to three years, or with fine which may extend upto two lakh rupees, or with both.

67. Publishing of information which is obscene in electronic form.

Whoever publishes or transmits or causes to be published in the electronic form, any material which is lascivious or appeals to the prurient interest or if its effect is such as to tend to deprave and corrupt persons who are likely, having regard to all relevant circumstances, to read, see or hear the matter contained or embodied in it, shall be punished on first conviction with imprisonment of either description for a term which may extend to five years and with fine which may extend to one lakh rupees and in the event of a second or subsequent conviction with imprisonment of either description for a term which may extend to ten years and also with fine which may extend to two lakh rupees.

68. Power of Controller to give directions.

(1) The Controller may, by order, direct a Certifying Authority or any employee of such Authority to take such measures or cease carrying on such activities as specified in the order if those are necessary to ensure compliance with the provisions of this Act, rules or any regulations made thereunder.

(2) Any person who fails to comply with any order under sub-section (1) shall be guilty of an offence and shall be liable on conviction to imprisonment for a term not exceeding three years or to a Fine not exceeding two lakh rupees or to both.

69. Directions of Controller to a subscriber to extend facilities to decrypt information.

(1) If the Controller is satisfied that it is necessary or expedient so to do in the interest of the sovereignty or integrity of India, the security of the State, friendly relations with foreign Stales or public order or for preventing incitement to the commission of any cognizable offence, for reasons to be recorded in writing, by order, direct any agency of the Government to intercept any information transmitted through any computer resource.

(2) The subscriber or any person in-charge of the computer resource shall, when called upon by any agency which has been directed under sub-section (1), extend all facilities and technical assistance to decrypt the information.

(3) The subscriber or any person who fails to assist the agency referred to in sub-section (2) shall be punished with an imprisonment for a term which may extend to seven years.

70. Protected system.

(1) The appropriate Government may, by notification in the Official Gazette, declare that any computer, computer system or computer network to be a protected system.

(2) The appropriate Government may, by order in writing, authorise the persons who are authorised to access protected systems notified under sub-section (1).

(3) Any person who secures access or attempts to secure access to a protected system in contravention of the provisions of this section shall be punished with imprisonment of either description for a term which may extend to ten years and shall also be liable to fine.

71. Penalty for misrepresentation.

Whoever makes any misrepresentation to, or suppresses any material fact from, the Controller or the Certifying Authority for obtaining any licence or Digital Signature Certificate, as the case may be. shall be punished with imprisonment for a term which may extend to two years, or with fine which may extend to one lakh rupees, or with both.

72. Penalty for breach of confidentiality and privacy.

Save as otherwise provided in this Act or any other law for the time being in force, any person who, in pursuance of any of the powers conferred under this Act, rules or regulations made thereunder, has secured access to any electronic record, book, register, correspondence, information, document or other material without the consent of the person concerned discloses such electronic record, book. register, correspondence, information, document or other material to any other person shall be punished with imprisonment for a term which may extend to two years, or with fine which may extend to one lakh rupees, or with both.

73. Penalty for publishing Digital Signature Certificate false in certain particulars.

(1) No person shall publish a Digital Signature Certificate or otherwise make it available to any other person with the knowledge that-

(a) the Certifying Authority listed in the certificate has not issued it; or

(b) the subscriber listed in the certificate has not accepted it; or

(c) the certificate has been revoked or suspended,

unless such publication is for the purpose of verifying a digital signature created prior to such suspension or revocation.

(2) Any person who contravenes the provisions of sub-section (1) shall be punished with imprisonment for a term which may extend to two years, or with fine which may extend to one lakh rupees, or with both.

74. Publication for fraudulent purpose.

Whoever knowingly creates, publishes or otherwise makes available a Digital Signature Certificate for any fraudulent or unlawful purpose shall be punished with imprisonment for a term which may extend to two years, or with fine which may extend to one lakh rupees, or with both.

75. Act to apply for offence or contravention commited outside India.

(1) Subject to the provisions of sub-section (2), the provisions of this Act shall apply also to any offence or contravention committed outside India by any person irrespective of his nationality.

(2) For the purposes of sub-section (1), this Act shall apply to an offence or contravention committed outside India by any person if the act or conduct constituting the offence or contravention involves a computer, computer system or computer network located in India.

76. Confiscation.

Any computer, computer system, floppies, compact disks, tape drives or any other accessories related thereto, in respect of which any provision of this Act. rules, orders or regulations made thereunder has been or is being contravened, shall be liable to confiscation:

Provided that where it is established to the satisfaction of the court adjudicating the confiscation that the person in whose possession, power or control of any such computer, computer system, floppies, compact disks, tape drives or any other accessories relating thereto is found is not responsible for the contravention of the provisions of this Act, rules, orders or regulations made thereunder, the court may, instead of making an order for confiscation of such computer, computer system, floppies, compact disks, tape drives or any other accessories related thereto, make such other order authorised by this Act against the person contravening of the provisions of this Act, rules, orders or regulations made thereunder as it may think fit.

77. Penalties or confiscation not to interfere with other punishments.

No penalty imposed or confiscation made under this Act shall prevent the imposition of any other punishment to which the person affected thereby is liable under any other law for the time being in force.

78. Power to investigate offences.

Notwithstanding anything contained in the Code of Criminal Procedure, 1973, a police officer not below the rank of Deputy Superintendent of Police shall investigate any offence under this Act.

VARIOUS SECTION OF IPC REFERRED IN CHAPTERS

383. Extortion IPC

Whoever intentionally puts any person in fear of any injury to that person, or to any other, and thereby dishonestly induces the person so put in fear to deliver to any property or valuable security, or anything signed or sealed which may be converted into a valuable security, commits "extortion".

420. Cheating and dishonestly inducing delivery of property

Whoever cheats and thereby dishonestly induces the person deceived any property to any person, or to make, alter or destroy the whole or any part of a valuable security, or anything which is signed or sealed, and which is capable of being converted into a valuable security, shall be punished with imprisonment of either description for a term which may extend to seven years, and shall also be liable to fine.

463. Forgery.

Whoever makes any false documents or electronic record part of a document or electronic record with, intent to cause damage or injury, to the public or to any person, or to support any claim or title, or to cause any person to part with property, or to enter into any express or implied contract, or with intent to commit fraud or that fraud may be committed, commits forgery.

470. Forged document or electronic record.

A false document or Electronic Record made wholly or in part by forgery is designated "a forged document or electronic record".

471. Using as genuine a forged document or electronic record

Whoever fraudulently or dishonestly uses as genuine any document or electronic record which he knows or has reason to believe to be a forged document or electronic record, shall be punished in the same manner as if he had forged such document or electronic record.

499. Defamation

Whoever, by words either spoken or intended to be read, or by signs or by visible representations, makes or publishes any imputation concerning any person intending to harm, or knowing or having reason to believe that such imputation will harm, the reputation of such person, is said, except in the cases hereinafter expected, of defame that person.

Explanation 1: It may amount to defamation to impute anything to a deceased person, if the imputation would harm the reputation of that person if living, and is intended to be hurtful to the feelings of his family or other near relatives.

Explanation 2: It may amount to defamation to make an imputation concerning a company or an association or collection of persons as such.

Explanation 3: An imputation in the form of an alternative or expressed ironically, may amount to defamation.

Explanation 4: No imputation is said to harm a person's reputation, unless that imputation directly or indirectly, in the estimation of others, lowers the moral or intellectual character of that person, or lowers the character of that person in respect of his caste or of his calling, or lowers the credit of that person, or causes it to be believed that the body of that person is in a loathsome state, or in a state generally considered as disgraceful.

500. Punishment for defamation

Whoever defames another shall be punished with simple imprisonment for a term which may extend to two years, or with fine, or with both.

503. Criminal intimidation

Whoever threatens another with any injury to his person, reputation or property, or to the person or reputation of any one in whom that person is interested, with intent to cause alarm to that person, or to cause that person to do any act which he is not legally bound to do, or to omit to do any act which that person is legally entitled to do, as the means of avoiding the execution of such threat, commits criminal intimidation.

Explanation: A threat to inure the reputation of any deceased person in whom the person threatened is interested, is within this section.

THE FIRST SCHEDULE

(See section 91)

Amendments to the Indian penal code

(45 of 1860)

1. After section 29, the following section shall be inserted, namely: —

Electronic record.

"29A. The words "electronic record" shall have the meaning assigned to them in clause *(t)* of sub-section (1) of section 2 of the Information Technology Act, 2000.".

2. In section 167, for the words "such public servant, charged with the preparation or translation of any document, frames or translates that document", the words "such public servant, charged with the preparation or translation of any document or electronic record, frames, prepares or translates that document or electronic record" shall be substituted.

3. In section 172, for the words "produce a document in a Court of Justice", the words "produce a document or an electronic record in a Court of Justice" shall be substituted.

4. In section 173, for the words "to produce a document in a Court of Justice", the words "to produce a document or electronic record in a Court of Justice" shall be substituted.

5. In section 175, for the word "document" at both the places where it occurs, the words "document or electronic record" shall be substituted.

6. In section 192, for the words "makes any false entry in any book or record, or makes any document containing a false statement", the words "makes any false entry in any book or record, or electronic record or

makes any document or electronic record containing a false statement" shall be substituted.

7. In section 204, for the word "document" at both the places where it occurs, the words "document or electronic record" shall be substituted.

8. In section 463, for the words "Whoever makes any false documents or part of a document with intent to cause damage or injury", the words "Whoever makes any false documents or false electronic record or part of a document or electronic record, with intent to cause damage or injury" shall be substituted.

9. In section 464, —

(a) for the portion beginning with the words "A person is said to make a false document" and ending with the words "by reason of deception practised upon him, he does not know the contents of the document or the nature of the alteration", the following shall be substituted, namely: —

"A person is said to make a false document or false electronic record —

First" Who dishonestly or fraudulently"

(a) makes, signs, seals or executes a document or part of a document;

(b) makes or transmits any electronic record or part of any electronic record;

(c) affixes any digital signature on any electronic record;

(d) makes any mark denoting the execution of a document or the authenticity of the digital signature,

with the intention of causing it to be believed that such document or part of document, electronic record or digital signature was made, signed, sealed, executed, transmitted or affixed by or by the authority of a person by whom or by whose authority he knows that it was not made, signed, sealed, executed or affixed; or

Secondly - Who, without lawful authority, dishonestly or fraudulently, by cancellation or otherwise, alters a document or an electronic record in any material part thereof, after it has been made, executed or affixed with digital signature either by himself or by any other person, whether such person be living or dead at the time of such alteration; or

Thirdly - Who dishonestly or fraudulently causes any person to sign, seal, execute or alter a document or an electronic record or to affix his digital signature on any electronic record knowing that such person by reason of unsoundness of mind or intoxication cannot, or that by reason of deception practised upon him, he does not know the contents of the document or electronic record or the nature of the alteration. " ;

(b) after *Explanation* 2, the following *Explanation* shall be inserted at the end, namely: —

'*Explanation* 3. — For the purposes of this section, the expression "affixing digital signature" shall have the meaning assigned to it in clause (d) of subsection (1) of section 2 of the Information Technology Act, 2000.'.

10. In section 466, —

(a) for the words "Whoever forges a document", the words "Whoever forges a document or an electronic record" shall be substituted;

(b) the following *Explanation* shall be inserted at the end, namely:-

'*Explanation*. — For the purposes of this section, "register" includes any list, data or record of any entries maintained in the electronic form as defined in clause *(r)* of sub-section (1) of section 2 of the Information Technology Act, 2000.'.

11. In section 468, for the words "document forged", the words "document or electronic record forged" shall be substituted.

12. In section 469, for the words "intending that the document forged", the words "intending that the document or electronic record forged" shall be substituted.

13. In section 470, for the word "document" in both the places where it occurs, the words "document or electronic record" shall be substituted.

14. In section 471, for the word "document" wherever it occurs, the words "document or electronic record" shall be substituted.

15. In section 474, for the portion beginning with the words "Whoever has in his possession any document" and ending with the words "if the document is one of the description mentioned in section 466 of this Code", the following shall be substituted, namely:—

"Whoever has in his possession any document or electronic record, knowing the same to be forged and intending that the same shall fraudulently or dishonestly be used as a genuine, shall, if the document or electronic record is one of the description mentioned in section 466 of this Code.".

16. In section 476, for the words "any document", the words "any document or electronic record" shall be substituted.

17. In section 477A, for the words "book, paper, writing" at both the places where they occur, the words "book, electronic record, paper, writing" shall be substituted.

Annexure 3   Various Amendments in Indian Evidence Act, 1872

THE SECOND SCHEDULE

(*See* section 92)

(1 of 1872)

1. In section 3, —

(a) in the definition of "Evidence", for the words "all documents produced for the inspection of the Court", the words "all documents including electronic records produced for the inspection of the Court" shall be substituted;

(b) after the definition of "India", the following shall be inserted, namely:— 'the expressions "Certifying Authority", "digital signature", "Digital Signature Certificate", "electronic form", "electronic records", "information", "secure electronic record", "secure digital signature" and "subscriber" shall have the meanings respectively assigned to them in the Information Technology Act, 2000.'.

2. In section 17, for the words "oral or documentary,", the words "oral or documentary or contained in electronic form" shall be substituted.

3. After section 22, the following section shall be inserted, namely:—

"22A. **When oral admission as to contents of electronic records are relevant**. — Oral admissions as to the contents of electronic records are not relevant, unless the genuineness of the electronic record produced is in question.".

4. In section 34, for the words "Entries in the books of account", the words "Entries in the books of account, including those maintained in an electronic form" shall be substituted.

5. In section 35, for the word "record", in both the places where it occurs, the words "record or an electronic record" shall be substituted.

6. For section 39, the following section shall be substituted, namely:-

"39. What evidence to be given when statement forms part of a conversation, document, electronic record, book or series of letters or papers. — When any statement of which evidence is given forms part of a longer statement, or of a conversation or pan of an isolated document, or is contained in a document which forms part of a book, or is contained in part of electronic record or of a connected series of letters or papers, evidence shall be given of so much and no more of the statement, conversation, document, electronic record, book or series of letters or papers as the Court considers necessary in that particular case to the full understanding of the nature and effect of the statement, and of the circumstances under which it was made.".

7. After section 47, the following section shall be inserted, namely: —

"47A. Opinion as to digital signature where relevant. — When the Court has 10 form an opinion as to the digital signature of any person, the opinion of the Certifying Authority which has issued the Digital Signature Certificate is a relevant fact.".

8. In section 59, for the words "contents of documents" the words "contents of documents or electronic records" shall be substituted.

9. After section 65, the following sections shall be inserted, namely: —

'65A. Special provisions as to evidence relating to electronic record. — The contents of electronic records may be proved in accordance with the provisions of section 65B.

65B. Admissibility of electronic records. — (1) Notwithstanding anything contained in this Act, any information contained in an electronic record which is printed on a paper, stored, recorded or copied in optical or magnetic media produced by a computer (hereinafter referred to as the computer output) shall be deemed to be also a document, if the conditions mentioned in this section are satisfied in relation to the information and computer in question and shall be admissible in any proceedings, without further proof or production of the original, as evidence of any contents of the original or of any fact stated therein of which direct evidence would be admissible.

(2) The conditions referred to in sub-section (1) in respect of a computer output shall be the following, namely:—

(a) the computer output containing the information was produced by the computer during the period over which the computer was used regularly to store or process information for the purposes of any activities regularly carried on over that period by the person having lawful control over the use of the computer;

(b) during the said period, information of the kind contained in the electronic record or of the kind from which the information so contained is derived was regularly fed into the computer in the ordinary course of the said activities;

(c) throughout the material part of the said period, the computer was operating properly or, if not, then in respect of any period in which it was not operating properly or was out of operation during that part of the period, was not such as to affect the electronic record or the accuracy of its contents; and

(d) the information contained in the electronic record reproduces or is derived from such information fed into the computer in the ordinary course of the said activities.

(3) Where over any period, the function of storing or processing information for the purposes of any activities regularly carried on over that period as mentioned in clause (a) of sub-section (2) was regularly performed by computers, whether-

(a) by a combination of computers operating over that period; or

(b) by different computers operating in succession over that period; or

(c) by different combinations of computers operating in succession over that period; or

(d) in any other manner involving the successive operation over that period, in whatever order, of one or more computers and one or more combinations of computers,

all the computers used for that purpose during that period shall be treated for the purposes of this section as constituting a single computer; and references in this section to a computer shall be construed accordingly.

(4) In any proceedings where it is desired to give a statement in evidence by virtue of this section, a certificate doing any of the following things, that is to say, —

(a) identifying the electronic record containing the statement and describing the manner in which it was produced;

(b) giving such particulars of any device involved in the production of that electronic record as may be appropriate for the purpose of showing that the electronic record was produced by a computer;

(c) dealing with any of the matters to which the conditions mentioned in sub-section (2) relate,

and purporting to be signed by a person occupying a responsible official position in relation to the operation of the relevant device or the management of the relevant activities (whichever is appropriate) shall be evidence of any matter stated in the certificate; and for the purposes of this sub-section it shall be sufficient for a matter to be stated to the best of the knowledge and belief of the person stating it.

(5) For the purposes of this section, —

(a) information shall be taken to be supplied to a computer if it is supplied thereto in any appropriate form and whether it is so supplied directly or (with or without human intervention) by means of any appropriate equipment;

(b) whether in the course of activities carried on by any official, information is supplied with a view to its being stored or processed for the purposes of those activities by a computer operated otherwise than in the course of those activities, that information, if duly supplied to that computer, shall be taken to be supplied to it in the course of those activities;

(c) a computer output shall be taken to have been produced by a computer

whether it was produced by it directly or (with or without human intervention) by means of any appropriate equipment.

Explanation. – For the purposes of this section any reference to information being derived from other information shall be a reference to its being derived there from by calculation, comparison or any other process.

10. After section 67, the following section shall be inserted, namely:-

"67A. *Proof as to digital signature.* – Except in the case of a secure digital signature, if the digital signature of any subscriber is alleged to have been affixed to an electronic record the fact that such digital signature is the digital signature of the subscriber must be proved.".

11. After section 73, the following section shall be inserted, namely: –

'**73A. *Proof as to verification of digital signature.*** – In order to ascertain whether a digital signature is that of the person by whom it purports to have been affixed, the Court may direct-

(a) that person or the Controller or the Certifying Authority to produce the Digital Signature Certificate;

(b) any other person to apply the public key listed in the Digital Signature Certificate and verify the digital signature purported to have been affixed by that person.

Explanation. – For the purposes of this section, "Controller" means the Controller appointed under sub-section (1) of section 17 of the Information Technology Act, 2000'.

12. Presumption as to Gazettes in electronic forms. – After section 81, the following section shall be inserted, namely:-

"*81A*. The Court shall presume the genuineness of every electronic record purporting to be the Official Gazette, or purporting to be electronic record directed by any law to be kept by any person, if such electronic record is kept substantially in the form required by law and is produced from proper custody.".

13. Presumption as to electronic agreements. — After section 85, the following sections shall be inserted, namely:-

"*85A*. The Court shall presume that every electronic record purporting to be an agreement containing the digital signatures of the parties was so concluded by affixing the digital signature of the parties.

85B. Presumption as to electronic records and digital signatures. — (1) In any proceedings involving a secure electronic record, the Court shall presume unless contrary is proved, that the secure electronic record has not been altered since the specific point of time to which the secure status relates.

(2) In any proceedings, involving secure digital signature, the Court shall presume unless the contrary is proved that —

(a) the secure digital signature is affixed by subscriber with the intention of signing or approving the electronic record;

(b) except in the case of a secure electronic record or a secure digital signature, nothing in this section shall create any presumption relating to authenticity and integrity of the electronic record or any digital signature.

85C. Presumption as to Digital Signature Certificates. — The Court shall presume, unless contrary is proved, that the information listed in a Digital Signature Certificate is correct, except for information specified as subscriber information which has not been verified, if the certificate was accepted by the subscriber.".

14. Presumption as to electronic messages. — After section 88, the following section shall be inserted, namely: —

'*88A.* The Court may presume that an electronic message forwarded by the originator through an electronic mail server to the addressee to whom the message purports to be addressed corresponds with the message as fed into his computer for transmission; but the Court shall not make any presumption as to the person by whom such message was sent.

Explanation. – For the purposes of this section, the expressions "addressee" and "originator" shall have the same meanings respectively assigned to them in clauses *(b)* and (za) of sub-section (1) of section 2 of the Information Technology Act, 2000.'.

15. Presumption as to electronic records five years old. – After section 90, the following section shall be inserted, namely: –

"90A. Where any electronic record, purporting or proved to be five years old, is produced from any custody which the Court in the particular case considers proper, the Court may presume that the digital signature which purports to be the digital signature of any particular person was so affixed by him or any person authorised by him in this behalf.

Explanation. – Electronic records are said to be in proper custody if they are in the place in which, and under the care of the person with whom, they naturally be; but no custody is improper if it is proved to have had a legitimate origin, or the circumstances of the particular case are such as to render such an origin probable.

This *Explanation* applies also to section 81A.".

16. For section 131, the following section shall be substituted, namely: –

"*131. Production of documents or electronic records which another person, having possession, could refuse to produce.* – No one shall be compelled to produce documents in his possession or electronic records under his control, which any other person would be entitled to refuse to produce if they were in his possession or control, unless such last-mentioned person consents to their production.".

13. When foreign judgment not conclusive.

A foreign judgment shall be conclusive as to any matter thereby directly adjudicated upon between the same parties or between parties under whom they or any of them claim litigating under the same title except—

   (a)   where it has not been pronounced by a Court of competent jurisdiction;

   (b)   where it has not been given on the merits of the case;

   (c)   where it appears on the face of the proceedings to be founded on an incorrect view of international law or a refusal to recognise the law of India in cases in which such law is applicable;

   (d)   where the proceedings in which the judgment was obtained are opposed to natural justice;

   (e)   where it has been obtained by fraud;

   (f)   where it sustains a claim founded on a breach of any law in force in India.

15. Court in which suits to be instituted.

Every suit shall be instituted in the Court of the lowest grade competent to try it.

44A. Execution of decrees passed by Courts in reciprocating territory.

44A. Execution of decrees passed by Courts in reciprocating territory.

(1) Where a certified copy of decree of any of the superior Courts of any reciprocating territory has been filed in a District Court, the decree may be executed in India as if it had been passed by the District Court.

(2) Together with the certified copy of the decree shall be filed a certificate from such superior Court stating the extent, if any, to which the decree has been satisfied or adjusted and such certificate shall, for the purposes of proceedings under this section, be conclusive proof of the extent of such satisfaction or adjustment.

(3) The provisions of section 47 shall as from the filing of the certified copy of the decree apply to the proceedings of a District Court executing a decree under this section, and the District Court shall refuse execution of any such decree, if it is shown to the satisfaction of the Court that the decree falls within any of the exceptions specified in clauses (a) to (f) of section 13.

Explanation 1.—"Reciprocating territory" means any country or territory outside India which the Central Government may, by notification in the Official Gazette, declare to be a reciprocating territory for the purposes of this section; and "superior Courts", with reference to any such territory, means such Courts as may be specified in the said notification.

Explanation 2.—"Decree" with reference to a superior Court means any decree or judgment of such Court under which a sum of money is payable, not being a sum payable in respect of taxes or other charges of a like nature or in respect to a fine or other penalty, but shall in no case include an arbitration award, even if such an award is enforceable as a decree or judgment.

Annexure 5   Data Protection Act

To make provision for the protection of individuals against the violation of their privacy by the processing of personal data and for matters connected therewith or ancillary thereto.

PART I

PRELIMINARY

Short title

1. The short title of this Act is the Data Protection Act.

Interpretation

2. In this Act, unless the context otherwise requires:

"blocking" in relation to personal data, means the operation to suspend modification of data or suspend or restrict the provision of information to a third party when such provision is so suspended or restricted in accordance with the provisions of this Act;

"Commissioner" means the Data Protection Commissioner appointed under article 36 and includes any officer or employee of the Commissioner authorised by him in that behalf;

"consent" means any freely given specific and informed indication of the wishes of the data subject by which he signifies his agreement to personal data relating to him being processed;

"controller of personal data" or "controller" means a person who alone or jointly with others determines the purposes and means of the processing of personal data;

"data subject" means a natural person to whom the personal data

relates;

"identity card number" means the identifying number contained in an identity card as provided in the Identity Card Act;

"Minister" means the Minister responsible for data protection;

"personal data" means any information relating to an identified or identifiable natural person; an identifiable person is one who can be identified, directly or indirectly, in particular by reference to an identification number or to one or more factors specific to his physical, physiological, mental, economic, cultural or social identity;

"personal data filing system" or "filing system" means any structured set of personal data which is accessible according to specific criteria, whether centralised, decentralised or dispersed on a functional or geographical basis;

"personal data representative" means a person, appointed by the controller of personal data, who shall independently ensure that the personal data is processed in a correct and lawful manner;

"prescribed" means prescribed by regulations made by the Minister in accordance with the provisions of this Act, after consultation with the Commissioner;

"processing" and "processing of personal data" mean any operation or set of operations which is taken in regard to personal data, whether or not it occurs by automatic means, and includes the collection, recording, organisation, storage, adaptation, alteration,

retrieval, gathering, use, disclosure by transmission, dissemination or otherwise making information available, alignment or combination, blocking, erasure or destruction of such data;

"processor" means a person who processes personal data on behalf of a controller;

"recipient" means a person to whom personal data is provided;

however, when personal data is provided in order that the Commissioner may perform such supervision, control or audit that it is under a duty to attend to, the Commissioner shall not be regarded as a recipient;

"sensitive personal data" means personal data that reveals race or ethnic origin, political opinions, religious or philosophical beliefs, membership of a trade union, health, or sex life;

"third country" means a state that is not included in an Order issued for the purpose of determining which states are not to be considered as a third country for the purposes of this Act as may be prescribed from time to time under this Act;

"third party" means a person other than the data subject, the controller of personal data, the personal data representative, the processor and such persons who under the direct responsibility of the controller of personal data or the processor are authorised to process personal data.

PART II

APPLICABILITY

Mode of Processing

3. The provisions of this Act shall apply to the processing of personal data, wholly or partly, by automated means and to such processing other than by automated means where such personal data forms part of a filing system or is intended to form part of a filing system.

Territorial scope

4. (1) This Act shall also apply:

(*a*) to the processing of personal data carried out in the context of the activities of an establishment of a controller in Malta or in a Maltese Embassy or High Commission abroad;

(*b*) to the processing of personal data where the controller is established in a third country provided that the equipment used for the processing of the personal data is situated in Malta.

(2) Without prejudice to the following proviso, the provisions of sub-article (1)(*b*) shall not apply if the equipment is used only for purposes of transit of information between a third country and another such country:

Provided that the controller in such a case shall appoint a person established in Malta to act as his representative.

Non-applicability of the Act

5. This Act shall not apply —

(*a*) to processing of personal data where such processing is undertaken by a natural person in the course of a purely personal activity; and

(*b*) to processing operations concerning public security, defence, State security (including the economic well being of the State when the processing operation relates to security matters) and activities of the State in areas of criminal law:

Provided that the Minister may, after consultation with the Commissioner and with the concurrence of the Minister responsible for the Police, by regulations make provisions extending the application of this Act or adding to or derogating from the provisions of this subarticle to enforce the provisions of any international obligation, convention or treaty relating to the protection of personal data, to which Malta is a party, or may become a party.

Freedom of expression

6. (1) Subject to the following provisions of this article, nothing in this Act shall prejudice the application of the provisions of the European Convention Act relating to freedom of expression, or the provisions of the Press Act relating to journalistic freedoms.

(2) Notwithstanding the provisions of sub-article (1) the Commissioner shall encourage the drawing up of a suitable code of conduct to be applicable to journalists and to the media to regulate the processing of any personal data and the code of conduct shall provide appropriate measures and procedures to protect the data subject, having regard to the nature of the data.

(3) In the absence of such code of conduct, the Commissioner may establish specific measures and procedures to protect the data subjects; in

such a case journalists and the media are to comply with measures and procedures so established.

(4) If the measures and procedures contained in the code of conduct applicable to journalists and the media in terms of sub-article (2) or (3) are not complied with, the Commissioner may prohibit any person concerned from carrying out any processing, in whole or in part, and order the blocking of data when, having regard to the nature of the data, the means of the processing or the effects that it may have, there is a serious risk of a relevant damage to one or more data subjects.

PART III

REQUIREMENTS AND CRITERIA FOR PROCESSING

Requirements for processing.

7. The controller shall ensure that:

(a) personal data is processed fairly and lawfully;

(b) personal data is always processed in accordance with good practice;

(c) personal data is only collected for specific, explicitly stated and legitimate purposes;

(d) personal data is not processed for any purpose that is incompatible with that for which the information is collected;

(e) personal data that is processed is adequate and relevant in relation to the purposes of the processing;

(f) no more personal data is processed than is necessary having regard to the purposes of the processing;

(g) personal data that is processed is correct and, if necessary, up to date;

(h) all reasonable measures are taken to complete, correct, block or erase data to the extent that such data is incomplete or incorrect, having regard to the purposes for which they are processed;

(*i*) personal data is not kept for a period longer than is necessary, having regard to the purposes for which they are processed.

Processing for historical purposes, etc.

8. The processing of personal data for historical, statistical or scientific purposes shall not be regarded as incompatible with the purposes for which the information was collected:

Provided that the Controller shall ensure that:

(*a*) the appropriate safeguards are in place where personal data processed for historical, statistical or scientific purposes may be kept for a period longer than is necessary having regard to the purposes for which they are processed; or

(*b*) personal data kept for historical, statistical or scientific purposes shall not be used for any decision concerning a data subject.

Criteria for processing.

9. Personal data may be processed only if:

(*a*) the data subject has unambiguously given his consent; or

(*b*) processing is necessary for the performance of a contract to which the data subject is party or in order to take steps at the request of the data subject prior to entering into a contract; or

(*c*) processing is necessary for compliance with a legal obligation to which the controller is subject; or

(*d*) processing is necessary in order to protect the vital interests of the data subject; or

(*e*) processing is necessary for the performance of an activity that is carried out in the public interest or in the exercise of official authority vested in the controller or in a third party to whom the data is disclosed; or

(*f*) processing is necessary for a purpose that concerns a legitimate interest of the controller or of such a third party to whom personal data is provided, except where such interest is overridden by the interest to protect the fundamental rights and freedoms of the data subject and in particular the right to privacy.

Direct marketing

10. (1) Personal data may not be processed for purposes concerning direct marketing, if the data subject gives notice to the controller of personal data that he opposes such processing.

(2) The controller shall appropriately inform the data subject of his right to oppose, at no cost, the processing referred to sub-article (1) of this article.

Revocation of consent.

11. (1) In those cases where the processing of personal data is made in terms of article 9(e) and (f), the data subject, except where otherwise provided in any other law, shall be entitled to object at any time to the controller on compelling legitimate grounds to the processing of such data.

(2) Saving the provisions of article 10, where the processing of personal data takes place with the consent of the data subject, the data subject may at any time revoke his consent for compelling legitimate grounds relating to his particular situation.

Sensitive personal data.

12. (1) Subject to the other provisions of this Act no person shall process sensitive personal data:

Provided that such personal data may be processed in those cases provided for under sub-article (2) and under articles 13 to 16 or as may be prescribed by the Minister having regard to an important public interest.

(2) Sensitive personal data may be processed if the data subject:

(*a*) has given his explicit consent to processing; or

(*b*) has made the data public.

Necessary processing

13. Sensitive personal data may be processed if appropriate safeguards are adopted and the processing is necessary in order that:

(*a*) the controller will be able to comply with his duties or exercise his rights under any law regulating the conditions of employment; or

(*b*) the vital interests of the data subject or of some otherperson will be able to be protected and the data subject is physically or legally incapable of giving his consent; or

(*c*) legal claims will be able to be established, exercised or defended.

PART IV

PROCESSING FOR SPECIFIC PURPOSES

Processing by foundations, etc.

14. Any body of persons or other entity not being a commercial body or entity, with political, philosophical, religious or trade union objects may, in the course of its legitimate activities and with appropriate guarantees, process sensitive personal data

concerning the members of the respective body or entity and suchother persons who by reason of the objects of the body or entity have regular contact therewith:

Provided that sensitive personal data may be provided to a third party only if the data subject explicitly consents thereto.

Processing concerning health or medical purposes.

15. Sensitive personal data may be processed for health and hospital care purposes, provided that it is necessary for:

(*a*) preventive medicine and the protection of public health;

(*b*) medical diagnosis;

(*c*) health care or treatment; or

(*d*) management of health and hospital care services:

Provided that the data is processed by a health professional or other person subject to the obligation of professional secrecy.

For the purposes of this article "health professional" means a person in possession of a warrant to exercise a profession regulated by the Medical and Kindred Professions Ordinance and any person acting under the personal direction and supervision of such person.

Processing concerning research and statistics

16. (1) Sensitive personal data may be processed for research and statistics purposes, provided that the processing is necessary as stipulated in article 9(e).

(2) If the processing referred to in subarticle (1) has been approved:

(a) in the case of statistics, by the Commissioner himself;

(b) in the case of research, by the Commissioner on the advice of a research ethics committee of an institution recognised by the Commissioner for the purposes of this paragraph;the provisions of subarticle (1) shall be deemed to be satisfied.

(3) Personal data may be provided to be used for the purposes referred to in subarticle (1), unless otherwise provided by applicable rules on secrecy and confidentiality.

Processing concerning legal offences.

17. (1) Data relating to offences, criminal convictions or security measures may only be processed under the control of a public authority.

(2) For this purpose, the Minister may by regulations authorize any person to process the data referred to in subarticle (1) subject to such suitable specific safeguards as may be prescribed:

Provided that a complete register of criminal convictions may only be kept under the control of a public authority.

Processing of identity card number.

18. The identity card number may, in the absence of consent, only be processed when such processing is clearly justified having regard to:

(*a*) the purpose of the processing;

(*b*) the importance of a secure identification;

(*c*) some other valid reason as may be prescribed.

PART V

DATA COLLECTION AND RIGHT OF ACCESS

Information to data subject.

19. The Controller or any other person authorised by him in that behalf must provide a data subject from whom data relating to the data subject himself are collected, with at least the following information, except, where the data subject already has it:

(*a*) the identity and habitual residence or principal place of business of the controller and of any other person authorised by him in that behalf, if any;

(*b*) the purposes of the processing for which the data are intended; and

(*c*) any further information relating to matters such as:

(i)   the recipients or categories of the recipients of data;

(ii) whether the reply to any questions made to the data subject is obligatory or voluntary, as well as the possible consequence of failure to reply; and

(iii) the existence of the right to access, the right to rectify, and, where applicable, the right to erase the data concerning him, and, insofar as such further information is necessary, having regard to the specific circumstances in which the data is collected, to guarantee fair processing in respect of the data subject.

Data collected from other sources.

20. (1) Where the data have not been obtained from the data subject, the controller or any other person authorised by him in that behalf shall provide the data subject with at least the following information, except where the data subject already has it:

(a) the identity and habitual residence or principal place of business of the controller and of any other person authorised by him in that behalf;

(b) the purposes of the processing;

(c) any further information including:

(i) the categories of data concerned;

(ii) the recipients or categories of recipients;

(iii) the existence of the right of access, the right to rectify, and, where applicable, the right to erase the data concerning him;

and insofar as such further information is necessary, having regard to the specific circumstances in which the data is processed, to guarantee fair processing in respect of the data subject.

(2) The information referred to in subarticle (1) shall be provided at the time of undertaking the recording of personal data or, if a disclosure to a third party is envisaged, not later than the time when the data are first disclosed.

(3) Information referred to in subarticle (1) need not be provided if there are provisions concerning the registration or disclosure of any such personal data in any other law and appropriate safeguards are adopted.

(4) Information under subarticle (1) need not be provided if the personal data is required:

(a) for processing for statistical purposes;

(b) for purposes of historical or scientific research;

and insofar as the provision of such information proves impossible or would involve a disproportionate effort.

Right of access.

21. (1) The controller of personal data at the request of the data subject shall provide to the data subject, without excessive delay and without expense, written information as to whether personal data concerning the data subject is processed:

Provided that a request by the data subject under this subarticle shall only be made by the data subject at reasonable intervals.

(2) If such data is processed the data controller shall provide to the data subject written information in an intelligible form about:

(i)   actual information about the data subject which is processed;

(ii)   where this information has been collected;

(iii)   the purpose of the processing;

(iv)   to which recipients or categories of recipients the information is disclosed; and

(v)   knowledge of the logic involved in any automatic processing of data concerning the data subject.

(3) An application under subarticle (1) shall be made in writing to the controller of personal data and is to be signed by the data subject.

Rectification

22. (1) The controller shall be liable at the request of the data subject to immediately rectify, block or erase such personal data that has not been processed in accordance with this Act or with regulations made under this Act.

(2) The controller shall notify the third party to whom the data has been disclosed about the measures undertaken under subarticle (1) of this article:

Provided that no such notification need be provided if it is shown to be impossible or it will involve a disproportionate effort.

PART VI

EXEMPTIONS, RESTRICTIONS AND OTHER MEASURES

Exemptions and restrictions in case of secrecy, etc.

23. (1) The provisions of articles 7, 19, 20 (1), 21 and 35 shall not apply when a law specifically provides for the provision of information as a necessary measure in the interest of:

(*a*) national security;

(*b*) defence;

(*c*) public security;

(*d*) the prevention, investigation, detection and prosecution of criminal offences, or of breaches of ethics for regulated professions;

(*e*) an important economic or financial interest including monetary, budgetary and taxation matters;

(*f*) a monitoring, inspection or regulatory function connected, even occasionally, with the exercise of official authority referred to in paragraphs (*c*), (*d*) and (*e*); or

(*g*) such information being prejudicial to the protection of the data subject or of the rights and freedoms of others.

(2) The provisions of article 21 shall not apply when data is processed solely for purposes of scientific research or is kept in personal form for a period which does not exceed the period necessary for the sole purpose of compiling statistics:

Provided that the provisions of this subarticle shall not apply where the data is used for taking measures or decisions regarding any particular individual or where there is a risk of breaching the privacy of the data subject.

Decisions based on automated processing.

24. (1) If a decision is based solely on automated processing of such personal data as is intended to assess the qualities of a natural person, and such decision has a legal or other significant effect for that person, that person shall have the right to request that the decision be reconsidered other than in a manner based solely on automated processing, and such reconsideration shall be obligatory on the person making such decision.

(2) The provisions of subarticle (1) shall not apply where the decision is taken in the course of the entering into or performance of a contract with the data subject, provided that the request for the entering into or the performance of the contract, lodged by the data subject, has been satisfied or that there are suitable measures to safeguard his legitimate interests such as the right to be heard.

(3) A person who is the subject of a decision referred to in sub-article (1) shall be entitled to obtain upon representation information from the controller about what has controlled the automated processing that resulted in the decision:

Provided that information made available by the controller shall be subject to the provisions of article 21.

Persons authorized to process data.

25. (1) Any person acting under the authority of the controller or of the processor, including the processor himself, who has access to personal data may only process personal data in accordance with instructions from the controller unless the person is otherwise required to do so by law.

(2) The carrying out of processing by way of a processor is to be governed by a contract or other legally binding instrument in a written or in an equivalent form binding the processor to the controller and stipulating in particular that the processor:

(*a*) shall act only on instructions from the controller;

(*b*) shall take those measures referred to in article 26(1).

Security measures relating to processing.

26. (1) The controller shall implement appropriate technical and organisational measures to protect the personal data that is processed against accidental destruction or loss or unlawful forms of processing thereby providing an adequate level of security that gives regard to the:

(*a*) technical possibilities available;

(*b*) cost of implementing the security measures;

(*c*) special risks that exist in the processing of personal data;

(*d*) sensitivity of the personal data being processed.

(2) If the controller engages a processor, the controller shall ensure that the processor:

(*a*) can implement the security measures that must be taken;

(*b*) actually takes the measures so identified by the controller.

Transfer of data to a third country.

27. (1) Without prejudice to the provisions of article 28, the transfer to a third country of personal data that is undergoing processing or intended processing, may only take place subject to the provisions of this Act and provided that the third country to which the data is transferred ensures an adequate level of protection.

(2) The adequacy of the level of protection of a third country shall be assessed in the light of all the circumstances surrounding a data transfer operation or a set of data transfer operations; particular consideration shall be given to the nature of the data, the purpose and duration of the proposed processing operation or operations, the country of origin and country of final destination, the rules of law, both general and sectoral, in force in the third country in question and the professional rules and security measures which are complied with in that country.

(3) It is for the Commissioner to decide whether a third country ensures an adequate level of protection.

(4) The transfer of personal data to a third country that does not ensure adequate protection is prohibited.

Exemptions from the prohibition of the transfer of data to third country

28. (1) For the purpose of implementing any international convention to which Malta is a party or any other international obligation of Malta, the Minister may by Order designate that the transfer of personal data to any country listed in the said Order shall not, notwithstanding the provisions of this Act or any other law, be restricted on grounds of protection of privacy. In making such Order the Minister may include conditions and restrictions provided for in any said international instrument.

(2) A transfer of personal data to a third country that does not ensure an adequate level of protection within the meaning of article 27(2) may be effected by the controller if the data subject has given his unambiguous consent to the proposed transfer or if the transfer —

(*a*) is necessary for the performance of a contract between the data subject and the controller or the implementation of precontractual measures taken in response to the data subject's request;

(*b*) is necessary for the performance or conclusion of a contract concluded or to be concluded in the interests of the data subject between the controller and a third party;

(*c*) is necessary or legally required on public interest grounds, or for the establishment, exercise or defence of legal claims;

(*d*) is necessary in order to protect the vital interests of the data subject; or

(*e*) is made from a register that according to laws or regulations is intended to provide information to the public and which is open to consultation either by the public in general or by any person who can demonstrate legitimate interest, provided that the conditions laid down in law for consultation are fulfilled in the particular case.

(3) Without prejudice to subarticle (1) the Commissioner may authorise a transfer or a set of transfers of personal data to a third country that does not ensure an adequate level of protection within the meaning of article 27(2):

Provided that the controller provides adequate safeguards, which may result particularly by means of appropriate contractual provisions, with respect to the protection of the privacy and fundamental rights and freedoms of individuals and with respect to their exercise.

PART VII

NOTIFICATION AND OTHER PROCEDURES

Obligation for notification

29. (1) The controller shall notify the Commissioner before carrying out any wholly or partially automated processing operation or set of such operations intended to serve a single purpose or several related purposes.

(2) The Minister may prescribe on any matter relating to the form of notification to be made under this subarticle in respect of–

(*a*) processing whose sole purpose is the keeping of a register which according to laws or regulations is intended to provide information to the public and which is open to consultation either by the public in general or by any person demonstrating a legitimate interest; and

(*b*) processing operations referred to in article 14.

(3) The notification referred to in subarticle (1) must specify:

(*a*) the name and address of the data controller and of any other person authorised by him in that behalf, if any;

(*b*) the purpose or purposes of the processing;

(*c*) a description of the category or categories of data subject and of the data or categories of data relating to them;

(*d*) the recipients or categories of recipient to whom the data might be disclosed;

(*e*) proposed transfers of data to third countries; and

(*f*) a general description allowing a preliminary assessment to be made of the appropriateness of the measures taken pursuant to article 26 to ensure security of processing:

> Provided that the controller shall notify the Commissioner of any changes affecting the information referred to under this subarticle and the Minister may prescribe any matter related to the form of such notification.

(4) The Commissioner may allow the simplification of or the exemption from the notification obligations provided for under this Part of this Act only in respect of categories of processing operations—

(i) which are unlikely, due account being taken of the data being processed, to prejudice the rights and freedoms of data subjects, and

(ii) in respect of which the Commissioner specifies the purposes of the processing, the data or categories of data being processed, the category or categories of data subjects affected by such processing, the recipients or categories of recipients to whom the data is to be disclosed and the length of time for which the data is to be stored.

Derogation from the obligation for notification.

30. (1) The controller shall notify the Commissioner on the appointment or removal of a personal data representative.

(2) Where a personal data representative has been so appointed the notification required in terms of article 29(1) and (3) shall not be required.

Function of data representative.

31. (1) The personal data representative shall have the function of independently ensuring that the controller processes personal data in a lawful and correct manner and in accordance with good practice and in t h e event of the persona l data representative identifying any inadequacies, he shall bring these to the attention of the controller.

(2) If the personal data representative has reason to suspect that the controller has contravened the provisions applicable for processing personal data and if rectification is not implemented as soon as practicable after such contravention has been pointed out, the personal data representative shall notify this situation to the Commissioner.

(3) The personal data representative shall also consult with the Commissioner in the event of doubt about how the rules applicable to processing of personal data are to be applied.

Register of processing subject to notification.

32. The personal data representative shall maintain a register of the processing that the controller implements and which would have been subject to the duty of notification if the representative had not been appointed. The register shall comprise at least the information that a notification under article 29 would have contained.

Assistance to data subject.

33. The personal data representative shall assist the data subject to exercise his rights under this Act.

Mandatory notification.

34. (1) (*a*) Processing of personal data that involves particular risks of improper interference with the rights and freedoms of data subjects shall be submitted for prior checking to the Commissioner.

(*b*) The Minister may by regulation define the processing operations involving particular risks as referred to in paragraph (*a*) and prescribe rules in relation thereto.

(2) The prior checking referred to in subarticle (1) shall be carried out by the Commissioner following receipt of a notification from either the controller or the personal data representative:

Provided that in the case of doubt, the controller or personal data representative shall consult the Commissioner.

Register of processing operations.

35. (1) The Commissioner shall maintain a register of processing operations notified in accordance with article 29(1). The register shall contain the information listed in article 29(3)(*a*) to (*e*).

(2) The controller or the personal data representative, if so instructed by the controller, shall provide at least the information referred to in article 29(3)(*a*) to (*e*) to any person who requests it expeditiously and in an appropriate manner about such automated or other processing of personal data that have not been notified to the Commissioner under article 29(3):

Provided that the provisions of this subarticle shall not apply to the information specified in article 29(2)(*a*).

PART VIII

THE DATA PROTECTION COMMISSIONER

Data Protection Commissioner.

36. (1) There shall be a Data Protection Commissioner who shall be appointed by the Prime Minister after he has consulted the Leader of the Opposition.

(2) A person shall not be qualified to hold office as Commissioner if he:

(*a*) is a Minister, Parliamentary Secretary, or a Member of the House of Representatives; or

(*b*) is a judge or magistrate of the courts of justice; or

(*c*) is an officer in the public service; or

(*d*) is a member of a local council; or

(*e*) has a financial or other interest in any enterprise or activity which is likely to affect the discharge of his functions as a Commissioner:

Provided that the disqualification of a person under this paragraph may be waived if such person declares the interest and such declaration and waiver are published in the Gazette.

Independence of functions.

37. (1) In the exercise of his functions under this Act the Commissioner shall act independently and shall not be subject to the direction or control of any other person or authority. Commissioner may not hold other offices of profit. Exceptions.

(2) It shall not be lawful for the Commissioner to carry out any other profession, business or trade or to hold any other office of profit whatsoever, even though of a temporary nature, with the exception of any temporary judicial office on any international court or tribunal or any international adjudicating body, and the office of examiner at a University.

Legal personality and representation of the Commissioner.

38. (1) The Commissioner shall have a distinct legal personality and shall be capable, subject to the provisions of this Act, of entering into contracts, of acquiring, holding and disposing of any kind of property for the purposes of his functions, of suing and being sued, and of doing all such things and entering into all such transactions as are incidental or conducive to the exercise or performance of his functions under this Act.

(2) Any document purporting to be an instrument made or issued by the Commissioner and signed by him shall be received in evidence and shall, until the contrary is proved, be deemed to be an instrument made or issued by the Commissioner.

Tenure of office.

39. (1) The Commissioner shall hold office for a term of five years and shall be eligible for reappointment on the expiration of his term of office.

(2) The Commissioner shall not be removed from his office except by the Prime Minister upon an address of the House of Representatives supported by the votes of not less than two thirds of all the members thereof and praying for such removal on the ground of proved inability to perform the functions of his office (whether arising from infirmity of body or mind or any other cause) or proved misbehaviour.

(3) If the Commissioner resigns or if his office is otherwise vacant or if the Commissioner is for any reason unable to perform the functions of his office, or for any other temporary purpose where the Commissioner considers it necessary not to carry out any of his functions because of such circumstances, that were he a judge of the superior courts, he would abstain, the Prime Minister shall, after he has consulted the Leader of the Opposition, appoint a person who is qualified to be appointed as a temporary Commissioner, if such person is qualified to be a Commissioner; and any person so appointed shall cease to be such a Commissioner when a Commissioner is appointed to fill the vacancy or, as the case may be, when the Commissioner who was unable to perform the functions of his office resumes those functions or, in the case of a temporary purpose, the temporary Commissioner has performed the function assigned to him.

(4) The appointment of a temporary Commissioner for a temporary purpose as provided in subarticle (3) shall be exercised only on a certificate signed by the Commissioner to the effect that, in his opinion, it is necessary for the due conduct of the business of the Commissioner under this Act, that a temporary Commissioner be appointed.

Functions of the Commissioner

40. The Commissioner shall have the following functions:

(*a*) to create and maintain a public register of all processing operations according to notifications submitted to him as specified in this Act;

(*b*) to exercise control and, either of his own motion or at the request of a data subject, verify whether the processing is carried on in accordance with the provisions of this Act or regulations made thereunder;

(*c*) to instruct the processor and controller to take such measures as may be necessary to ensure that the processing is in accordance with this Act or regulations made thereunder;

(*d*) to receive reports and claims from data subjects or associations representing them on violations of this Act or regulations made thereunder, to take such remedial action as he deems necessary or as may be prescribed under this Act, and to inform such data subjects or associations of the outcome;

(e) to issue such directions as may be required of him for the purposes of this Act;

(f) to institute civil legal proceedings in cases where the provisions of this Act have been or are about to be violated and to refer to the competent public authority any criminal offence encountered in the course of or by reason of his functions;

(g) to encourage the drawing up of suitable codes of conduct by the various sectors affected by the provisions of this Act and to ascertain that the provisions of such codes are in accordance with the provisions of this Act and for such purpose the Commissioner may seek the views of data subjects or their representatives;

(h) to take such measures as may be necessary so as to bring to the knowledge of the general public the provisions of this Act and for such purpose to give advice to any person where it is required;

(i) to order the blocking, erasure or destruction of data, to impose a temporary or definitive ban on processing, or to warn or admonish the controller;

(j) to advise the Government on any legislative measures that are required to be taken to enable him carry out his functions appropriately;

(k) to draw up annual reports of his activities at regular intervals, at least once a year, which reports shall be made public;

(l) at the request of a data subject to verify that the processing of the personal data described in article 23 of this Act is compliant with the provisions of this Act or of any law as specified in subarticle (1) of the said article 23 and in such a case the data subject shall be informed accordingly; and

(m) to collaborate with supervisory authorities of other countries to the extent necessary for the performance of his duties, in particular by exchanging all useful information, in accordance with any convention to which Malta is a party or other any international obligation of Malta.

Commissioner's right of access to information.

41. (1) The Commissioner shall be entitled to obtain on request:

(*a*) access to the personal data that is processed, and;

(*b*) information about and documentation of the processing of personal data and security of such processing:

> Provided that where the personal data is processed for the purpose of compliance with a legal obligation to which the controller is subject, the Minister may by regulation prescribe rules and procedures for the purposes of the implementation of subarticle (1)(*a*).

(2) Without prejudice to any other provision of any other law, any person who does not comply with any lawful request relevant to an investigation by the Commissioner shall be guilty of an offence against this article.

(3) The investigations on the data processing described in article 23 are subject to the written authorisation of the Commissioner.

(4) If the Commissioner cannot, pursuant to a request under subarticle (1), obtain sufficient information in order to conclude that the processing of personal data is lawful, the Commissioner may prohibit the controller of personal data from processing personal data in any other manner than by storing them.

(5) In the exercise of his functions under this article the Commissioner shall have the same powers to enter and search any premises as are vested in the executive police by any law as may from time to time be in force.

Commissioner to seek rectification.

42. (1) If the Commissioner concludes that personal data is processed or may be processed in an unlawful manner, the Commissioner shall order rectification, and if rectification is not effected or if the matter is urgent, the Commissioner may prohibit the controller of personal data to continue processing the personal data in any manner other than to store that data.

(2) If the controller does not implement security measures in terms of article 26, the Commissioner may impose an administrative fine as stipulated in the following subarticle.

(3) In any of the cases mentioned in the preceding subarticles or in article 41(2), the Commissioner may, by order in writing, require the controller of personal data to pay such administrative fine as may be prescribed, provided that if the controller fails to comply with such requirement the Commissioner shall commence proceedings against the controller:

Provided that such administrative fine shall be due to the Commissioner as a civil debt, constituting an executive title for the purposes of Title VII of the Code of Organisation and Civil

Procedure as if payment of the amount of the fine had been ordered by a judgement of a court of civil jurisdiction.

Application for erasure.

43. (1) Where the Commissioner decides that personal data has been unlawfully processed, the Commissioner shall by notice order the controller of personal data to erase the personal data.

(2) If the controller of personal data feels aggrieved by the decision of the Commissioner, he may, within fifteen days from the receipt of the notice referred to in subarticle (1), by application request the Court of Appeal as constituted in accordance with article 41(6) of the Code of Organisation and Civil Procedure, to revoke the order of the Commissioner.

Collaboration with other authorities.

44. The Commissioner, before taking a decision in the exercise of his functions under article 40(c) or (e) which may significantly impact the operation of any government department or of any public or private enterprise, shall consult the interested party or parties who may be directly affected by the decision and he shall give reasons for his decisions.

Oath of secrecy.

45. The Commissioner and any officer and employee of the Commissioner shall, before assuming their duties, take an oath of office contained in the Schedule to this Act to carry out their duties with equity and impartiality and in accordance with the provisions of this Act and shall be subject to the provisions of the Official Secrets Act, and the Code of Ethics applicable to public officers.

The oath of office shall be taken before the Attorney General.

Compensation for damages.

46. (1) The data subject may, by sworn application filed in the competent court, exercise an action for damages against the controller who processes data in contravention of this Act or regulations made thereunder.

(2) An action under this article shall be commenced within a period of twelve months from the date when the data subject becomes aware or could have become aware of such a contravention, which ever is the earlier.

Penalties.

47. (1) Any person who:

(a) provides untrue information to data subjects as is prescribed by this Act, or in the notification to the Commissioner under article 29 or to the Commissioner when the Commissioner requests information in accordance with article 41;

(b) processes personal data in contravention of the provisions of articles 12 to 17;

(c) transfers personal data to a third country in contravention of article 27 and 28;

(*d*) omits to give notification under article 29(1) or in accordance with regulations issued under article 34;

shall be guilty of an offence and shall on conviction be liable to a fine (*multa*) not exceeding twenty-three thousand and two hundred and ninety-three euro and seventy-three cents (☐23,293.73) or to imprisonment for six months or to both such fine and imprisonment.

(2) Any person who fails to comply with an order in writing to pay an administrative fine in accordance with the provisions of article 41(2) or of article 42(1), shall not be subject to the payment of a penalty under the provisions of this article.

Data Protection Appeals Tribunal.

48. (1) There shall be a Tribunal to be known as the Data Protection Appeals Tribunal, in this Act referred to as "the Tribunal", having the functions and powers assigned to it by this Act or by any other law.

(2) The Tribunal shall consist of a chairman and two other members appointed by the Minister.

(3) The chairman shall be an advocate with a minimum of twelve years legal experience.

(4) The two other members mentioned in subarticle (2) shall be persons who in the opinion of the Minister represent the interests of data subjects and of data controllers.

(5) The chairman and other members of the Tribunal shall hold office for such period being of not less than three years as may be determined in their appointment and cannot be removed during their term of office except on grounds of proved inability to perform the functions of their office whether arising from infirmity of body or mind or any other cause, or proved misbehaviour.

(6) A member of the Tribunal may be challenged or abstain for any of the reasons for which a judge may be challenged or abstain in accordance with article 734 of the Code of Organisation and Civil Procedure. In any such case the Minister shall appoint a person, having the qualifications of the member challenged or abstaining, to sit as a member of the Tribunal in substitution of the said member.

(7) A member of the House of Representatives or of a Loc Council, a Judge or a Magistrate, or an officer in the public service shall be disqualified from being appointed or continuing to be a member of the Tribunal for so long as he holds that office.

(8) The Minister shall also designate a person to serve as secretary to the Tribunal.

49. (1) Any person aggrieved by a decision of the Appeals. Commissioner shall have the right to appeal in writing to the Tribunal within thirty days from the notification to him of the said decision.

(2) An appeal to the Tribunal may be made on any of the following grounds:

(*a*) that a material error as to the facts has been made;

(*b*) that there was a material procedural error;

(*c*) that an error of law has been made;

(*d*) that there was some material illegality, including unreasonableness or lack of proportionality.

(3) The Tribunal shall give reasons for its decision and shall cause such decisions to be made public omitting, if it deems it appropriate for reasons of confidentiality, the names of the persons involved.

(4) In determining an appeal under this article the Tribunal may:

(i)   dismiss the appeal;

(ii) annul the decision;

and where the Tribunal annuls the decision it may refer the matter to the competent authority with a direction to reconsider it and reach a decision in accordance with the findings of the Tribunal.

(5) The effect of a decision to which an appeal relates shall not except where the Tribunal or the Court of Appeal, as the case may be, so orders, be suspended in consequence of the bringing of the appeal.

Powers and procedures of the Tribunal.

50. (1) The Tribunal shall be competent to hear and decide any appeal made to it in accordance with the provisions of this Act and any regulations made thereunder; and subject to article 51, the decisions of the Tribunal shall be final and binding.

(2) For the exercise of its functions, the Tribunal may summon any person to appear before it and give evidence and produce documents; and the chairperson shall have the power to administer the oath. The Tribunal may also appoint experts to advice the Tribunal on any technical issue that may be relevant to its decision.

(3) For the purposes aforesaid the Tribunal shall have the same powers as are competent to the First Hall, Civil Court according to law.

(4) Save as may be prescribed, the Tribunal may regulate its own procedure.

Appeal to the Court of Appeal.

51. Any party to an appeal to the Tribunal who feels aggrieved by a decision of the Tribunal, or the Commissioner if he feels aggrieved with any such decision, may on a question of law appeal to the Court of Appeal as constituted in accordance with article 41(6) of the Code of Organisation and Civil Procedure by means of an application filed in the registry of that court within thirty days from the date on which that decision has been notified.

Financial provision.

52. (1) The expenses required by the Commissioner to exercise his functions under this Act as may be fixed by the House of Representatives in accordance with this article shall be a charge on the Consolidated Fund without the need of any further appropriation other than this Act.

(2) Where during the course of any financial year the sum fixed by the House of Representatives is in the opinion of the Commissioner insufficient to enable him to efficiently fulfil his functions the Commissioner shall prepare supplementary estimates for consideration by the House of Representatives.

(3) The Commissioner shall cause to be prepared in every financial year, and shall not later than six weeks after the end of each such year adopt, estimates of the income and expenditure of the Commissioner for the next following financial year:

Provided that the estimates for the first financial year of the Commissioner shall be prepared and adopted within such time as the Minister may by notice in writing to the Commissioner specify.

(4) A copy of the estimates shall, upon their adoption by the Commissioner, be sent forthwith by the Commissioner to the Minister and to the Minister responsible for finance.

(5) The Minister shall at the earliest opportunity and not later than six weeks after he has received a copy of the estimates from the Commissioner, approve the same with or without amendment after consultation with the Minister responsible for finance.

Accounts and audit.

53. (1) The Commissioner shall cause to be kept proper accounts and other records in respect of his operations and shall cause to be prepared a statement of accounts in respect of each financial year.

(2) The accounts of the Commissioner shall be audited by an auditor or auditors to be appointed by the Commissioner and approved by the Minister:

Provided that the Minister responsible for finance may after consultation with the Minister require the books or the accounts of the Commissioner to be audited or examined by the Auditor General who shall for the purpose have the power to carry out such physical checking and other certifications as he may deem necessary.

(3) After the end of each financial year, and not later than the date on which the estimates of the Commissioner are forwarded to the Minister under article 52(3), the Commissioner shall cause a copy of the statement of account duly audited to be transmitted to the Minister and to the Minister responsible for finance together with a copy of any report made by the auditors on that statement or on the accounts of the Commissioner.

(4) The Minister shall, at the earliest opportunity and not later than eight weeks after he has received a copy of every such statement and report, or if at any time during that period the House of Representatives is not in session, within eight weeks from the beginning of the next following session, cause every such statement and report to be laid on the Table of the House of Representatives.

(5) The Commissioner shall, not later than six weeks after the end of each financial year, make and transmit to the Minister and to the Minister responsible for finance a report dealing generally with the activities of the Commissioner during the financial year and contain such information relating to the proceedings and policy of the Commissioner as either of the said Ministers may from time to time require. The Minister shall, at the earliest opportunity and not later than eight weeks after he has received a copy of every such report, or if at any time during that period the House of Representatives is not in session, within eight weeks from the beginning of the next following session cause a copy of every such report to be laid on the Table of the House of Representatives.

PART IX

GENERAL

Power to make regulations.

54. The Minister may, after consultation with the Commissioner, prescribe regulations for the better carrying out of the provisions of this Act, and without prejudice to the generality of the foregoing may in particular prescribe regulations concerning:

(a) the cases in which processing of personal data is permitted;

(b) the requirements which are imposed on the controller when processing personal data;

(c) what a notification or application to a controller should contain;

(d) which information shall be provided to the data subject and how information shall be provided;

(e) notification to the Commissioner and the procedure when information notified has been altered;

(f) rules and procedures relating to access by the Commissioner of data held in instances where the controller processes data for compliance with a legal obligation;

(g) the qualifications required for a person to be appointed as a personal data representative;

(h) the minimum guarantees to be provided by the bodies of persons or other entities referred to in article 14 in the processing of personal data;

(i) the fees that may be levied by the Commissioner;

(j) the administrative fines that may be imposed by the Commissioner and the administrative violations in respect of which such fines be imposed; provided that such fines shall not be in an amount exceeding twenty-three thousand and two hundred and ninety-three euro and seventy-three cents (□23,293.73) for each violation and two thousand and three hundred and twenty-nine euro and thirty-seven cents (□2,329.37) for each day during which such violation persists;

(k) the penalties that may be imposed under this Act;

(l) for establishing rules, procedures, formalities and time limits in respect of any matter provided for under this Act;

(m) the extension of the application of this Act to any particular activity or sector and to provide for the manner in which data protection is to be implemented in specific sectors or in respect of specific activities; and

(n) for anything that may be prescribed under any of the provisions of this Act.

English text to prevail.

55. In the case of conflict between the Maltese and English text of this Act, the English text shall prevail.

Communications Authority Act.

56. The First Schedule to the Malta Communications Authority Act shall be amended as follows:

(*a*) paragraph 2 thereof shall be deleted; and

(*b*) paragraph 3 thereof shall be re-numbered as paragraph.

Annexure 6   OECD Guidelines on the Protection of Privacy and Transborder Flows of Personal Data

PREFACE

The development of automatic data processing, which enables vast quantities of data to be transmitted within seconds across national frontiers, and indeed across continents, has made it necessary to consider privacy protection in relation to personal data. Privacy protection laws have been introduced, or will be introduced shortly, in approximately one half of OECD Member countries (Austria, Canada, Denmark, France, Germany, Luxembourg, Norway, Sweden and the United States have passed legislation. Belgium, Iceland, the Netherlands, Spain and Switzerland have prepared draft bills) to prevent what are considered to be violations of fundamental human rights, such as the unlawful storage of personal data, the storage of inaccurate personal data, or the abuse or unauthorised disclosure of such data.

On the other hand, there is a danger that disparities in national legislations could hamper the free flow of personal data across frontiers; these flows have greatly increased in recent years and are bound to grow further with the widespread introduction of new computer and communications technology. Restrictions on these flows could cause serious disruption in important sectors of the economy, such as banking and insurance.

For this reason OECD Member countries considered it necessary to develop Guidelines which would help to harmonise national privacy legislation and, while upholding such human rights, would at the same time prevent interruptions in international flows of data. They represent a consensus on basic principles which can be built into existing national legislation, or serve as a basis for legislation in those countries which do not yet have it.

The Guidelines, in the form of a Recommendation by the Council of the OECD, were developed by a group of government experts under the chairmanship of The Hon. Mr. Justice M.D. Kirby, Chairman of the Australian Law Reform Commission. The Recommendation was adopted and became applicable on 23rd September, 1980.

The Guidelines are accompanied by an Explanatory Memorandum intended to provide information on the discussion and reasoning underlining their formulation.

RECOMMENDATION OF THE COUNCIL CONCERNING GUIDELINES GOVERNING THE PROTECTION OF PRIVACY AND TRANSBORDER FLOWS OF PERSONAL DATA (23rd September, 1980)

THE COUNCIL,

Having regard to articles 1(c), 3(a) and 5(b) of the Convention on the Organisation for Economic Co-operation and Development of 14th December, 1960;

RECOGNISING:

- that, although national laws and policies may differ, Member countries have a common interest in protecting privacy and individual liberties, and in reconciling fundamental but competing values such as privacy and the free flow of information;

- that automatic processing and transborder flows of personal data create new forms of relationships among countries and require the development of compatible rules and practices;

- that transborder flows of personal data contribute to economic and social development;

- that domestic legislation concerning privacy protection and transborder flows of personal data may hinder such transborder flows;

Determined to advance the free flow of information between Member countries and to avoid the creation of unjustified obstacles to the development of economic and social relations among Member countries;

RECOMMENDS:

1. That Member countries take into account in their domestic legislation the principles concerning the protection of privacy and individual liberties set forth in the Guidelines contained in the Annex to this Recommendation which is an integral part thereof;

2. That Member countries endeavour to remove or avoid creating, in the name of privacy protection, unjustified obstacles to transborder flows of personal data;

3. That Member countries co-operate in the implementation of the Guidelines set forth in the Annex;

4. That Member countries agree as soon as possible on specific procedures of consultation and co-operation for the application of these Guidelines.

Annex to the Recommendation of the Council of 23rd September 1980
GUIDELINES GOVERNING THE PROTECTION OF PRIVACY AND TRANSBORDER FLOWS OF PERSONAL DATA

PART ONE

GENERAL DEFINITIONS

1. For the purposes of these Guidelines:

(a) "data controller" means a party who, according to domestic law, is competent to decide about the contents and use of personal data regardless of whether or not such data are collected, stored, processed or disseminated by that party or by an agent on its behalf;

(b) "personal data" means any information relating to an identified or identifiable individual (data subject);

(c) "transborder flows of personal data" means movements of personal data across national borders.

Scope of Guidelines

2. These Guidelines apply to personal data, whether in the public or private sectors, which, because of the manner in which they are processed, or because of their nature or the context in which they are used, pose a danger to privacy and individual liberties.

3. These Guidelines should not be interpreted as preventing:

(a) the application, to different categories of personal data, of different protective measures depending upon their nature and the context in which they are collected, stored, processed or disseminated;

(b) the exclusion from the application of the Guidelines of personal data which obviously do not contain any risk to privacy and individual liberties; or

(c) the application of the Guidelines only to automatic processing of personal data.

4. Exceptions to the Principles contained in Parts Two and Three of these Guidelines, including those relating to national sovereignty, national security and public policy ("order public"), should be:

(a) as few as possible, and

(b) made known to the public.

5 . In the particular case of Federal countries the observance of these Guidelines may be affected by the division of powers in the Federation.

6. These Guidelines should be regarded as minimum standards which are capable of being supplemented by additional measures for the protection of privacy and individual liberties.

PART TWO

BASIC PRINCIPLES OF NATIONAL APPLICATION.

Collection Limitation Principle

7. There should be limits to the collection of personal data and any such data should be obtained by lawful and fair means and, where appropriate, with the knowledge or consent of the data subject.

Data Quality Principle

8. Personal data should be relevant to the purposes for which they are to be used, and, to the extent necessary for those purposes, should be accurate, complete and kept up-to-date.

Purpose Specification Principle

9. The purposes for which personal data are collected should be specified not later than at the time of data collection and the subsequent use limited to the fulfilment of those purposes or such others as are not incompatible with those purposes and as are specified on each occasion of change of purpose.

Use Limitation Principle

10. Personal data should not be disclosed, made available or otherwise used for purposes other than those specified in accordance with Paragraph 9 except:

(a) with the consent of the data subject; or

(b) by the authority of law.

Security Safeguards Principle

11. Personal data should be protected by reasonable security safeguards against such risks as loss or unauthorised access, destruction, use, modification or disclosure of data.

Openness Principle

12. There should be a general policy of openness about developments, practices and policies with respect to personal data. Means should be

readily available of establishing the existence and nature of personal data, and the main purposes of their use, as well as the identity and usual residence of the data controller.

Individual Participation Principle

13. An individual should have the right:

(a) to obtain from a data controller, or otherwise, confirmation of whether or not the data controller has data relating to him;

(b) to have communicated to him, data relating to him

- o within a reasonable time;

- o at a charge, if any, that is not excessive;

- o in a reasonable manner; and

- o in a form that is readily intelligible to him;

(c) to be given reasons if a request made under subparagraphs(a) and (b) is denied, and to be able to challenge such denial; and

(d) to challenge data relating to him and, if the challenge is successful to have the data erased, rectified, completed or amended.

Accountability Principle

14. A data controller should be accountable for complying with measures which give effect to the principles stated above.

PART THREE

BASIC PRINCIPLES OF INTERNATIONAL APPLICATION: FREE FLOW AND LEGITIMATE RESTRICTIONS

15. Member countries should take into consideration the implications for other Member countries of domestic processing and re-export of personal data.

16. Member countries should take all reasonable and appropriate steps to ensure that transborder flows of personal data, including transit through a Member country, are uninterrupted and secure.

17. A Member country should refrain from restricting transborder flows of personal data between itself and another Member country except where the latter does not yet substantially observe these Guidelines or where the re-export of such data would circumvent its domestic privacy legislation. A Member country may also impose restrictions in respect of certain categories of personal data for which its domestic privacy legislation includes specific regulations in view of the nature of those data and for which the other Member country provides no equivalent protection.

18. Member countries should avoid developing laws, policies and practices in the name of the protection of privacy and individual liberties, which would create obstacles to transborder flows of personal data that would exceed requirements for such protection.

PART FOUR

NATIONAL IMPLEMENTATION

19. In implementing domestically the principles set forth in Parts Two and Three, Member countries should establish legal, administrative or other procedures or institutions for the protection of privacy and individual liberties in respect of personal data. Member countries should in particular endeavour to:

(a) adopt appropriate domestic legislation;

(b) encourage and support self-regulation, whether in the form of codes of conduct or otherwise;

(c) provide for reasonable means for individuals to exercise their rights;

(d) provide for adequate sanctions and remedies in case of failures to comply with measures which implement the principles set forth in Parts Two and Three; and

(e) ensure that there is no unfair discrimination against data subjects.

PART FIVE

INTERNATIONAL CO-OPERATION

20. Member countries should, where requested, make known to other Member countries details of the observance of the principles set forth in these Guidelines. Member countries should also ensure that procedures for transborder flows of personal data and for the protection of privacy and individual liberties are simple and compatible with those of other Member countries which comply with these Guidelines.

21. Member countries should establish procedures to facilitate:

- information exchange related to these Guidelines, and

- mutual assistance in the procedural and investigative matters involved.

22. Member countries should work towards the development of principles, domestic and international, to govern the applicable law in the case of transborder flows of personal data.

EXPLANATORY MEMORANDUM: INTRODUCTION

A feature of OECD Member countries over the past decade has been the development of laws for the protection of privacy. These laws have tended to assume different forms in different countries, and in many countries are still in the process of being developed. The disparities in legislation may create obstacles to the free flow of information between countries. Such flows have greatly increased in recent years and are bound to continue to grow as a result of the introduction of new computer and communication technology.

The OECD, which had been active in this field for some years past, decided to address the problems of diverging national legislation and in 1978 instructed a Group of Experts to develop Guidelines on basic rules governing the transborder flow and the protection of personal data and privacy, in order to facilitate the harmonization of national legislation. The Group has now completed its work.

The Guidelines are broad in nature and reflect the debate and legislative work which has been going on for several years in Member countries. The Expert Group which prepared the Guidelines has considered it essential to issue an accompanying Explanatory Memorandum. Its purpose is to explain and elaborate the Guidelines and the basic problems of protection of privacy and individual liberties. It draws attention to key issues that have emerged in the discussion of the Guidelines and spells out the reasons for the choice of particular solutions.

The first part of the Memorandum provides general background information on the area of concern as perceived in Member countries. It explains the need for international action and summarises the work carried out so far by the OECD and certain other international organisations. It concludes with a list of the main problems encountered by the Expert Group in its work.

Part Two has two subsections. The first contains comments on certain general features of the Guidelines, the second detailed comments on individual paragraphs.

This Memorandum is an information document, prepared to explain and describe generally the work of the Expert Group. It is subordinate to the Guidelines themselves. It cannot vary the meaning of the Guidelines but is supplied to help in their interpretation and application.

I. GENERAL BACKGROUND

The Problems

1. The 1970s may be described as a period of intensified investigative and legislative activities concerning the protection of privacy with respect to the collection and use of personal data. Numerous official reports show that the problems are taken seriously at the political level and at the same time that the task of balancing opposing interests is delicate and unlikely to be accomplished once and for all. Public interest has tended to focus on the risks and implications associated with the computerised processing of personal data and some countries have chosen to enact statutes which deal exclusively with computers and computer-supported activities. Other countries have preferred a more general approach to privacy

protection issues irrespective of the particular data processing technology involved.

2. The remedies under discussion are principally safeguards for the individual which will prevent an invasion of privacy in the classical sense, i.e. abuse or disclosure of intimate personal data; but other, more or less closely related needs for protection have become apparent. Obligations of record-keepers to inform the general public about activities concerned with the processing of data, and rights of data subjects to have data relating to them supplemented or amended, are two random examples. Generally speaking, there has been a tendency to broaden the traditional concept of privacy ("the right to be left alone") and to identify a more complex synthesis of interests which can perhaps more correctly be termed privacy and individual liberties.

3. As far as the legal problems of automatic data processing (ADP) are concerned, the protection of privacy and individual liberties constitutes perhaps the most widely debated aspect. Among the reasons for such widespread concern are the ubiquitous use of computers for the processing of personal data, vastly expanded possibilities of storing, comparing, linking, selecting and accessing personal data, and the combination of computers and telecommunications technology which may place personal data simultaneously at the disposal of thousands of users at geographically dispersed locations and enables the pooling of data and the creation of complex national and international data networks. Certain problems require particularly urgent attention, e.g. those relating to emerging international data networks, and to the need of balancing competing interests of privacy on the one hand and freedom of information on the other, in order to allow a full exploitation of the potentialities of modern data processing technologies in so far as this is desirable.

Activities at national level

4. Of the OECD Member countries more than one-third have so far enacted one or several laws which, among other things, are intended to protect individuals against abuse of data relating to them and to give them the right of access to data with a view to checking their accuracy and appropriateness. In federal states, laws of this kind may be found

both at the national and at the state or provincial level. Such laws are referred to differently in different countries. Thus, it is common practice in continental Europe to talk about "data laws" or "data protection laws" (*lois sur la protection des données*), whereas in English speaking countries they are usually known as "privacy protection laws". Most of the statutes were enacted after 1973 and this present period may be described as one of continued or even widened legislative activity. Countries which already have statutes in force are turning to new areas of protection or are engaged in revising or complementing existing statutes. Several other countries are entering the area and have bills pending or are studying the problems with a view to preparing legislation. These national efforts, and not least the extensive reports and research papers prepared by public committees or similar bodies, help to clarify the problems and the advantages and implications of various solutions. At the present stage, they provide a solid basis for international action.

5. The approaches to protection of privacy and individual liberties adopted by the various countries have many common features. Thus, it is possible to identify certain basic interests or values which are commonly considered to be elementary components of the area of protection. Some core principles of this type are: setting limits to the collection of personal data in accordance with the objectives of the data collector and similar criteria; restricting the usage of data to conform with openly specified purposes; creating facilities for individuals to learn of the existence and contents of data and have data corrected; and the identification of parties who are responsible for compliance with the relevant privacy protection rules and decisions. Generally speaking, statutes to protect privacy and individual liberties in relation to personal data attempt to cover the successive stages of the cycle beginning with the initial collection of data and ending with erasure or similar measures, and to ensure to the greatest possible extent individual awareness, participation and control.

6. Differences between national approaches as apparent at present in laws, bills or proposals for legislation refer to aspects such as the scope of legislation, the emphasis placed on different elements of protection, the detailed implementation of the broad principles indicated above, and the machinery of enforcement. Thus, opinions vary with respect to licensing requirements and control mechanisms in the form of special supervisory

bodies ("data inspection authorities"). Categories of sensitive data are defined differently, the means of ensuring openness and individual participation vary, to give just a few instances. Of course, existing traditional differences between legal systems are a cause of disparity, both with respect to legislative approaches and the detailed formulation of the regulatory framework for personal data protection.

International aspects of privacy and data banks

7. For a number of reasons the problems of developing safeguards for the individual in respect of the handling of personal data cannot be solved exclusively at the national level. The tremendous increase in data flows across national borders and the creation of international data banks (collections of data intended for retrieval and other purposes) have highlighted the need for concerted national action and at the same time support arguments in favour of free flows of information which must often be balanced against requirements for data protection and for restrictions on their collection, processing and dissemination.

8. One basic concern at the international level is for consensus on the fundamental principles on which protection of the individual must be based. Such a consensus would obviate or diminish reasons for regulating the export of data and facilitate resolving problems of conflict of laws. Moreover, it could constitute a first step towards the development of more detailed, binding international agreements.

9. There are other reasons why the regulation of the processing of personal data should be considered in an international context: the principles involved concern values which many nations are anxious to uphold and see generally accepted; they may help to save costs in international data traffic; countries have a common interest in preventing the creation of locations where national regulations on data processing can easily be circumvented; indeed, in view of the international mobility of people, goods and commercial and scientific activities, commonly accepted practices with regard to the processing of data may be advantageous even where no transborder data traffic is directly involved.

Relevant international activities

10. There are several international agreements on various aspects of telecommunications which, while facilitating relations and co-operation between countries, recognise the sovereign right of each country to regulate its own telecommunications (The International Telecommunications Convention of 1973). The protection of computer data and programmes has been investigated by, among others, the World Intellectual Property Organisation which has developed draft model provisions for national laws on the protection of computer software. Specialised agreements aiming at informational co-operation may be found in a number of areas, such as law enforcement, health services, statistics and judicial services (e.g. with regard to the taking of evidence).

11. A number of international agreements deal in a more general way with the issues which are at present under discussion, viz. the protection of privacy and the free dissemination of information. They include the European Convention of Human Rights of 4th November, 1950 and the International Covenant on Civil and Political Rights (United Nations, 19th December, 1966).

12. However, in view of the inadequacy of existing international instruments relating to the processing of data and individual rights, a number of international organisations have carried out detailed studies of the problems involved in order to find more satisfactory solutions.

13. In 1973 and 1974 the Committee of Ministers of the Council of Europe adopted two resolutions concerning the protection of the privacy of individuals vis-à-vis electronic data banks in the private and public sectors respectively. Both resolutions recommend that the governments of the Member states of the Council of Europe take steps to give effect to a number of basic principles of protection relating to the obtaining of data, the quality of data, and the rights of individuals to be informed about data and data processing activities.

14. Subsequently the Council of Europe, on the instructions of its Committee of Ministers, began to prepare an international Convention on privacy protection in relation to data processing abroad and transfrontier data processing. It also initiated work on model regulations for medical

data banks and rules of conduct for data processing professionals. The Convention was adopted by the Committee of Ministers on 17th September 1980. It seeks to establish basic principles of data protection to be enforced by Member countries, to reduce restrictions on transborder data flows between the Contracting Parties on the basis of reciprocity, to bring about co-operation between national data protection authorities, and to set up a Consultative Committee for the application and continuing development of the convention.

15. The European Community has carried out studies concerning the problems of harmonization of national legislations within the Community, in relation to transborder data flows and possible distortions of competition, the problems of data security and confidentiality, and the nature of transborder data flows. A sub-committee of the European Parliament held a public hearing on data processing and the rights of the individual in early 1978. Its work has resulted in a report to the European Parliament in spring 1979. The report, which was adopted by the European Parliament in May 1979, contains a resolution on the protection of the rights of the individual in the face of technical developments in data processing.

Activities of the OECD

16. The OECD programme on transborder data flows derives from computer utilisation studies in the public sector which were initiated in 1969. A Group of Experts, the Data Bank Panel, analysed and studied different aspects of the privacy issue, e.g. in relation to digital information, public administration, transborder data flows, and policy implications in general. In order to obtain evidence on the nature of the problems, the Data Bank Panel organised a Symposium in Vienna in 1977 which provided opinions and experience from a diversity of interests, including government, industry, users of international data communication networks, processing services, and interested intergovernmental organisations.

17. A number of guiding principles were elaborated in a general framework for possible international action. These principles recognised (a) the need for generally continuous and uninterrupted flows of information between countries, (b) the legitimate interests of countries in

preventing transfers of data which are dangerous to their security or contrary to their laws on public order and decency or which violate the rights of their citizens, (c) the economic value of information and the importance of protecting "data trade" by accepted rules of fair competition, (d) the needs for security safeguards to minimise violations of proprietary data and misuse of personal information, and (e) the significance of a commitment of countries to a set of core principles for the protection of personal information.

18. Early in 1978 a new ad hoc Group of Experts on Transborder Data Barriers and Privacy Protection was set up within the OECD which was instructed to develop guidelines on basic rules governing the transborder flow and the protection of personal data and privacy, in order to facilitate a harmonization of national legislations, without this precluding at a later date the establishment of an international Convention. This work was to be carried out in close co-operation with the Council of Europe and the European Community and to be completed by lst July 1979.

19. The Expert Group, under the chairmanship of the Honourable Mr. Justice Kirby, Australia, and with the assistance of Dr. Peter Seipel (Consultant), produced several drafts and discussed various reports containing, for instance, comparative analyses of different approaches to legislation in this field. It was particularly concerned with a number of key issues set out below.

(a) The specific, sensitive facts issue

The question arose as to whether the Guidelines should be of a general nature or whether they should be structured to deal with different types of data or activities (e.g. credit reporting). Indeed, it is probably not possible to identify a set of data which are universally regarded as being sensitive.

(b) The ADP issue

The argument that ADP is the main cause for concern is doubtful and, indeed, contested.

(c) The legal persons issue

Some, but by no means all, national laws protect data relating to legal persons in a similar manner to data related to physical persons.

(d) The remedies and sanctions issue

The approaches to control mechanisms vary considerably: for instance, schemes involving supervision and licensing by specially constituted authorities might be compared to schemes involving voluntary compliance by record-keepers and reliance on traditional judicial remedies in the Courts.

(e) The basic machinery or implementation issue

The choice of core principles and their appropriate level of detail presents difficulties. For instance, the extent to which data security questions (protection of data against unauthorised interference, fire, and similar occurrences) should be regarded as part of the privacy protection complex is debatable; opinions may differ with regard to time limits for the retention, or requirements for the erasure, of data and the same applies to requirements that data be relevant to specific purposes. In particular, it is difficult to draw a clear dividing line between the level of basic principles or objectives and lower level "machinery" questions which should be left to domestic implementation.

(f) The choice of law issue

The problems of choice of jurisdiction, choice of applicable law and recognition of foreign judgements have proved to be complex in the context of transborder data flows. The question arose, however, whether and to what extent it should be attempted at this stage to put forward solutions in Guidelines of a non-binding nature.

(g) The exceptions issue

Similarly, opinions may vary on the question of exceptions. Are they required at all? If so, should particular categories of exceptions be provided for or should general limits to exceptions be formulated?

(h) The bias issue

Finally, there is an inherent conflict between the protection and the free transborder flow of personal data. Emphasis may be placed on one or the other, and interests in privacy protection may be difficult to distinguish from other interests relating to trade, culture, national sovereignty, and so forth.

20. During its work the Expert Group maintained close contacts with corresponding organs of the Council of Europe. Every effort was made to avoid unnecessary differences between the texts produced by the two organisations; thus, the set of basic principles of protection are in many respects similar. On the other hand, a number of differences do occur. To begin with, the OECD Guidelines are not legally binding, whereas the Council of Europe has produced a convention which will be legally binding among those countries which ratify it. This in turn means that the question of exceptions has been dealt with in greater detail by the Council of Europe. As for the area of application, the Council of Europe Convention deals primarily with the automatic processing of personal data whereas the OECD Guidelines apply to personal data which involve dangers to privacy and individual liberties, irrespective of the methods and machinery used in their handling. At the level of details, the basic principles of protection proposed by the two organisations are not identical and the terminology employed differs in some respects. The institutional framework for continued co-operation is treated in greater detail in the Council of Europe Convention than in the OECD Guidelines.

21. The Expert Group also maintained co-operation with the Commission of the European Communities as required by its mandate.

II. THE GUIDELINES

A. PURPOSE AND SCOPE

General

22. The Preamble of the Recommendation expresses the basic concerns calling for action. The Recommendation affirms the commitment of Member countries to protect privacy and individual liberties and to respect the transborder flows of personal data.

23. The Guidelines set out in the Annex to the Recommendation consist of five parts. Part One contains a number of definitions and specifies the scope of the Guidelines, indicating that they represent minimum standards. Part Two contains eight basic principles (Paragraphs 7-14) relating to the protection of privacy and individual liberties at the national level. Part Three deals with principles of international application, i.e. principles which are chiefly concerned with relationships between Member countries.

24. Part Four deals, in general terms, with means of implementing the basic principles set out in the preceding parts and specifies that these principles should be applied in a non-discriminatory manner. Part Five concerns matters of mutual assistance between Member countries, chiefly through the exchange of information and by avoiding incompatible national procedures for the protection of personal data. It concludes with a reference to issues of applicable law which may arise when flows of personal data involve several Member countries.

Objectives

25. The core of the Guidelines consists of the principles set out in Part Two of the Annex. It is recommended to Member countries that they adhere to these principles with a view to:

(a) achieving acceptance by Member countries of certain minimum standards of protection of privacy and individual liberties with regard to personal data;

(b) reducing differences between relevant domestic rules and practices of Member countries to a minimum;

(c) ensuring that in protecting personal data they take into consideration the interests of other Member countries and the need to avoid undue interference with flows of personal data between Member countries; and

(d) eliminating, as far as possible, reasons which might induce Member countries to restrict transborder flows of personal data because of the possible risks associated with such flows.

As stated in the Preamble, two essential basic values are involved: the protection of privacy and individual liberties and the advancement of free flows of personal data. The Guidelines attempt to balance the two values against one another; while accepting certain restrictions to free transborder flows of personal data, they seek to reduce the need for such restrictions and thereby strengthen the notion of free information flows between countries.

26. Finally, Parts Four and Five of the Guidelines contain principles seeking to ensure:

(a) effective national measures for the protection of privacy and individual liberties;

(b) avoidance of practices involving unfair discrimination between individuals; and

(c) bases for continued international co-operation and compatible procedures in any regulation of transborder flows of personal data.

Level of detail

27. The level of detail of the Guidelines varies depending upon two main factors, viz. (a) the extent of consensus reached concerning the solutions put forward, and (b) available knowledge and experience pointing to solutions to be adopted at this stage. For instance, the Individual Participation Principle (Paragraph 13) deals specifically with various aspects of protecting an individual's interest, whereas the provision on problems of choice of law and related matters (Paragraph 22) merely states a starting-point for a gradual development of detailed common approaches and international agreements. On the whole, the Guidelines constitute a general framework for concerted actions by Member countries: objectives put forward by the Guidelines may be pursued in different ways, depending on the legal instruments and strategies preferred by Member countries for their implementation. To conclude, there is a need for a continuing review of the Guidelines, both by Member countries and the OECD. As and when experience is gained, it may prove desirable to develop and adjust the Guidelines accordingly.

Non-Member countries

28. The Recommendation is addressed to Member countries and this is reflected in several provisions which are expressly restricted to relationships between Member countries (see Paragraphs 15, 17 and 20 of the Guidelines). Widespread recognition of the Guidelines is, however, desirable and nothing in them should be interpreted as preventing the application of relevant provisions by Member countries to non-Member countries. In view of the increase in transborder data flows and the need to ensure concerted solutions, efforts will be made to bring the Guidelines to the attention of non-Member countries and appropriate international organisations.

The broader regulatory perspective

29. It has been pointed out earlier that the protection of privacy and individual liberties constitutes one of many overlapping legal aspects involved in the processing of data. The Guidelines constitute a new instrument, in addition to other, related international instruments governing such issues as human rights, telecommunications, international trade, copyright, and various information services. If the need arises, the principles set out in the Guidelines could be further developed within the framework of activities undertaken by the OECD in the area of information, computer and communications policies.

30. Some Member countries have emphasized the advantages of a binding international Convention with a broad coverage. The Mandate of the Expert Group required it to develop guidelines on basic rules governing the transborder flow and the protection of personal data and privacy, without this precluding at a later stage the establishment of an international Convention of a binding nature. The Guidelines could serve as a starting-point for the development of an international Convention when the need arises.

Legal persons, groups and similar entities

31. Some countries consider that the protection required for data relating to individuals may be similar in nature to the protection required for data relating to business enterprises, associations and groups which may or may not possess legal personality. The experience of a number of

countries also shows that it is difficult to define clearly the dividing line between personal and non-personal data. For example, data relating to a small company may also concern its owner or owners and provide personal information of a more or less sensitive nature. In such instances it may be advisable to extend to corporate entities the protection offered by rules relating primarily to personal data.

32. Similarly, it is debatable to what extent people belonging to a particular group (i.e. mentally disabled persons immigrants, ethnic minorities) need additional protection against the dissemination of information relating to that group.

33. On the other hand, the Guidelines reflect the view that the notions of individual integrity and privacy are in many respects particular and should not be treated the same way as the integrity of a group of persons, or corporate security and confidentiality. The needs for protection are different and so are the policy frameworks within which solutions have to be formulated and interests balanced against one another. Some members of the Expert Group suggested that the possibility of extending the Guidelines to legal persons (corporations, associations) should be provided for. This suggestion has not secured a sufficient consensus. The scope of the Guidelines is therefore confined to data relating to individuals and it is left to Member countries to draw dividing lines and decide policies with regard to corporations, groups and similar bodies (cf. paragraph 49 below).

Automated and non-automated data

34. In the past, OECD activities in privacy protection and related fields have focused on automatic data processing and computer networks. The Expert Group has devoted special attention to the issue of whether or not these Guidelines should be restricted to the automatic and computer-assisted processing of personal data. Such an approach may be defended on a number of grounds, such as the particular dangers to individual privacy raised by automation and computerised data banks, and increasing dominance of automatic data processing methods, especially in transborder data flows, and the particular framework of information, computer and communications policies within which the Expert Group has set out to fulfil its Mandate.

35. On the other hand, it is the conclusion of the Expert Group that limiting the Guidelines to the automatic processing of personal data would have considerable drawbacks. To begin with, it is difficult, at the level of definitions, to make a clear distinction between the automatic and non-automatic handling of data. There are, for instance, "mixed" data processing systems, and there are stages in the processing of data which may or may not lead to automatic treatment. These difficulties tend to be further complicated by ongoing technological developments, such as the introduction of advanced semi-automated methods based on the use of microfilm, or microcomputers which may increasingly be used for private purposes that are both harmless and impossible to control. Moreover, by concentrating exclusively on computers the Guidelines might lead to inconsistency and lacunae, and opportunities for record-keepers to circumvent rules which implement the Guidelines by using non-automatic means for purposes which may be offensive.

36. Because of the difficulties mentioned, the Guidelines do not put forward a definition of "automatic data processing" although the concept is referred to in the preamble and in paragraph 3 of the Annex. It may be assumed that guidance for the interpretation of the concept can be obtained from sources such as standard technical vocabularies.

37. Above all, the principles for the protection of privacy and individual liberties expressed in the Guidelines are valid for the processing of data in general, irrespective of the particular technology employed. The Guidelines therefore apply to personal data in general or, more precisely, to personal data which, because of the manner in which they are processed, or because of their nature or context, pose a danger to privacy and individual liberties.

38. It should be noted, however, that the Guidelines do not constitute a set of general privacy protection principles; invasions of privacy by, for instance, candid photography, physical maltreatment, or defamation are outside their scope unless such acts are in one way or another associated with the handling of personal data. Thus, the Guidelines deal with the building-up and use of aggregates of data which are organised for retrieval, decision-making, research, surveys and similar purposes. It should be emphasized that the Guidelines are neutral with regard to the

particular technology used; automatic methods are only one of the problems raised in the Guidelines although, particularly in the context of transborder data flows, this is clearly an important one.

B. DETAILED COMMENTS

General

39. The comments which follow relate to the actual Guidelines set out in the Annex to the Recommendation. They seek to clarify the debate in the Expert Group.

Paragraph 1: Definitions

40. The list of definitions has been kept short. The term "data controller" is of vital importance. It attempts to define a subject who, under domestic law, should carry ultimate responsibility for activities concerned with the processing of personal data. As defined, the data controller is a party who is legally competent to decide about the contents and use of data, regardless of whether or not such data are collected, stored, processed or disseminated by that party or by an agent on its behalf. The data controller may be a legal or natural person, public authority, agency or any other body. The definition excludes at least four categories which may be involved in the processing of data, viz. (a) licensing authorities and similar bodies which exist in some Member countries and which authorise the processing of data but are not entitled to decide (in the proper sense of the word) what activities should be carried out and for what purposes; (b) data processing service bureaux which carry out data processing on behalf of others; (c) telecommunications authorities and similar bodies which act as mere conduits; and (d) "dependent users" who may have access to data but who are not authorised to decide what data should be stored, who should be able to use them, etc. In implementing the Guidelines, countries may develop more complex schemes of levels and types of responsibilities. Paragraphs 14 and 19 of the Guidelines provide a basis for efforts in this direction.

41. The terms "personal data" and "data subject" serve to underscore that the Guidelines are concerned with physical persons. The precise dividing line between personal data in the sense of information relating

to identified or identifiable individuals and anonymous data may be difficult to draw and must be left to the regulation of each Member country. In principle, personal data convey information which by direct (e.g. a civil registration number) or indirect linkages (e.g. an address) may be connected to a particular physical person.

42. The term "transborder flows of personal data" restricts the application of certain provisions of the Guidelines to international data flows and consequently omits the data flow problems particular to federal states. The movements of data will often take place through electronic transmission but other means of data communication may also be involved. Transborder flows as understood in the Guidelines includes the transmission of data by satellite.

Paragraph 2: Area of application

43. The Section of the Memorandum dealing with the scope and purpose of the Guidelines introduces the issue of their application to the automatic as against non-automatic processing of personal data. Paragraph 2 of the Guidelines, which deals with this problem, is based on two limiting criteria. The first is associated with the concept of personal data: the Guidelines apply to data which can be related to identified or identifiable individuals. Collections of data which do not offer such possibilities (collections of statistical data in anonymous form) are not included. The second criterion is more complex and relates to a specific risk element of a factual nature, viz. that data pose a danger to privacy and individual liberties. Such dangers can arise because of the use of automated data processing methods (the manner in which data are processed), but a broad variety of other possible risk sources is implied. Thus, data which are in themselves simple and factual may be used in a context where they become offensive to a data subject. On the other hand, the risks as expressed in Paragraph 2 of the Guidelines are intended to exclude data collections of an obviously innocent nature (e.g. personal notebooks). The dangers referred to in Paragraph 2 of the Guidelines should relate to privacy and individual liberties. However, the protected interests are broad (cf. paragraph 2 above) and may be viewed differently by different Member countries and at different times. A delimitation as far as the Guidelines are concerned and a common basic approach are

provided by the principles set out in Paragraphs 7 to 13.

44. As explained in Paragraph 2 of the Guidelines, they are intended to cover both the private and the public sector. These notions may be defined differently by different Member countries.

Paragraph 3: Different degrees of sensitivity

45. The Guidelines should not be applied in a mechanistic way irrespective of the kind of data and processing activities involved. The framework provided by the basic principles in Part Two of the Guidelines permits Member countries to exercise their discretion with respect to the degree of stringency with which the Guidelines are to be implemented, and with respect to the scope of the measures to be taken. In particular, Paragraph 3(b) provides for many "trivial" cases of collection and use of personal data (cf. above) to be completely excluded from the application of the Guidelines. Obviously this does not mean that Paragraph 3 should be regarded as a vehicle for demolishing the standards set up by the Guidelines. But, generally speaking, the Guidelines do not presuppose their uniform implementation by Member countries with respect to details. For instance, different traditions and different attitudes by the general public have to be taken into account. Thus, in one country universal personal identifiers may be considered both harmless and useful whereas in another country they may be regarded as highly sensitive and their use restricted or even forbidden. In one country, protection may be afforded to data relating to groups and similar entities whereas such protection is completely non-existent in another country, and so forth. To conclude, some Member countries may find it appropriate to restrict the application of the Guidelines to the automatic processing of personal data. Paragraph 3(c) provides for such a limitation.

Paragraph 4: Exceptions to the Guidelines

46. To provide formally for exceptions in Guidelines which are part of a non-binding Recommendation may seem superfluous. However, the Expert Group has found it appropriate to include a provision dealing with this subject and stating that two general criteria ought to guide national policies in limiting the application of the Guidelines: exceptions should be as few as possible, and they should be made known to the

public (e.g. through publication in an official government gazette). General knowledge of the existence of certain data or files would be sufficient to meet the second criterion, although details concerning particular data etc. may have to be kept secret. The formula provided in Paragraph 4 is intended to cover many different kinds of concerns and limiting factors, as it was obviously not possible to provide an exhaustive list of exceptions - hence the wording that they include national sovereignty, national security and public policy ("order public"). Another overriding national concern would be, for instance, the financial interests of the State ("crédit public"). Moreover, Paragraph 4 allows for different ways of implementing the Guidelines: it should be borne in mind that Member countries are at present at different stages of development with respect to privacy protection rules and institutions and will probably proceed at different paces, applying different strategies, e.g. the regulation of certain types of data or activities as compared to regulation of a general nature ("omnibus approach").

47. The Expert Group recognised that Member countries might apply the Guidelines differentially to different kinds of personal data. There may be differences in the permissible frequency of inspection, in ways of balancing competing interests such as the confidentiality of medical records versus the individual's right to inspect data relating to him, and so forth. Some examples of areas which may be treated differently are credit reporting, criminal investigation and banking. Member countries may also choose different solutions with respect to exceptions associated with, for example, research and statistics. An exhaustive enumeration of all such situations and concerns is neither required nor possible. Some of the subsequent paragraphs of the Guidelines and the comments referring to them provide further clarification of the area of application of the Guidelines and of the closely related issues of balancing opposing interests (compare with Paragraphs 7, 8, 17 and 18 of the Guidelines). To summarise, the Expert Group has assumed that exceptions will be limited to those which are necessary in a democratic society.

Paragraph 5: Federal countries

48. In Federal countries, the application of the Guidelines is subject to various constitutional limitations. Paragraph 5, accordingly, serves to

underscore that no commitments exist to apply the Guidelines beyond the limits of constitutional competence.

Paragraph 6: Minimum standards

49. First, Paragraph 6 describes the Guidelines as minimum standards for adoption in domestic legislation. Secondly, and in consequence, it has been agreed that the Guidelines are capable of being supplemented by additional measures for the protection of privacy and individual liberties at the national as well as the international level.

Paragraph 7: Collection Limitation Principle

50. As an introductory comment on the principles set out in Paragraphs 7 to 14 of the Guidelines it should be pointed out that these principles are interrelated and partly overlapping. Thus, the distinctions between different activities and stages involved in the processing of data which are assumed in the principles, are somewhat artificial and it is essential that the principles are treated together and studied as a whole. Paragraph 7 deals with two issues, viz. (a) limits to the collection of data which, because of the manner in which they are to be processed, their nature, the context in which they are to be used or other circumstances, are regarded as specially sensitive; and (b) requirements concerning data collection methods. Different views are frequently put forward with respect to the first issue. It could be argued that it is both possible and desirable to enumerate types or categories of data which are per se sensitive and the collection of which should be restricted or even prohibited. There are precedents in European legislation to this effect (race, religious beliefs, criminal records, for instance). On the other hand, it may be held that no data are intrinsically "private" or "sensitive" but may become so in view of their context and use. This view is reflected, for example, in the privacy legislation of the United States.

51. The Expert Group discussed a number of sensitivity criteria, such as the risk of discrimination, but has not found it possible to define any set of data which are universally regarded as sensitive. Consequently, Paragraph 7 merely contains a general statement that there should be limits to the collection of personal data. For one thing, this represents an affirmative recommendation to lawmakers to decide on limits which

would put an end to the indiscriminate collection of personal data. The nature of the limits is not spelt out but it is understood that the limits may relate to:

o   data quality aspects (i.e. that it should be possible to derive information of sufficiently high quality from the data collected, that data should be collected in a proper information framework, etc.);

o   limits associated with the purpose of the processing of data (i.e. that only certain categories of data ought to be collected and, possibly, that data collection should be restricted to the minimum necessary to fulfil the specified purpose);

o   "earmarking" of specially sensitive data according to traditions and attitudes in each Member country;

o   limits to data collection activities of certain data controllers;

o   civil rights concerns.

52. The second part of Paragraph 7 (data collection methods) is directed against practices which involve, for instance, the use of hidden data registration devices such as tape recorders, or deceiving data subjects to make them supply information. The knowledge or consent of the data subject is as a rule essential, knowledge being the minimum requirement. On the other hand, consent cannot always be imposed, for practical reasons. In addition, Paragraph 7 contains a reminder ("where appropriate") that there are situations where for practical or policy reasons the data subject's knowledge or consent cannot be considered necessary. Criminal investigation activities and the routine up-dating of mailing lists may be mentioned as examples. Finally, Paragraph 7 does not exclude the possibility of a data subject being represented by another party, for instance in the case of minors, mentally disabled person, etc.

Paragraph 8: Data Quality Principle

53. Requirements that data be relevant can be viewed in different ways. In fact, some members of the Expert Group hesitated as to whether such requirements actually fitted into the framework of privacy

protection. The conclusion of the Group was to the effect, however, that data should be related to the purpose for which they are to be used. For instance, data concerning opinions may easily be misleading if they are used for purposes to which they bear no relation, and the same is true of evaluative data. Paragraph 8 also deals with accuracy, completeness and up-to-dateness which are all important elements of the data quality concept. The requirements in this respect are linked to the purposes of data, i.e. they are not intended to be more far-reaching than is necessary for the purposes for which the data are used. Thus, historical data may often have to be collected or retained; cases in point are social research, involving so-called longitudinal studies of developments in society, historical research, and the activities of archives. The "purpose test" will often involve the problem of whether or not harm can be caused to data subjects because of lack of accuracy, completeness and up-dating.

Paragraph 9: Purpose Specification Principle

54. The Purpose Specification Principle is closely associated with the two surrounding principles, i.e. the Data Quality Principle and the Use Limitation Principle. Basically, Paragraph 9 implies that before, and in any case not later than at the time data collection it should be possible to identify the purposes for which these data are to be used, and that later changes of purposes should likewise be specified. Such specification of purposes can be made in a number of alternative or complementary ways, e.g. by public declarations, information to data subjects, legislation, administrative decrees, and licences provided by supervisory bodies. According to Paragraphs 9 and 10, new purposes should not be introduced arbitrarily; freedom to make changes should imply compatibility with the original purposes. Finally, when data no longer serve a purpose, and if it is practicable, it may be necessary to have them destroyed (erased) or given an anonymous form. The reason is that control over data may be lost when data are no longer of interest; this may lead to risks of theft, unauthorised copying or the like.

Paragraph 10: Use Limitation Principle

55. This paragraph deals with uses of different kinds, including disclosure, which involve deviations from specified purposes. For instance, data may be transmitted from one computer to another where

they can be used for unauthorised purposes without being inspected and thus disclosed in the proper sense of the word. As a rule the initially or subsequently specified purposes should be decisive for the uses to which data can be put. Paragraph 10 foresees two general exceptions to this principle: the consent of the data subject (or his representative - see Paragraph 52 above) and the authority of law (including, for example, licences granted by supervisory bodies). For instance, it may be provided that data which have been collected for purposes of administrative decision-making may be made available for research, statistics and social planning.

Paragraph 11: Security Safeguards Principle

56. Security and privacy issues are not identical. However, limitations on data use and disclosure should be reinforced by security safeguards. Such safeguards include physical measures (locked doors and identification cards, for instance), organisational measures (such as authority levels with regard to access to data) and, particularly in computer systems, informational measures (such as enciphering and threat monitoring of unusual activities and responses to them). It should be emphasized that the category of organisational measures includes obligations for data processing personnel to maintain confidentiality. Paragraph 11 has a broad coverage. The cases mentioned in the provision are to some extent overlapping (e.g. access/ disclosure). "Loss" of data encompasses such cases as accidental erasure of data, destruction of data storage media (and thus destruction of data) and theft of data storage media. "Modified" should be construed to cover unauthorised input of data, and "use" to cover unauthorised copying.

Paragraph 12: Openness Principle

57. The Openness Principle may be viewed as a prerequisite for the Individual Participation Principle (Paragraph 13); for the latter principle to be effective, it must be possible in practice to acquire information about the collection, storage or use of personal data. Regular information from data controllers on a voluntary basis, publication in official registers of descriptions of activities concerned with the processing of personal data, and registration with public bodies are some, though not all, of the ways by which this may be brought about. The reference to means which are

"readily available" implies that individuals should be able to obtain information without unreasonable effort as to time, advance knowledge, travelling, and so forth, and without unreasonable cost.

Paragraph 13: Individual Participation Principle

58. The right of individuals to access and challenge personal data is generally regarded as perhaps the most important privacy protection safeguard. This view is shared by the Expert Group which, although aware that the right to access and challenge cannot be absolute, has chosen to express it in clear and fairly specific language. With respect to the individual sub-paragraphs, the following explanations are called for:

59. The right to access should as a rule be simple to exercise. This may mean, among other things, that it should be part of the day-to-day activities of the data controller or his representative and should not involve any legal process or similar measures. In some cases it may be appropriate to provide for intermediate access to data; for example, in the medical area a medical practitioner can serve as a go-between. In some countries supervisory organs, such as data inspection authorities, may provide similar services. The requirement that data be communicated within reasonable time may be satisfied in different ways. For instance, a data controller who provides information to data subjects at regular intervals may be exempted from obligations to respond at once to individual requests. Normally, the time is to be counted from the receipt of a request. Its length may vary to some extent from one situation to another depending on circumstances such as the nature of the data processing activity. Communication of such data "in a reasonable manner" means, among other things, that problems of geographical distance should be given due attention. Moreover, if intervals are prescribed between the times when requests for access must be met, such intervals should be reasonable. The extent to which data subjects should be able to obtain copies of data relating to them is a matter of implementation which must be left to the decision of each Member country.

60. The right to reasons in Paragraph 13(c) is narrow in the sense that it is limited to situations where requests for information have been refused. A broadening of this right to include reasons for adverse

decisions in general, based on the use of personal data, met with sympathy in the Expert Group. However, on final consideration a right of this kind was thought to be too broad for insertion in the privacy framework constituted by the Guidelines. This is not to say that a right to reasons for adverse decisions may not be appropriate, e.g. in order to inform and alert a subject to his rights so that he can exercise them effectively.

61. The right to challenge in 13(c) and (d) is broad in scope and includes first instance challenges to data controllers as well as subsequent challenges in courts, administrative bodies, professional organs or other institutions according to domestic rules of procedure (compare with Paragraph 19 of the Guidelines). The right to challenge does not imply that the data subject can decide what remedy or relief is available (rectification, annotation that data are in dispute, etc.): such matters will be decided by domestic law and legal procedures. Generally speaking, the criteria which decide the outcome of a challenge are those which are stated elsewhere in the Guidelines.

Paragraph 14: Accountability Principle

62. The data controller decides about data and data processing activities. It is for his benefit that the processing of data is carried out. Accordingly. it is essential that under domestic law accountability for complying with privacy protection rules and decisions should be placed on the data controller who should not be relieved of this obligation merely because the processing of data is carried out on his behalf by another party, such as a service bureau. On the other hand, nothing in the Guidelines prevents service bureaux personnel, "dependent users" (see paragraph 40) and others from also being held accountable. For instance, sanctions against breaches of confidentiality obligations may be directed against all parties entrusted with the handling of personal information (cf. paragraph 19 of the Guidelines). Accountability under Paragraph 14 refers to accountability supported by legal sanctions, as well as to accountability established by codes of conduct, for instance.

Paragraphs 15-18: Basic Principles of International Application

63. The principles of international application are closely interrelated. Generally speaking, Paragraph 15 concerns respect by Member countries for each other's interest in protecting personal data, and the privacy and individual liberties of their nationals and residents. Paragraph 16 deals with security issues in a broad sense and may be said to correspond, at the international level, to Paragraph 11 of the Guidelines. Paragraphs 17 and 18 deal with restrictions on free flows of personal data between Member countries; basically, as far as protection of privacy and individual liberties is concerned, such flows should be admitted as soon as requirements of the Guidelines for the protection of these interests have been substantially, i.e. effectively, fulfilled. The question of other possible bases of restricting transborder flows of personal data is not dealt with in the Guidelines.

64. For domestic processing Paragraph 15 has two implications. First, it is directed against liberal policies which are contrary to the spirit of the Guidelines and which facilitate attempts to circumvent or violate protective legislation of other Member countries. However, such circumvention or violation, although condemned by all Member countries, is not specifically mentioned in this Paragraph as a number of countries felt it to be unacceptable that one Member country should be required to directly or indirectly enforce, extraterritorially, the laws of other Member countries. -- It should be noted that the provision explicitly mentions the re-export of personal data. In this respect, Member countries should bear in mind the need to support each other's efforts to ensure that personal data are not deprived of protection as a result of their transfer to territories and facilities for the processing of data where control is slack or non-existent.

65. Secondly, Member countries are implicitly encouraged to consider the need to adapt rules and practices for the processing of data to the particular circumstances which may arise when foreign data and data on non-nationals are involved. By way of illustration, a situation may arise where data on foreign nationals are made available for purposes which serve the particular interests of their country of nationality (e.g. access to the addresses of nationals living abroad).

66. As far as the Guidelines are concerned, the encouragement of international flows of personal data is not an undisputed goal in itself. To the extent that such flows take place they should, however, according to Paragraph 16, be uninterrupted and secure, i.e. protected against unauthorised access, loss of data and similar events. Such protection should also be given to data in transit, i.e. data which pass through a Member country without being used or stored with a view to usage in that country. The general commitment under Paragraph 16 should, as far as computer networks are concerned, be viewed against the background of the International Telecommunications Convention of Malaga-Torremolinos (25th October, 1973). According to that convention, the members of the International Telecommunications Union, including the OECD Member countries, have agreed, inter alia, to ensure the establishment, under the best technical conditions, of the channels and installations necessary to carry on the rapid and uninterrupted exchange of international telecommunications. Moreover, the members of ITU have agreed to take all possible measures compatible with the telecommunications system used to ensure the secrecy of international correspondence. As regards exceptions, the right to suspend international telecommunications services has been reserved and so has the right to communicate international correspondence to the competent authorities in order to ensure the application of internal laws or the execution of international conventions to which members of the ITU are parties. These provisions apply as long as data move through telecommunications lines. In their context, the Guidelines constitute a complementary safeguard that international flows of personal data should be uninterrupted and secure.

67. Paragraph 17 reinforces Paragraph 16 as far as relationships between Member countries are concerned. It deals with interests which are opposed to free transborder flows of personal data but which may nevertheless constitute legitimate grounds for restricting such flows between Member countries. A typical example would be attempts to circumvent national legislation by processing data in a Member country which does not yet substantially observe the Guidelines. Paragraph 17 establishes a standard of equivalent protection, by which is meant protection which is substantially similar in effect to that of the exporting

country, but which need not be identical in form or in all respects. As in Paragraph 15, the re-export of personal data is specifically mentioned - in this case with a view to preventing attempts to circumvent the domestic privacy legislation of Member countries. - The third category of grounds for legitimate restrictions mentioned in Paragraph 17, concerning personal data of a special nature, covers situations where important interests of Member countries could be affected. Generally speaking, however, paragraph 17 is subject to Paragraph 4 of the Guidelines which implies that restrictions on flows of personal data should be kept to a minimum.

68. Paragraph 18 attempts to ensure that privacy protection interests are balanced against interests of free transborder flows of personal data. It is directed in the first place against the creation of barriers to flows of personal data which are artificial from the point of view of protection of privacy and individual liberties and fulfil restrictive purposes of other kinds which are thus not openly announced. However, Paragraph 18 is not intended to limit the rights of Member countries to regulate transborder flows of personal data in areas relating to free trade, tariffs, employment, and related economic conditions for intentional data traffic. These are matters which were not addressed by the Expert Group, being outside its Mandate.

Paragraph 19: National Implementation

69. The detailed implementation of Parts Two and Three of the Guidelines is left in the first place to Member countries. It is bound to vary according to different legal systems and traditions, and Paragraph 19 therefore attempts merely to establish a general framework indicating in broad terms what kind of national machinery is envisaged for putting the Guidelines into effect. The opening sentence shows the different approaches which might be taken by countries, both generally and with respect to control mechanisms (e.g. specially set up supervisory bodies, existing control facilities such as courts, public authorities, etc.).

70. In Paragraph 19(a) countries are invited to adopt appropriate domestic legislation, the word "appropriate" foreshadowing the judgement by individual countries of the appropriateness or otherwise of legislative solutions. Paragraph 19(b) concerning self-regulation is

addressed primarily to common law countries where non-legislative implementation of the Guidelines would complement legislative action. Paragraph 19(c) should be given a broad interpretation; it includes such means as advice from data controllers and the provision of assistance, including legal aid. Paragraph 19(d) permits different approaches to the issue of control mechanisms: briefly, either the setting-up of special supervisory bodies, or reliance on already existing control facilities, whether in the form of courts, existing public authorities or otherwise. Paragraph 19(e) dealing with discrimination is directed against unfair practices but leaves open the possibility of "benign discrimination" to support disadvantaged groups, for instance. The provision is directed against unfair discrimination on such bases as nationality and domicile, sex, race, creed, or trade union affiliation.

Paragraph 20: Information Exchange and Compatible Procedures

71. Two major problems are dealt with here, viz. (a) the need to ensure that information can be obtained about rules, regulations, decisions, etc. which implement the Guidelines, and (b) the need to avoid transborder flows of personal data being hampered by an unnecessarily complex and disparate framework of procedures and compliance requirements. The first problem arises because of the complexity of privacy protection regulation and data policies in general. There are often several levels of regulation (in a broad sense) and many important rules cannot be laid down permanently in detailed statutory provisions; they have to be kept fairly open and left to the discretion of lower-level decision-making bodies.

72. The importance of the second problem is, generally speaking, proportional to the number of domestic laws which affect transborder flows of personal data. Even at the present stage, there are obvious needs for co-ordinating special provisions on transborder data flows in domestic laws, including special arrangements relating to compliance control and, where required, licences to operate data processing systems.

Paragraph 2 1: Machinery for Co-operation

73. The provision on national procedures assumes that the Guidelines will form a basis for continued co-operation. Data protection authorities

and specialised bodies dealing with policy issues in information and data communications are obvious partners in such a co-operation. In particular, the second purpose of such measures, contained in Paragraph 21(ii), i.e. mutual aid in procedural matters and requests for information, is future-oriented: its practical significance is likely to grow as international data networks and the complications associated with them become more numerous.

Paragraph 22: Conflicts of Laws

74. The Expert Group has devoted considerable attention to issues of conflicts of laws, and in the first place to the questions as to which courts should have jurisdiction over specific issues (choice of jurisdiction) and which system of law should govern specific issues (choice of law). The discussion of different strategies and proposed principles has confirmed the view that at the present stage, with the advent of such rapid changes in technology, and given the non-binding nature of the Guidelines, no attempt should be made to put forward specific, detailed solutions. Difficulties are bound to arise with respect to both the choice of a theoretically sound regulatory model and the need for additional experience about the implications of solutions which in themselves are possible.

75. As regards the question of choice of law, one way of approaching these problems is to identify one or more connecting factors which, at best, indicate one applicable law. This is particularly difficult in the case of international computer networks where, because of dispersed location and rapid movement of data, and geographically dispersed data processing activities, several connecting factors could occur in a complex manner involving elements of legal novelty. Moreover, it is not evident what value should presently be attributed to rules which by mechanistic application establish the specific national law to be applied. For one thing, the appropriateness of such a solution seems to depend upon the existence of both similar legal concepts and rule structures, and binding commitments of nations to observe certain standards of personal data protection. In the absence of these conditions, an attempt could be made to formulate more flexible principles which involve a search for a "proper law" and are linked to the purpose of ensuring effective protection of

privacy and individual liberties. Thus, in a situation where several laws may be applicable, it has been suggested that one solution could be to give preference to the domestic law offering the best protection of personal data. On the other hand, it may be argued that solutions of this kind leave too much uncertainty, not least from the point of view of the data controllers who may wish to know, where necessary in advance, by which national systems of rules an international data processing system will be governed.

76. In view of these difficulties, and considering that problems of conflicts of laws might best be handled within the total framework of personal and non-personal data, the Expert Group has decided to content itself with a statement which merely signals the issues and recommends that Member countries should work towards their solution.

77. The Expert Group called attention to the terms of Recommendation 4 on the Guidelines which suggests that Member countries agree as soon as possible on specific procedures of consultation and co-operation for the application of the Guidelines.

Data Protection Act, 1998 (International Law)

[16th July 1998]

An Act to make new provision for the regulation of the processing of information relating to individuals, including the obtaining, holding, use or disclosure of such information.

Be it enacted by the Queen's most Excellent Majesty, by and with the advice and consent of the Lords Spiritual and Temporal, and Commons, in this present Parliament assembled, and by the authority of the same, as follows: —

Part I

Preliminary

1. Basic interpretative provisions

(1) In this Act, unless the context otherwise requires —

- "data" means information which —

    (a) is being processed by means of equipment operating automatically in response to instructions given for that purpose,

    (b) is recorded with the intention that it should be processed by means of such equipment,

    (c) is recorded as part of a relevant filing system or with the intention that it should form part of a relevant filing system, or

    (d) does not fall within paragraph (a), (b) or (c) but forms part of an accessible record as defined by section 68;

- "data controller" means, subject to subsection (4), a person who (either alone or jointly or in common with other persons) determines the purposes for which and the manner in which any personal data are, or are to be, processed;

- "data processor", in relation to personal data, means any person (other than an employee of the data controller) who processes the data on behalf of the data controller;

- "data subject" means an individual who is the subject of personal data;

- "personal data" means data which relate to a living individual who can be identified —

  (a) from those data, or

  (b) from those data and other information which is in the possession of, or is likely to come into the possession of, the data controller, and includes any expression of opinion about the individual and any indication of the intentions of the data controller or any other person in respect of the individual;

- "processing", in relation to information or data, means obtaining, recording or holding the information or data or carrying out any operation or set of operations on the information or data, including —

  (a) organisation, adaptation or alteration of the information or data,

  (b) retrieval, consultation or use of the information or data,

  (c) disclosure of the information or data by transmission, dissemination or otherwise making available, or

  (d) alignment, combination, blocking, erasure or destruction of the information or data;

- "relevant filing system" means any set of information relating to individuals to the extent that, although the information is not processed by means of equipment operating automatically in response to instructions given for that purpose, the set is structured, either by reference to individuals or by reference to criteria relating to individuals, in such a way that specific information relating to a particular individual is readily accessible.

(2) In this Act, unless the context otherwise requires —

(a) "obtaining" or "recording", in relation to personal data, includes obtaining or recording the information to be contained in the data, and

(b) "using" or "disclosing", in relation to personal data, includes using or disclosing the information contained in the data.

(3) In determining for the purposes of this Act whether any information is recorded with the intention —

(a) that it should be processed by means of equipment operating automatically in response to instructions given for that purpose, or

(b) that it should form part of a relevant filing system, it is immaterial that it is intended to be so processed or to form part of such a system only after being transferred to a country or territory outside the European Economic Area.

(4) Where personal data are processed only for purposes for which they are required by or under any enactment to be processed, the person on whom the obligation to process the data is imposed by or under that enactment is for the purposes of this Act the data controller.

2. Sensitive personal data

In this Act "sensitive personal data" means personal data consisting of information as to —

(a) the racial or ethnic origin of the data subject,

(b) his political opinions,

(c) his religious beliefs or other beliefs of a similar nature,

(d) whether he is a member of a trade union (within the meaning of the [1992 c. 52.] Trade Union and Labour Relations (Consolidation) Act 1992),

(e) his physical or mental health or condition,

(f) his sexual life,

(g) the commission or alleged commission by him of any offence, or

(h) any proceedings for any offence committed or alleged to have been committed by him, the disposal of such proceedings or the sentence of any court in such proceedings.

3. The special purposes

In this Act "the special purposes" means any one or more of the following—

(a) the purposes of journalism,

(b) artistic purposes, and

(c) literary purposes.

4. The data protection principles

(1) References in this Act to the data protection principles are to the principles set out in Part I of Schedule 1.

(2) Those principles are to be interpreted in accordance with Part II of Schedule 1.

(3) Schedule 2 (which applies to all personal data) and Schedule 3 (which applies only to sensitive personal data) set out conditions applying for the purposes of the first principle; and Schedule 4 sets out cases in which the eighth principle does not apply.

(4) Subject to section 27(1), it shall be the duty of a data controller to comply with the data protection principles in relation to all personal data with respect to which he is the data controller.

5. Application of Act

(1) Except as otherwise provided by or under section 54, this Act applies to a data controller in respect of any data only if—

(a) the data controller is established in the United Kingdom and the data are processed in the context of that establishment, or

(b) the data controller is established neither in the United Kingdom nor in any other EEA State but uses equipment in the United Kingdom for processing the data otherwise than for the purposes of transit through the United Kingdom.

(2) A data controller falling within subsection (1)(b) must nominate for the purposes of this Act a representative established in the United Kingdom.

(3) For the purposes of subsections (1) and (2), each of the following is to be treated as established in the United Kingdom —

(a) an individual who is ordinarily resident in the United Kingdom,

(b) a body incorporated under the law of, or of any part of, the United Kingdom,

(c) a partnership or other unincorporated association formed under the law of any part of the United Kingdom, and

(d) any person who does not fall within paragraph (a), (b) or (c) but maintains in the United Kingdom —

(i) an office, branch or agency through which he carries on any activity, or

(ii) a regular practice;

and the reference to establishment in any other EEA State has a corresponding meaning.

6. The Commissioner and the Tribunal

(1) The office originally established by section 3(1)(a) of the [1984 c. 35.] Data Protection Act 1984 as the office of Data Protection Registrar shall continue to exist for the purposes of this Act but shall be known as the office of Data Protection Commissioner; and in this Act the Data Protection Commissioner is referred to as "the Commissioner".

(2) The Commissioner shall be appointed by Her Majesty by Letters Patent.

(3) For the purposes of this Act there shall continue to be a Data Protection Tribunal (in this Act referred to as "the Tribunal").

(4) The Tribunal shall consist of —

(a) a chairman appointed by the Lord Chancellor after consultation with the Lord Advocate,

(b) such number of deputy chairmen so appointed as the Lord Chancellor may determine, and

(c) such number of other members appointed by the Secretary of State as he may determine.

(5) The members of the Tribunal appointed under subsection (4)(a) and (b) shall be —

(a) persons who have a 7 year general qualification, within the meaning of section 71 of the [1990 c. 41.] Courts and Legal Services Act 1990,

(b) advocates or solicitors in Scotland of at least 7 years' standing, or

(c) members of the bar of Northern Ireland or solicitors of the Supreme Court of Northern Ireland of at least 7 years' standing.

(6) The members of the Tribunal appointed under subsection (4)(c) shall be —

(a) persons to represent the interests of data subjects, and

(b) persons to represent the interests of data controllers.

(7) Schedule 5 has effect in relation to the Commissioner and the Tribunal

Part II

Rights of data subjects and others

7. Right of access to personal data

(1) Subject to the following provisions of this section and to sections 8 and 9, an individual is entitled —

(a) to be informed by any data controller whether personal data of which that individual is the data subject are being processed by or on behalf of that data controller,

(b) if that is the case, to be given by the data controller a description of —

   (i) the personal data of which that individual is the data subject,

   (ii) the purposes for which they are being or are to be processed, and

   (iii) the recipients or classes of recipients to whom they are or may be disclosed,

(c) to have communicated to him in an intelligible form —

   (i) the information constituting any personal data of which that individual is the data subject, and

   (ii) any information available to the data controller as to the source of those data, and

(d) where the processing by automatic means of personal data of which that individual is the data subject for the purpose of evaluating matters relating to him such as, for example, his performance at work, his creditworthiness, his reliability or his conduct, has constituted or is likely to constitute the sole basis for any decision significantly affecting him, to be informed by the data controller of the logic involved in that decision-taking.

(2) A data controller is not obliged to supply any information under subsection (1) unless he has received —

(a) a request in writing, and

(b) except in prescribed cases, such fee (not exceeding the prescribed maximum) as he may require.

(3) A data controller is not obliged to comply with a request under this section unless he is supplied with such information as he may reasonably require in order to satisfy himself as to the identity of the

person making the request and to locate the information which that person seeks.

(4) Where a data controller cannot comply with the request without disclosing information relating to another individual who can be identified from that information, he is not obliged to comply with the request unless—

  (a) the other individual has consented to the disclosure of the information to the person making the request, or

  (b) it is reasonable in all the circumstances to comply with the request without the consent of the other individual.

(5) In subsection (4) the reference to information relating to another individual includes a reference to information identifying that individual as the source of the information sought by the request; and that subsection is not to be construed as excusing a data controller from communicating so much of the information sought by the request as can be communicated without disclosing the identity of the other individual concerned, whether by the omission of names or other identifying particulars or otherwise.

(6) In determining for the purposes of subsection (4)(b) whether it is reasonable in all the circumstances to comply with the request without the consent of the other individual concerned, regard shall be had, in particular, to—

  (a) any duty of confidentiality owed to the other individual,

  (b) any steps taken by the data controller with a view to seeking the consent of the other individual,

  (c) whether the other individual is capable of giving consent, and

  (d) any express refusal of consent by the other individual.

(7) An individual making a request under this section may, in such cases as may be prescribed, specify that his request is limited to personal data of any prescribed description.

(8) Subject to subsection (4), a data controller shall comply with a request under this section promptly and in any event before the end of the prescribed period beginning with the relevant day.

(9) If a court is satisfied on the application of any person who has made a request under the foregoing provisions of this section that the data controller in question has failed to comply with the request in contravention of those provisions, the court may order him to comply with the request.

(10) In this section —

- "prescribed" means prescribed by the Secretary of State by regulations;

- "the prescribed maximum" means such amount as may be prescribed;

- "the prescribed period" means forty days or such other period as may be prescribed;

- "the relevant day", in relation to a request under this section, means the day on which the data controller receives the request or, if later, the first day on which the data controller has both the required fee and the information referred to in subsection (3).

(11) Different amounts or periods may be prescribed under this section in relation to different cases.

8. Provisions supplementary to section 7

(1) The Secretary of State may by regulations provide that, in such cases as may be prescribed, a request for information under any provision of subsection (1) of section 7 is to be treated as extending also to information under other provisions of that subsection.

(2) The obligation imposed by section 7(1)(c)(i) must be complied with by supplying the data subject with a copy of the information in permanent form unless —

- (a) the supply of such a copy is not possible or would involve disproportionate effort, or

(b) the data subject agrees otherwise;

and where any of the information referred to in section 7(1)(c)(i) is expressed in terms which are not intelligible without explanation the copy must be accompanied by an explanation of those terms.

(3) Where a data controller has previously complied with a request made under section 7 by an individual, the data controller is not obliged to comply with a subsequent identical or similar request under that section by that individual unless a reasonable interval has elapsed between compliance with the previous request and the making of the current request.

(4) In determining for the purposes of subsection (3) whether requests under section 7 are made at reasonable intervals, regard shall be had to the nature of the data, the purpose for which the data are processed and the frequency with which the data are altered.

(5) Section 7(1)(d) is not to be regarded as requiring the provision of information as to the logic involved in any decision-taking if, and to the extent that, the information constitutes a trade secret.

(6) The information to be supplied pursuant to a request under section 7 must be supplied by reference to the data in question at the time when the request is received, except that it may take account of any amendment or deletion made between that time and the time when the information is supplied, being an amendment or deletion that would have been made regardless of the receipt of the request.

(7) For the purposes of section 7(4) and (5) another individual can be identified from the information being disclosed if he can be identified from that information, or from that and any other information which, in the reasonable belief of the data controller, is likely to be in, or to come into, the possession of the data subject making the request.

9. Application of section 7 where data controller is credit reference agency

(1) Where the data controller is a credit reference agency, section 7 has effect subject to the provisions of this section.

(2) An individual making a request under section 7 may limit his request to personal data relevant to his financial standing, and shall be taken to have so limited his request unless the request shows a contrary intention.

(3) Where the data controller receives a request under section 7 in a case where personal data of which the individual making the request is the data subject are being processed by or on behalf of the data controller, the obligation to supply information under that section includes an obligation to give the individual making the request a statement, in such form as may be prescribed by the Secretary of State by regulations, of the individual's rights —

(a) under section 159 of the [1974 c. 39.] Consumer Credit Act 1974, and

(b) to the extent required by the prescribed form, under this Act.

10. Right to prevent processing likely to cause damage or distress

(1) Subject to subsection (2), an individual is entitled at any time by notice in writing to a data controller to require the data controller at the end of such period as is reasonable in the circumstances to cease, or not to begin, processing, or processing for a specified purpose or in a specified manner, any personal data in respect of which he is the data subject, on the ground that, for specified reasons —

(a) the processing of those data or their processing for that purpose or in that manner is causing or is likely to cause substantial damage or substantial distress to him or to another, and

(b) that damage or distress is or would be unwarranted.

(2) Subsection (1) does not apply —

(a) in a case where any of the conditions in paragraphs 1 to 4 of Schedule 2 is met, or

(b) in such other cases as may be prescribed by the Secretary of State by order.

(3) The data controller must within twenty-one days of receiving a notice under subsection (1) ("the data subject notice") give the individual who gave it a written notice —

(a) stating that he has complied or intends to comply with the data subject notice, or

(b) stating his reasons for regarding the data subject notice as to any extent unjustified and the extent (if any) to which he has complied or intends to comply with it.

(4) If a court is satisfied, on the application of any person who has given a notice under subsection (1) which appears to the court to be justified (or to be justified to any extent), that the data controller in question has failed to comply with the notice, the court may order him to take such steps for complying with the notice (or for complying with it to that extent) as the court thinks fit.

(5) The failure by a data subject to exercise the right conferred by subsection (1) or section 11(1) does not affect any other right conferred on him by this Part.

11. Right to prevent processing for purposes of direct marketing

(1) An individual is entitled at any time by notice in writing to a data controller to require the data controller at the end of such period as is reasonable in the circumstances to cease, or not to begin, processing for the purposes of direct marketing personal data in respect of which he is the data subject.

(2) If the court is satisfied, on the application of any person who has given a notice under subsection (1), that the data controller has failed to comply with the notice, the court may order him to take such steps for complying with the notice as the court thinks fit.

(3) In this section "direct marketing" means the communication (by whatever means) of any advertising or marketing material which is directed to particular individuals.

12. Rights in relation to automated decision-taking

(1) An individual is entitled at any time, by notice in writing to any data controller, to require the data controller to ensure that no decision taken by or on behalf of the data controller which significantly affects that individual is based solely on the processing by automatic means of personal data in respect of which that individual is the data subject for the purpose of evaluating matters relating to him such as, for example, his performance at work, his creditworthiness, his reliability or his conduct.

(2) Where, in a case where no notice under subsection (1) has effect, a decision which significantly affects an individual is based solely on such processing as is mentioned in subsection (1) —

   (a) the data controller must as soon as reasonably practicable notify the individual that the decision was taken on that basis, and

   (b) the individual is entitled, within twenty-one days of receiving that notification from the data controller, by notice in writing to require the data controller to reconsider the decision or to take a new decision otherwise than on that basis.

(3) The data controller must, within twenty-one days of receiving a notice under subsection (2)(b) ("the data subject notice") give the individual a written notice specifying the steps that he intends to take to comply with the data subject notice.

(4) A notice under subsection (1) does not have effect in relation to an exempt decision; and nothing in subsection (2) applies to an exempt decision.

(5) In subsection (4) "exempt decision" means any decision —

   (a) in respect of which the condition in subsection (6) and the condition in subsection (7) are met, or

   (b) which is made in such other circumstances as may be prescribed by the Secretary of State by order.

(6) The condition in this subsection is that the decision —

(a) is taken in the course of steps taken —

    (i) for the purpose of considering whether to enter into a contract with the data subject,

    (ii) with a view to entering into such a contract, or

    (iii) in the course of performing such a contract, or

(b) is authorised or required by or under any enactment.

(7) The condition in this subsection is that either —

(a) the effect of the decision is to grant a request of the data subject, or

(b) steps have been taken to safeguard the legitimate interests of the data subject (for example, by allowing him to make representations).

(8) If a court is satisfied on the application of a data subject that a person taking a decision in respect of him ("the responsible person") has failed to comply with subsection (1) or (2)(b), the court may order the responsible person to reconsider the decision, or to take a new decision which is not based solely on such processing as is mentioned in subsection (1).

(9) An order under subsection (8) shall not affect the rights of any person other than the data subject and the responsible person.

13. Compensation for failure to comply with certain requirements

(1) An individual who suffers damage by reason of any contravention by a data controller of any of the requirements of this Act is entitled to compensation from the data controller for that damage.

(2) An individual who suffers distress by reason of any contravention by a data controller of any of the requirements of this Act is entitled to compensation from the data controller for that distress if —

(a) the individual also suffers damage by reason of the contravention, or

(b) the contravention relates to the processing of personal data for the special purposes.

(3) In proceedings brought against a person by virtue of this section it is a defence to prove that he had taken such care as in all the circumstances was reasonably required to comply with the requirement concerned.

14. Rectification, blocking, erasure and destruction

(1) If a court is satisfied on the application of a data subject that personal data of which the applicant is the subject are inaccurate, the court may order the data controller to rectify, block, erase or destroy those data and any other personal data in respect of which he is the data controller and which contain an expression of opinion which appears to the court to be based on the inaccurate data.

(2) Subsection (1) applies whether or not the data accurately record information received or obtained by the data controller from the data subject or a third party but where the data accurately record such information, then—

(a) if the requirements mentioned in paragraph 7 of Part II of Schedule 1 have been complied with, the court may, instead of making an order under subsection (1), make an order requiring the data to be supplemented by such statement of the true facts relating to the matters dealt with by the data as the court may approve, and

(b) if all or any of those requirements have not been complied with, the court may, instead of making an order under that subsection, make such order as it thinks fit for securing compliance with those requirements with or without a further order requiring the data to be supplemented by such a statement as is mentioned in paragraph (a).

(3) Where the court—

(a) makes an order under subsection (1), or

(b) is satisfied on the application of a data subject that personal data
of which he was the data subject and which have been rectified,
blocked, erased or destroyed were inaccurate, it may, where it
considers it reasonably practicable, order the data controller to
notify third parties to whom the data have been disclosed of the
rectification, blocking, erasure or destruction.

(4) If a court is satisfied on the application of a data subject—

(a) that he has suffered damage by reason of any contravention by a
data controller of any of the requirements of this Act in respect of
any personal data, in circumstances entitling him to compensation
under section 13, and

(b) that there is a substantial risk of further contravention in respect
of those data in such circumstances, the court may order the
rectification, blocking, erasure or destruction of any of those data.

(5) Where the court makes an order under subsection (4) it may,
where it considers it reasonably practicable, order the data controller to
notify third parties to whom the data have been disclosed of the
rectification, blocking, erasure or destruction.

(6) In determining whether it is reasonably practicable to require such
notification as is mentioned in subsection (3) or (5) the court shall have
regard, in particular, to the number of persons who would have to be
notified.

15. Jurisdiction and procedure

(1) The jurisdiction conferred by sections 7 to 14 is exercisable by the
High Court or a county court or, in Scotland, by the Court of Session or
the sheriff.

(2) For the purpose of determining any question whether an applicant
under subsection (9) of section 7 is entitled to the information which he
seeks (including any question whether any relevant data are exempt from
that section by virtue of Part IV) a court may require the information
constituting any data processed by or on behalf of the data controller and
any information as to the logic involved in any decision-taking as

mentioned in section 7(1)(d) to be made available for its own inspection but shall not, pending the determination of that question in the applicant's favour, require the information sought by the applicant to be disclosed to him or his representatives whether by discovery (or, in Scotland, recovery) or otherwise.

Part III

Notification by data controllers

16. Preliminary

(1) In this Part "the registrable particulars", in relation to a data controller, means —

(a) his name and address,

(b) if he has nominated a representative for the purposes of this Act, the name and address of the representative,

(c) a description of the personal data being or to be processed by or on behalf of the data controller and of the category or categories of data subject to which they relate,

(d) a description of the purpose or purposes for which the data are being or are to be processed,

(e) a description of any recipient or recipients to whom the data controller intends or may wish to disclose the data,

(f) the names, or a description of, any countries or territories outside the European Economic Area to which the data controller directly or indirectly transfers, or intends or may wish directly or indirectly to transfer, the data, and

(g) in any case where —

(i) personal data are being, or are intended to be, processed in circumstances in which the prohibition in subsection (1) of section 17 is excluded by subsection (2) or (3) of that section, and

(ii) the notification does not extend to those data,

a statement of that fact.

(2) In this Part—

- "fees regulations" means regulations made by the Secretary of State under section 18(5) or 19(4) or (7);

- "notification regulations" means regulations made by the Secretary of State under the other provisions of this Part;

- "prescribed", except where used in relation to fees regulations, means prescribed by notification regulations.

(3) For the purposes of this Part, so far as it relates to the addresses of data controllers—

(a) the address of a registered company is that of its registered office, and

(b) the address of a person (other than a registered company) carrying on a business is that of his principal place of business in the United Kingdom.

17. Prohibition on processing without registration

(1) Subject to the following provisions of this section, personal data must not be processed unless an entry in respect of the data controller is included in the register maintained by the Commissioner under section 19 (or is treated by notification regulations made by virtue of section 19(3) as being so included).

(2) Except where the processing is assessable processing for the purposes of section 22, subsection (1) does not apply in relation to personal data consisting of information which falls neither within paragraph (a) of the definition of "data" in section 1(1) nor within paragraph (b) of that definition.

(3) If it appears to the Secretary of State that processing of a particular description is unlikely to prejudice the rights and freedoms of data subjects, notification regulations may provide that, in such cases as may be prescribed, subsection (1) is not to apply in relation to processing of that description.

(4) Subsection (1) does not apply in relation to any processing whose sole purpose is the maintenance of a public register.

18. Notification by data controllers

(1) Any data controller who wishes to be included in the register maintained under section 19 shall give a notification to the Commissioner under this section.

(2) A notification under this section must specify in accordance with notification regulations —

(a) the registrable particulars, and

(b) a general description of measures to be taken for the purpose of complying with the seventh data protection principle.

(3) Notification regulations made by virtue of subsection (2) may provide for the determination by the Commissioner, in accordance with any requirements of the regulations, of the form in which the registrable particulars and the description mentioned in subsection (2)(b) are to be specified, including in particular the detail required for the purposes of section 16(1)(c), (d), (e) and (f) and subsection (2)(b).

(4) Notification regulations may make provision as to the giving of notification —

(a) by partnerships, or

(b) in other cases where two or more persons are the data controllers in respect of any personal data.

(5) The notification must be accompanied by such fee as may be prescribed by fees regulations.

(6) Notification regulations may provide for any fee paid under subsection (5) or section 19(4) to be refunded in prescribed circumstances.

19. Register of notifications

(1) The Commissioner shall —

(a) maintain a register of persons who have given notification under section 18, and

(b) make an entry in the register in pursuance of each notification received by him under that section from a person in respect of whom no entry as data controller was for the time being included in the register.

(2) Each entry in the register shall consist of —

(a) the registrable particulars notified under section 18 or, as the case requires, those particulars as amended in pursuance of section 20(4), and

(b) such other information as the Commissioner may be authorised or required by notification regulations to include in the register.

(3) Notification regulations may make provision as to the time as from which any entry in respect of a data controller is to be treated for the purposes of section 17 as having been made in the register.

(4) No entry shall be retained in the register for more than the relevant time except on payment of such fee as may be prescribed by fees regulations.

(5) In subsection (4) "the relevant time" means twelve months or such other period as may be prescribed by notification regulations; and different periods may be prescribed in relation to different cases.

(6) The Commissioner —

(a) shall provide facilities for making the information contained in the entries in the register available for inspection (in visible and legible form) by members of the public at all reasonable hours and free of charge, and

(b) may provide such other facilities for making the information contained in those entries available to the public free of charge as he considers appropriate.

(7) The Commissioner shall, on payment of such fee, if any, as may be prescribed by fees regulations, supply any member of the public with a duly certified copy in writing of the particulars contained in any entry made in the register.

20. Duty to notify changes

(1) For the purpose specified in subsection (2), notification regulations shall include provision imposing on every person in respect of whom an entry as a data controller is for the time being included in the register maintained under section 19 a duty to notify to the Commissioner, in such circumstances and at such time or times and in such form as may be prescribed, such matters relating to the registrable particulars and measures taken as mentioned in section 18(2)(b) as may be prescribed.

(2) The purpose referred to in subsection (1) is that of ensuring, so far as practicable, that at any time —

(a) the entries in the register maintained under section 19 contain current names and addresses and describe the current practice or intentions of the data controller with respect to the processing of personal data, and

(b) the Commissioner is provided with a general description of measures currently being taken as mentioned in section 18(2)(b).

(3) Subsection (3) of section 18 has effect in relation to notification regulations made by virtue of subsection (1) as it has effect in relation to notification regulations made by virtue of subsection (2) of that section.

(4) On receiving any notification under notification regulations made by virtue of subsection (1), the Commissioner shall make such amendments of the relevant entry in the register maintained under section 19 as are necessary to take account of the notification.

21. Offences

(1) If section 17(1) is contravened, the data controller is guilty of an offence.

(2) Any person who fails to comply with the duty imposed by notification regulations made by virtue of section 20(1) is guilty of an offence.

(3) It shall be a defence for a person charged with an offence under subsection (2) to show that he exercised all due diligence to comply with the duty.

22. Preliminary assessment by Commissioner

(1) In this section "assessable processing" means processing which is of a description specified in an order made by the Secretary of State as appearing to him to be particularly likely —

(a) to cause substantial damage or substantial distress to data subjects, or

(b) otherwise significantly to prejudice the rights and freedoms of data subjects.

(2) On receiving notification from any data controller under section 18 or under notification regulations made by virtue of section 20 the Commissioner shall consider —

(a) whether any of the processing to which the notification relates is assessable processing, and

(b) if so, whether the assessable processing is likely to comply with the provisions of this Act.

(3) Subject to subsection (4), the Commissioner shall, within the period of twenty-eight days beginning with the day on which he receives a notification which relates to assessable processing, give a notice to the data controller stating the extent to which the Commissioner is of the opinion that the processing is likely or unlikely to comply with the provisions of this Act.

(4) Before the end of the period referred to in subsection (3) the Commissioner may, by reason of special circumstances, extend that period on one occasion only by notice to the data controller by such further period not exceeding fourteen days as the Commissioner may specify in the notice.

(5) No assessable processing in respect of which a notification has been given to the Commissioner as mentioned in subsection (2) shall be carried on unless either —

(a) the period of twenty-eight days beginning with the day on which the notification is received by the Commissioner (or, in a case falling within subsection (4), that period as extended under that subsection) has elapsed, or

(b) before the end of that period (or that period as so extended) the data controller has received a notice from the Commissioner under subsection (3) in respect of the processing.

(6) Where subsection (5) is contravened, the data controller is guilty of an offence.

(7) The Secretary of State may by order amend subsections (3), (4) and (5) by substituting for the number of days for the time being specified there a different number specified in the order.

23. Power to make provision for appointment of data protection supervisors

(1) The Secretary of State may by order —

(a) make provision under which a data controller may appoint a person to act as a data protection supervisor responsible in particular for monitoring in an independent manner the data controller's compliance with the provisions of this Act, and

(b) provide that, in relation to any data controller who has appointed a data protection supervisor in accordance with the provisions of the order and who complies with such conditions as may be specified in the order, the provisions of this Part are to have effect subject to such exemptions or other modifications as may be specified in the order.

(2) An order under this section may —

(a) impose duties on data protection supervisors in relation to the Commissioner, and

(b) confer functions on the Commissioner in relation to data protection supervisors.

24. Duty of certain data controllers to make certain information available

(1) Subject to subsection (3), where personal data are processed in a case where—

(a) by virtue of subsection (2) or (3) of section 17, subsection (1) of that section does not apply to the processing, and

(b) the data controller has not notified the relevant particulars in respect of that processing under section 18,

the data controller must, within twenty-one days of receiving a written request from any person, make the relevant particulars available to that person in writing free of charge.

(2) In this section "the relevant particulars" means the particulars referred to in paragraphs (a) to (f) of section 16(1).

(3) This section has effect subject to any exemption conferred for the purposes of this section by notification regulations.

(4) Any data controller who fails to comply with the duty imposed by subsection (1) is guilty of an offence.

(5) It shall be a defence for a person charged with an offence under subsection (4) to show that he exercised all due diligence to comply with the duty.

25. Functions of Commissioner in relation to making of notification regulations

(1) As soon as practicable after the passing of this Act, the Commissioner shall submit to the Secretary of State proposals as to the provisions to be included in the first notification regulations.

(2) The Commissioner shall keep under review the working of notification regulations and may from time to time submit to the Secretary of State proposals as to amendments to be made to the regulations.

(3) The Secretary of State may from time to time require the Commissioner to consider any matter relating to notification regulations and to submit to him proposals as to amendments to be made to the regulations in connection with that matter.

(4) Before making any notification regulations, the Secretary of State shall—

(a) consider any proposals made to him by the Commissioner under subsection (1), (2) or (3), and

(b) consult the Commissioner.

26. Fees regulations

(1) Fees regulations prescribing fees for the purposes of any provision of this Part may provide for different fees to be payable in different cases.

(2) In making any fees regulations, the Secretary of State shall have regard to the desirability of securing that the fees payable to the Commissioner are sufficient to offset—

(a) the expenses incurred by the Commissioner and the Tribunal in discharging their functions and any expenses of the Secretary of State in respect of the Commissioner or the Tribunal, and

(b) to the extent that the Secretary of State considers appropriate—

(i) any deficit previously incurred (whether before or after the passing of this Act) in respect of the expenses mentioned in paragraph (a), and

(ii) expenses incurred or to be incurred by the Secretary of State in respect of the inclusion of any officers or staff of the Commissioner in any scheme under section 1 of the [1972 c. 11.] Superannuation Act 1972

Part IV

Exemptions

27. Preliminary

(1) References in any of the data protection principles or any provision of Parts II and III to personal data or to the processing of personal data do not include references to data or processing which by virtue of this Part are exempt from that principle or other provision.

(2) In this Part "the subject information provisions" means—

(a) the first data protection principle to the extent to which it requires compliance with paragraph 2 of Part II of Schedule 1, and

(b) section 7.

(3) In this Part "the non-disclosure provisions" means the provisions specified in subsection (4) to the extent to which they are inconsistent with the disclosure in question.

(4) The provisions referred to in subsection (3) are—

(a) the first data protection principle, except to the extent to which it requires compliance with the conditions in Schedules 2 and 3,

(b) the second, third, fourth and fifth data protection principles, and

(c) sections 10 and 14(1) to (3).

(5) Except as provided by this Part, the subject information provisions shall have effect notwithstanding any enactment or rule of law prohibiting or restricting the disclosure, or authorising the withholding, of information.

28. National security

(1) Personal data are exempt from any of the provisions of—

(a) the data protection principles,

(b) Parts II, III and V, and

(c) section 55,

if the exemption from that provision is required for the purpose of safeguarding national security.

(2) Subject to subsection (4), a certificate signed by a Minister of the Crown certifying that exemption from all or any of the provisions mentioned in subsection (1) is or at any time was required for the purpose there mentioned in respect of any personal data shall be conclusive evidence of that fact.

(3) A certificate under subsection (2) may identify the personal data to which it applies by means of a general description and may be expressed to have prospective effect.

(4) Any person directly affected by the issuing of a certificate under subsection (2) may appeal to the Tribunal against the certificate.

(5) If on an appeal under subsection (4), the Tribunal finds that, applying the principles applied by the court on an application for judicial review, the Minister did not have reasonable grounds for issuing the certificate, the Tribunal may allow the appeal and quash the certificate.

(6) Where in any proceedings under or by virtue of this Act it is claimed by a data controller that a certificate under subsection (2) which identifies the personal data to which it applies by means of a general description applies to any personal data, any other party to the proceedings may appeal to the Tribunal on the ground that the certificate does not apply to the personal data in question and, subject to any determination under subsection (7), the certificate shall be conclusively presumed so to apply.

(7) On any appeal under subsection (6), the Tribunal may determine that the certificate does not so apply.

(8) A document purporting to be a certificate under subsection (2) shall be received in evidence and deemed to be such a certificate unless the contrary is proved.

(9) A document which purports to be certified by or on behalf of a Minister of the Crown as a true copy of a certificate issued by that Minister under subsection (2) shall in any legal proceedings be evidence (or, in Scotland, sufficient evidence) of that certificate.

(10) The power conferred by subsection (2) on a Minister of the Crown shall not be exercisable except by a Minister who is a member of the Cabinet or by the Attorney General or the Lord Advocate.

(11) No power conferred by any provision of Part V may be exercised in relation to personal data which by virtue of this section are exempt from that provision.

(12) Schedule 6 shall have effect in relation to appeals under subsection (4) or (6) and the proceedings of the Tribunal in respect of any such appeal.

29. Crime and taxation

(1) Personal data processed for any of the following purposes —

(a) the prevention or detection of crime,

(b) the apprehension or prosecution of offenders, or

(c) the assessment or collection of any tax or duty or of any imposition of a similar nature,

are exempt from the first data protection principle (except to the extent to which it requires compliance with the conditions in Schedules 2 and 3) and section 7 in any case to the extent to which the application of those provisions to the data would be likely to prejudice any of the matters mentioned in this subsection.

(2) Personal data which —

(a) are processed for the purpose of discharging statutory functions, and

(b) consist of information obtained for such a purpose from a person who had it in his possession for any of the purposes mentioned in subsection (1),

are exempt from the subject information provisions to the same extent as personal data processed for any of the purposes mentioned in that subsection.

(3) Personal data are exempt from the non-disclosure provisions in any case in which —

(a) the disclosure is for any of the purposes mentioned in subsection (1), and

(b) the application of those provisions in relation to the disclosure would be likely to prejudice any of the matters mentioned in that subsection.

(4) Personal data in respect of which the data controller is a relevant authority and which —

(a) consist of a classification applied to the data subject as part of a system of risk assessment which is operated by that authority for either of the following purposes —

(i) the assessment or collection of any tax or duty or any imposition of a similar nature, or

(ii) the prevention or detection of crime, or apprehension or prosecution of offenders, where the offence concerned involves any unlawful claim for any payment out of, or any unlawful application of, public funds, and

(b) are processed for either of those purposes,

are exempt from section 7 to the extent to which the exemption is required in the interests of the operation of the system.

(5) In subsection (4) —

• "public funds" includes funds provided by any Community institution;

• "relevant authority" means —

(a) a government department,

(b) a local authority, or

(c) any other authority administering housing benefit or council tax benefit.

30. Health, education and social work

(1) The Secretary of State may by order exempt from the subject information provisions, or modify those provisions in relation to, personal data consisting of information as to the physical or mental health or condition of the data subject.

(2) The Secretary of State may by order exempt from the subject information provisions, or modify those provisions in relation to —

(a) personal data in respect of which the data controller is the proprietor of, or a teacher at, a school, and which consist of information relating to persons who are or have been pupils at the school, or

(b) personal data in respect of which the data controller is an education authority in Scotland, and which consist of information relating to persons who are receiving, or have received, further education provided by the authority.

(3) The Secretary of State may by order exempt from the subject information provisions, or modify those provisions in relation to, personal data of such other descriptions as may be specified in the order, being information—

(a) processed by government departments or local authorities or by voluntary organisations or other bodies designated by or under the order, and

(b) appearing to him to be processed in the course of, or for the purposes of, carrying out social work in relation to the data subject or other individuals;

but the Secretary of State shall not under this subsection confer any exemption or make any modification except so far as he considers that the application to the data of those provisions (or of those provisions without modification) would be likely to prejudice the carrying out of social work.

(4) An order under this section may make different provision in relation to data consisting of information of different descriptions.

(5) In this section—

- "education authority" and "further education" have the same meaning as in the [1980 c. 44.] Education (Scotland) Act 1980 ("the 1980 Act"), and

- "proprietor"—

  (a) in relation to a school in England or Wales, has the same meaning as in the [1996 c. 56.] Education Act 1996,

(b) in relation to a school in Scotland, means—

(c) in the case of a self-governing school, the board of management within the meaning of the [1989 c. 39.] Self-Governing Schools etc. (Scotland) Act 1989,

    (ii) in the case of an independent school, the proprietor within the meaning of the 1980 Act,

    (iii) in the case of a grant-aided school, the managers within the meaning of the 1980 Act, and

    (iv) in the case of a public school, the education authority within the meaning of the 1980 Act, and

(g) in relation to a school in Northern Ireland, has the same meaning as in the [S.I. 1986/594 (N.I.3).] Education and Libraries (Northern Ireland) Order 1986 and includes, in the case of a controlled school, the Board of Governors of the school.

31. Regulatory activity

(1) Personal data processed for the purposes of discharging functions to which this subsection applies are exempt from the subject information provisions in any case to the extent to which the application of those provisions to the data would be likely to prejudice the proper discharge of those functions.

(2) Subsection (1) applies to any relevant function which is designed—

(a) for protecting members of the public against—

    (i) financial loss due to dishonesty, malpractice or other seriously improper conduct by, or the unfitness or incompetence of, persons concerned in the provision of banking, insurance, investment or other financial services or in the management of bodies corporate,

    (ii) financial loss due to the conduct of discharged or undischarged bankrupts, or

    (iii) dishonesty, malpractice or other seriously improper conduct by, or the unfitness or incompetence of, persons authorised to carry on any profession or other activity,

(b) for protecting charities against misconduct or mismanagement (whether by trustees or other persons) in their administration,

(c) for protecting the property of charities from loss or misapplication,

(d) for the recovery of the property of charities,

(e) for securing the health, safety and welfare of persons at work, or

(f) for protecting persons other than persons at work against risk to health or safety arising out of or in connection with the actions of persons at work.

(3) In subsection (2) "relevant function" means —

(a) any function conferred on any person by or under any enactment,

(b) any function of the Crown, a Minister of the Crown or a government department, or

(c) any other function which is of a public nature and is exercised in the public interest.

(4) Personal data processed for the purpose of discharging any function which —

(a) is conferred by or under any enactment on —

    (i) the Parliamentary Commissioner for Administration,

    (ii) the Commission for Local Administration in England, the Commission for Local Administration in Wales or the Commissioner for Local Administration in Scotland,

    (iii) the Health Service Commissioner for England, the Health Service Commissioner for Wales or the Health Service Commissioner for Scotland,

    (iv) the Welsh Administration Ombudsman,

    (v)   the Assembly Ombudsman for Northern Ireland, or

    (vi)   the Northern Ireland Commissioner for Complaints, and

  (b) is designed for protecting members of the public against —

    (i)   maladministration by public bodies,

    (ii)   failures in services provided by public bodies, or

    (iii)   a failure of a public body to provide a service which it was a function of the body to provide,

are exempt from the subject information provisions in any case to the extent to which the application of those provisions to the data would be likely to prejudice the proper discharge of that function.

(5) Personal data processed for the purpose of discharging any function which —

  (a) is conferred by or under any enactment on the Director General of Fair Trading, and

  (b) is designed —

    (i)   for protecting members of the public against conduct which may adversely affect their interests by persons carrying on a business,

    (ii)   for regulating agreements or conduct which have as their object or effect the prevention, restriction or distortion of competition in connection with any commercial activity, or

    (iii)   for regulating conduct on the part of one or more undertakings which amounts to the abuse of a dominant position in a market,

are exempt from the subject information provisions in any case to the extent to which the application of those provisions to the data would be likely to prejudice the proper discharge of that function.

32. Journalism, literature and art

(1) Personal data which are processed only for the special purposes are exempt from any provision to which this subsection relates if —

(a) the processing is undertaken with a view to the publication by any person of any journalistic, literary or artistic material,

(b) the data controller reasonably believes that, having regard in particular to the special importance of the public interest in freedom of expression, publication would be in the public interest, and

(c) the data controller reasonably believes that, in all the circumstances, compliance with that provision is incompatible with the special purposes.

(2) Subsection (1) relates to the provisions of —

(a) the data protection principles except the seventh data protection principle,

(b) section 7,

(c) section 10,

(d) section 12, and

(e) section 14(1) to (3).

(3) In considering for the purposes of subsection (1)(b) whether the belief of a data controller that publication would be in the public interest was or is a reasonable one, regard may be had to his compliance with any code of practice which —

(a) is relevant to the publication in question, and

(b) is designated by the Secretary of State by order for the purposes of this subsection.

(4) Where at any time ("the relevant time") in any proceedings against a data controller under section 7(9), 10(4), 12(8) or 14 or by virtue of section 13 the data controller claims, or it appears to the court, that any personal data to which the proceedings relate are being processed —

(a) only for the special purposes, and

(b) with a view to the publication by any person of any journalistic, literary or artistic material which, at the time twenty-four hours immediately before the relevant time, had not previously been published by the data controller,

the court shall stay the proceedings until either of the conditions in subsection (5) is met.

(5) Those conditions are—

(a) that a determination of the Commissioner under section 45 with respect to the data in question takes effect, or

(b) in a case where the proceedings were stayed on the making of a claim, that the claim is withdrawn.

(6) For the purposes of this Act "publish", in relation to journalistic, literary or artistic material, means make available to the public or any section of the public.

33. Research, history and statistics

(1) In this section—

- "research purposes" includes statistical or historical purposes;

- "the relevant conditions", in relation to any processing of personal data, means the conditions—

    (a) that the data are not processed to support measures or decisions with respect to particular individuals, and

    (b) that the data are not processed in such a way that substantial damage or substantial distress is, or is likely to be, caused to any data subject.

(2) For the purposes of the second data protection principle, the further processing of personal data only for research purposes in compliance with the relevant conditions is not to be regarded as incompatible with the purposes for which they were obtained.

(3) Personal data which are processed only for research purposes in compliance with the relevant conditions may, notwithstanding the fifth data protection principle, be kept indefinitely.

(4) Personal data which are processed only for research purposes are exempt from section 7 if —

(a) they are processed in compliance with the relevant conditions, and

(b) the results of the research or any resulting statistics are not made available in a form which identifies data subjects or any of them.

(5) For the purposes of subsections (2) to (4) personal data are not to be treated as processed otherwise than for research purposes merely because the data are disclosed —

(a) to any person, for research purposes only,

(b) to the data subject or a person acting on his behalf,

(c) at the request, or with the consent, of the data subject or a person acting on his behalf, or

(d) in circumstances in which the person making the disclosure has reasonable grounds for believing that the disclosure falls within paragraph (a), (b) or (c).

34. Information available to the public by or under enactment

Personal data are exempt from —

(a) the subject information provisions,

(b) the fourth data protection principle and section 14(1) to (3), and

(c) the non-disclosure provisions,

if the data consist of information which the data controller is obliged by or under any enactment to make available to the public, whether by publishing it, by making it available for inspection, or otherwise and whether gratuitously or on payment of a fee.

35. Disclosures required by law or made in connection with legal proceedings etc.

(1) Personal data are exempt from the non-disclosure provisions where the disclosure is required by or under any enactment, by any rule of law or by the order of a court.

(2) Personal data are exempt from the non-disclosure provisions where the disclosure is necessary —

(a)   for the purpose of, or in connection with, any legal proceedings (including prospective legal proceedings), or

(b)   for the purpose of obtaining legal advice,

or is otherwise necessary for the purposes of establishing, exercising or defending legal rights.

36. Domestic purposes

Personal data processed by an individual only for the purposes of that individual's personal, family or household affairs (including recreational purposes) are exempt from the data protection principles and the provisions of Parts II and III.

37. Miscellaneous exemptions

Schedule 7 (which confers further miscellaneous exemptions) has effect.

38. Powers to make further exemptions by order

(1) The Secretary of State may by order exempt from the subject information provisions personal data consisting of information the disclosure of which is prohibited or restricted by or under any enactment if and to the extent that he considers it necessary for the safeguarding of the interests of the data subject or the rights and freedoms of any other individual that the prohibition or restriction ought to prevail over those provisions.

(2) The Secretary of State may by order exempt from the non-disclosure provisions any disclosures of personal data made in circumstances specified in the order, if he considers the exemption is necessary for the safeguarding of the interests of the data subject or the rights and freedoms of any other individual.

39. Transitional relief

Part V

Enforcement

40. Enforcement notices

(1) If the Commissioner is satisfied that a data controller has contravened or is contravening any of the data protection principles, the Commissioner may serve him with a notice (in this Act referred to as "an enforcement notice") requiring him, for complying with the principle or principles in question, to do either or both of the following—

(a) to take within such time as may be specified in the notice, or to refrain from taking after such time as may be so specified, such steps as are so specified, or

(b) to refrain from processing any personal data, or any personal data of a description specified in the notice, or to refrain from processing them for a purpose so specified or in a manner so specified, after such time as may be so specified.

(2) In deciding whether to serve an enforcement notice, the Commissioner shall consider whether the contravention has caused or is likely to cause any person damage or distress.

(3) An enforcement notice in respect of a contravention of the fourth data protection principle which requires the data controller to rectify, block, erase or destroy any inaccurate data may also require the data controller to rectify, block, erase or destroy any other data held by him and containing an expression of opinion which appears to the Commissioner to be based on the inaccurate data.

(4) An enforcement notice in respect of a contravention of the fourth data protection principle, in the case of data which accurately record information received or obtained by the data controller from the data subject or a third party, may require the data controller either—

(a) to rectify, block, erase or destroy any inaccurate data and any other data held by him and containing an expression of opinion as mentioned in subsection (3), or

(b) to take such steps as are specified in the notice for securing compliance with the requirements specified in paragraph 7 of Part II of Schedule 1 and, if the Commissioner thinks fit, for supplementing the data with such statement of the true facts relating to the matters dealt with by the data as the Commissioner may approve.

(5) Where —

(a) an enforcement notice requires the data controller to rectify, block, erase or destroy any personal data, or

(b) the Commissioner is satisfied that personal data which have been rectified, blocked, erased or destroyed had been processed in contravention of any of the data protection principles,

an enforcement notice may, if reasonably practicable, require the data controller to notify third parties to whom the data have been disclosed of the rectification, blocking, erasure or destruction; and in determining whether it is reasonably practicable to require such notification regard shall be had, in particular, to the number of persons who would have to be notified.

(6) An enforcement notice must contain —

(a) a statement of the data protection principle or principles which the Commissioner is satisfied have been or are being contravened and his reasons for reaching that conclusion, and

(b) particulars of the rights of appeal conferred by section 48.

(7) Subject to subsection (8), an enforcement notice must not require any of the provisions of the notice to be complied with before the end of the period within which an appeal can be brought against the notice and, if such an appeal is brought, the notice need not be complied with pending the determination or withdrawal of the appeal.

(8) If by reason of special circumstances the Commissioner considers that an enforcement notice should be complied with as a matter of urgency he may include in the notice a statement to that effect and a statement of his reasons for reaching that conclusion; and in that event

subsection (7) shall not apply but the notice must not require the provisions of the notice to be complied with before the end of the period of seven days beginning with the day on which the notice is served.

(9) Notification regulations (as defined by section 16(2)) may make provision as to the effect of the service of an enforcement notice on any entry in the register maintained under section 19 which relates to the person on whom the notice is served.

(10) This section has effect subject to section 46(1).

41. Cancellation of enforcement notice

(1) If the Commissioner considers that all or any of the provisions of an enforcement notice need not be complied with in order to ensure compliance with the data protection principle or principles to which it relates, he may cancel or vary the notice by written notice to the person on whom it was served.

(2) A person on whom an enforcement notice has been served may, at any time after the expiry of the period during which an appeal can be brought against that notice, apply in writing to the Commissioner for the cancellation or variation of that notice on the ground that, by reason of a change of circumstances, all or any of the provisions of that notice need not be complied with in order to ensure compliance with the data protection principle or principles to which that notice relates.

42. Request for assessment

(1) A request may be made to the Commissioner by or on behalf of any person who is, or believes himself to be, directly affected by any processing of personal data for an assessment as to whether it is likely or unlikely that the processing has been or is being carried out in compliance with the provisions of this Act.

(2) On receiving a request under this section, the Commissioner shall make an assessment in such manner as appears to him to be appropriate, unless he has not been supplied with such information as he may reasonably require in order to—

(a) satisfy himself as to the identity of the person making the request, and

(b) enable him to identify the processing in question.

(3) The matters to which the Commissioner may have regard in determining in what manner it is appropriate to make an assessment include—

(a) the extent to which the request appears to him to raise a matter of substance,

(b) any undue delay in making the request, and

(c) whether or not the person making the request is entitled to make an application under section 7 in respect of the personal data in question.

(4) Where the Commissioner has received a request under this section he shall notify the person who made the request—

(a) whether he has made an assessment as a result of the request, and

(b) to the extent that he considers appropriate, having regard in particular to any exemption from section 7 applying in relation to the personal data concerned, of any view formed or action taken as a result of the request.

43. Information notices

(1) If the Commissioner—

(a) has received a request under section 42 in respect of any processing of personal data, or

(b) reasonably requires any information for the purpose of determining whether the data controller has complied or is complying with the data protection principles,

he may serve the data controller with a notice (in this Act referred to as "an information notice") requiring the data controller, within such time as is specified in the notice, to furnish the Commissioner, in such form as may be so specified, with such information relating to the request or to compliance with the principles as is so specified.

(2) An information notice must contain—

(a) in a case falling within subsection (1)(a), a statement that the Commissioner has received a request under section 42 in relation to the specified processing, or

(b) in a case falling within subsection (1)(b), a statement that the Commissioner regards the specified information as relevant for the purpose of determining whether the data controller has complied, or is complying, with the data protection principles and his reasons for regarding it as relevant for that purpose.

(3) An information notice must also contain particulars of the rights of appeal conferred by section 48.

(4) Subject to subsection (5), the time specified in an information notice shall not expire before the end of the period within which an appeal can be brought against the notice and, if such an appeal is brought, the information need not be furnished pending the determination or withdrawal of the appeal.

(5) If by reason of special circumstances the Commissioner considers that the information is required as a matter of urgency, he may include in the notice a statement to that effect and a statement of his reasons for reaching that conclusion; and in that event subsection (4) shall not apply, but the notice shall not require the information to be furnished before the end of the period of seven days beginning with the day on which the notice is served.

(6) A person shall not be required by virtue of this section to furnish the Commissioner with any information in respect of—

(a) any communication between a professional legal adviser and his client in connection with the giving of legal advice to the client with respect to his obligations, liabilities or rights under this Act, or

(b) any communication between a professional legal adviser and his client, or between such an adviser or his client and any other person, made in connection with or in contemplation of proceedings under or arising out of this Act (including proceedings before the Tribunal) and for the purposes of such proceedings.

(7) In subsection (6) references to the client of a professional legal adviser include references to any person representing such a client.

(8) A person shall not be required by virtue of this section to furnish the Commissioner with any information if the furnishing of that information would, by revealing evidence of the commission of any offence other than an offence under this Act, expose him to proceedings for that offence.

(9) The Commissioner may cancel an information notice by written notice to the person on whom it was served.

(10) This section has effect subject to section 46(3).

44 Special information notices

(1) If the Commissioner—

(a) has received a request under section 42 in respect of any processing of personal data, or

(b) has reasonable grounds for suspecting that, in a case in which proceedings have been stayed under section 32, the personal data to which the proceedings relate—

   (i)   are not being processed only for the special purposes, or

   (ii) are not being processed with a view to the publication by any person of any journalistic, literary or artistic material which has not previously been published by the data controller,

he may serve the data controller with a notice (in this Act referred to as a "special information notice") requiring the data controller, within such time as is specified in the notice, to furnish the Commissioner, in such form as may be so specified, with such information as is so specified for the purpose specified in subsection (2).

(2) That purpose is the purpose of ascertaining —

(a) whether the personal data are being processed only for the special purposes, or

(b) whether they are being processed with a view to the publication by any person of any journalistic, literary or artistic material which has not previously been published by the data controller.

(3) A special information notice must contain —

(a) in a case falling within paragraph (a) of subsection (1), a statement that the Commissioner has received a request under section 42 in relation to the specified processing, or

(b) in a case falling within paragraph (b) of that subsection, a statement of the Commissioner's grounds for suspecting that the personal data are not being processed as mentioned in that paragraph.

(4) A special information notice must also contain particulars of the rights of appeal conferred by section 48.

(5) Subject to subsection (6), the time specified in a special information notice shall not expire before the end of the period within which an appeal can be brought against the notice and, if such an appeal is brought, the information need not be furnished pending the determination or withdrawal of the appeal.

(6) If by reason of special circumstances the Commissioner considers that the information is required as a matter of urgency, he may include in the notice a statement to that effect and a statement of his reasons for reaching that conclusion; and in that event subsection (5) shall not apply, but the notice shall not require the information to be furnished before the end of the period of seven days beginning with the day on which the notice is served.

(7) A person shall not be required by virtue of this section to furnish the Commissioner with any information in respect of —

(a) any communication between a professional legal adviser and his client in connection with the giving of legal advice to the client with respect to his obligations, liabilities or rights under this Act, or

(b) any communication between a professional legal adviser and his client, or between such an adviser or his client and any other person, made in connection with or in contemplation of proceedings under or arising out of this Act (including proceedings before the Tribunal) and for the purposes of such proceedings.

(8) In subsection (7) references to the client of a professional legal adviser include references to any person representing such a client.

(9) A person shall not be required by virtue of this section to furnish the Commissioner with any information if the furnishing of that information would, by revealing evidence of the commission of any offence other than an offence under this Act, expose him to proceedings for that offence.

(10) The Commissioner may cancel a special information notice by written notice to the person on whom it was served.

45. Determination by Commissioner as to the special purposes

(1) Where at any time it appears to the Commissioner (whether as a result of the service of a special information notice or otherwise) that any personal data —

(a) are not being processed only for the special purposes, or

(b) are not being processed with a view to the publication by any person of any journalistic, literary or artistic material which has not previously been published by the data controller,

he may make a determination in writing to that effect.

(2) Notice of the determination shall be given to the data controller; and the notice must contain particulars of the right of appeal conferred by section 48.

(3) A determination under subsection (1) shall not take effect until the end of the period within which an appeal can be brought and, where an appeal is brought, shall not take effect pending the determination or withdrawal of the appeal.

46. Restriction on enforcement in case of processing for the special purposes

(1) The Commissioner may not at any time serve an enforcement notice on a data controller with respect to the processing of personal data for the special purposes unless —

(a) a determination under section 45(1) with respect to those data has taken effect, and

(b) the court has granted leave for the notice to be served.

(2) The court shall not grant leave for the purposes of subsection (1)(b) unless it is satisfied —

(a) that the Commissioner has reason to suspect a contravention of the data protection principles which is of substantial public importance, and

(b) except where the case is one of urgency, that the data controller has been given notice, in accordance with rules of court, of the application for leave.

(3) The Commissioner may not serve an information notice on a data controller with respect to the processing of personal data for the special purposes unless a determination under section 45(1) with respect to those data has taken effect.

47. Failure to comply with notice

(1) A person who fails to comply with an enforcement notice, an information notice or a special information notice is guilty of an offence.

(2) A person who, in purported compliance with an information notice or a special information notice —

(a) makes a statement which he knows to be false in a material respect, or

(b) recklessly makes a statement which is false in a material respect,

is guilty of an offence.

(3) It is a defence for a person charged with an offence under subsection (1) to prove that he exercised all due diligence to comply with the notice in question.

48. Rights of appeal

(1) A person on whom an enforcement notice, an information notice or a special information notice has been served may appeal to the Tribunal against the notice.

(2) A person on whom an enforcement notice has been served may appeal to the Tribunal against the refusal of an application under section 41(2) for cancellation or variation of the notice.

(3) Where an enforcement notice, an information notice or a special information notice contains a statement by the Commissioner in accordance with section 40(8), 43(5) or 44(6) then, whether or not the person appeals against the notice, he may appeal against —

(a) the Commissioner's decision to include the statement in the notice, or

(b) the effect of the inclusion of the statement as respects any part of the notice.

(4) A data controller in respect of whom a determination has been made under section 45 may appeal to the Tribunal against the determination.

(5) Schedule 6 has effect in relation to appeals under this section and the proceedings of the Tribunal in respect of any such appeal.

49. Determination of appeals

(1) If on an appeal under section 48(1) the Tribunal considers —

(a) that the notice against which the appeal is brought is not in accordance with the law, or

(b) to the extent that the notice involved an exercise of discretion by the Commissioner, that he ought to have exercised his discretion differently,

the Tribunal shall allow the appeal or substitute such other notice or decision as could have been served or made by the Commissioner; and in any other case the Tribunal shall dismiss the appeal.

(2) On such an appeal, the Tribunal may review any determination of fact on which the notice in question was based.

(3) If on an appeal under section 48(2) the Tribunal considers that the enforcement notice ought to be cancelled or varied by reason of a change in circumstances, the Tribunal shall cancel or vary the notice.

(4) On an appeal under subsection (3) of section 48 the Tribunal may direct—

(a) that the notice in question shall have effect as if it did not contain any such statement as is mentioned in that subsection, or

(b) that the inclusion of the statement shall not have effect in relation to any part of the notice,

and may make such modifications in the notice as may be required for giving effect to the direction.

(5) On an appeal under section 48(4), the Tribunal may cancel the determination of the Commissioner.

(6) Any party to an appeal to the Tribunal under section 48 may appeal from the decision of the Tribunal on a point of law to the appropriate court; and that court shall be—

(a) the High Court of Justice in England if the address of the person who was the appellant before the Tribunal is in England or Wales,

(b) the Court of Session if that address is in Scotland, and

(c) the High Court of Justice in Northern Ireland if that address is in Northern Ireland.

(7) For the purposes of subsection (6) —

(a) the address of a registered company is that of its registered office, and

(b) the address of a person (other than a registered company) carrying on a business is that of his principal place of business in the United Kingdom.

50. Powers of entry and inspection

Part VI

Miscellaneous and General

Functions of Commissioner

51. General duties of Commissioner

(1) It shall be the duty of the Commissioner to promote the following of good practice by data controllers and, in particular, so to perform his functions under this Act as to promote the observance of the requirements of this Act by data controllers.

(2) The Commissioner shall arrange for the dissemination in such form and manner as he considers appropriate of such information as it may appear to him expedient to give to the public about the operation of this Act, about good practice, and about other matters within the scope of his functions under this Act, and may give advice to any person as to any of those matters.

(3) Where —

(a) the Secretary of State so directs by order, or

(b) the Commissioner considers it appropriate to do so,

the Commissioner shall, after such consultation with trade associations, data subjects or persons representing data subjects as appears to him to be appropriate, prepare and disseminate to such persons as he considers appropriate codes of practice for guidance as to good practice.

(4) The Commissioner shall also —

(a) where he considers it appropriate to do so, encourage trade associations to prepare, and to disseminate to their members, such codes of practice, and

(b) where any trade association submits a code of practice to him for his consideration, consider the code and, after such consultation with data subjects or persons representing data subjects as appears to him to be appropriate, notify the trade association whether in his opinion the code promotes the following of good practice.

(5) An order under subsection (3) shall describe the personal data or processing to which the code of practice is to relate, and may also describe the persons or classes of persons to whom it is to relate.

(6) The Commissioner shall arrange for the dissemination in such form and manner as he considers appropriate of —

(a) any Community finding as defined by paragraph 15(2) of Part II of Schedule 1,

(b) any decision of the European Commission, under the procedure provided for in Article 31(2) of the Data Protection Directive, which is made for the purposes of Article 26(3) or (4) of the Directive, and

(c) such other information as it may appear to him to be expedient to give to data controllers in relation to any personal data about the protection of the rights and freedoms of data subjects in relation to the processing of personal data in countries and territories outside the European Economic Area.

(7) The Commissioner may, with the consent of the data controller, assess any processing of personal data for the following of good practice and shall inform the data controller of the results of the assessment.

(8) The Commissioner may charge such sums as he may with the consent of the Secretary of State determine for any services provided by the Commissioner by virtue of this Part.

(9) In this section —

- "good practice" means such practice in the processing of personal data as appears to the Commissioner to be desirable having regard to the interests of data subjects and others, and includes (but is not limited to) compliance with the requirements of this Act;

- "trade association" includes any body representing data controllers.

52. Reports and codes of practice to be laid before Parliament

(1) The Commissioner shall lay annually before each House of Parliament a general report on the exercise of his functions under this Act.

(2) The Commissioner may from time to time lay before each House of Parliament such other reports with respect to those functions as he thinks fit.

(3) The Commissioner shall lay before each House of Parliament any code of practice prepared under section 51(3) for complying with a direction of the Secretary of State, unless the code is included in any report laid under subsection (1) or (2).

53. Assistance by Commissioner in cases involving processing for the special purposes

(1) An individual who is an actual or prospective party to any proceedings under section 7(9), 10(4), 12(8) or 14 or by virtue of section 13 which relate to personal data processed for the special purposes may apply to the Commissioner for assistance in relation to those proceedings.

(2) The Commissioner shall, as soon as reasonably practicable after receiving an application under subsection (1), consider it and decide whether and to what extent to grant it, but he shall not grant the application unless, in his opinion, the case involves a matter of substantial public importance.

(3) If the Commissioner decides to provide assistance, he shall, as soon as reasonably practicable after making the decision, notify the applicant, stating the extent of the assistance to be provided.

(4) If the Commissioner decides not to provide assistance, he shall, as soon as reasonably practicable after making the decision, notify the applicant of his decision and, if he thinks fit, the reasons for it.

(5) In this section—

(a) references to "proceedings" include references to prospective proceedings, and

(b) "applicant", in relation to assistance under this section, means an individual who applies for assistance.

(6) Schedule 10 has effect for supplementing this section.

54. International co-operation

(1) The Commissioner—

(a) shall continue to be the designated authority in the United Kingdom for the purposes of Article 13 of the Convention, and

(b) shall be the supervisory authority in the United Kingdom for the purposes of the Data Protection Directive.

(2) The Secretary of State may by order make provision as to the functions to be discharged by the Commissioner as the designated authority in the United Kingdom for the purposes of Article 13 of the Convention.

(3) The Secretary of State may by order make provision as to co-operation by the Commissioner with the European Commission and with supervisory authorities in other EEA States in connection with the performance of their respective duties and, in particular, as to—

(a) the exchange of information with supervisory authorities in other EEA States or with the European Commission, and

(b) the exercise within the United Kingdom at the request of a supervisory authority in another EEA State, in cases excluded by section 5 from the application of the other provisions of this Act, of functions of the Commissioner specified in the order.

(4) The Commissioner shall also carry out any data protection functions which the Secretary of State may by order direct him to carry out for the purpose of enabling Her Majesty's Government in the United Kingdom to give effect to any international obligations of the United Kingdom.

(5) The Commissioner shall, if so directed by the Secretary of State, provide any authority exercising data protection functions under the law of a colony specified in the direction with such assistance in connection with the discharge of those functions as the Secretary of State may direct or approve, on such terms (including terms as to payment) as the Secretary of State may direct or approve.

(6) Where the European Commission makes a decision for the purposes of Article 26(3) or (4) of the Data Protection Directive under the procedure provided for in Article 31(2) of the Directive, the Commissioner shall comply with that decision in exercising his functions under paragraph 9 of Schedule 4 or, as the case may be, paragraph 8 of that Schedule.

(7) The Commissioner shall inform the European Commission and the supervisory authorities in other EEA States —

(a) of any approvals granted for the purposes of paragraph 8 of Schedule 4, and

(b) of any authorisations granted for the purposes of paragraph 9 of that Schedule.

(8) In this section —

- "the Convention" means the Convention for the Protection of Individuals with regard to Automatic Processing of Personal Data which was opened for signature on 28th January 1981;

- "data protection functions" means functions relating to the protection of individuals with respect to the processing of personal information.

Unlawful obtaining etc. of personal data

55. Unlawful obtaining etc. of personal data

(1) A person must not knowingly or recklessly, without the consent of the data controller —

(a) obtain or disclose personal data or the information contained in personal data, or

(b) procure the disclosure to another person of the information contained in personal data.

(2) Subsection (1) does not apply to a person who shows —

(a)   that the obtaining, disclosing or procuring —

(i)   was necessary for the purpose of preventing or detecting crime, or

(ii)   was required or authorised by or under any enactment, by any rule of law or by the order of a court,

(b)   that he acted in the reasonable belief that he had in law the right to obtain or disclose the data or information or, as the case may be, to procure the disclosure of the information to the other person,

(c)   that he acted in the reasonable belief that he would have had the consent of the data controller if the data controller had known of the obtaining, disclosing or procuring and the circumstances of it, or

(d)   that in the particular circumstances the obtaining, disclosing or procuring was justified as being in the public interest.

(3) A person who contravenes subsection (1) is guilty of an offence.

(4) A person who sells personal data is guilty of an offence if he has obtained the data in contravention of subsection (1).

(5) A person who offers to sell personal data is guilty of an offence if —

(a) he has obtained the data in contravention of subsection (1), or

(b) he subsequently obtains the data in contravention of that subsection.

(6) For the purposes of subsection (5), an advertisement indicating that personal data are or may be for sale is an offer to sell the data.

(7) Section 1(2) does not apply for the purposes of this section; and for the purposes of subsections (4) to (6), "personal data" includes information extracted from personal data.

(8) References in this section to personal data do not include references to personal data which by virtue of section 28 are exempt from this section.

Records obtained under data subject's right of access

56. Prohibition of requirement as to production of certain records

(1) A person must not, in connection with —

(a) the recruitment of another person as an employee,

(b) the continued employment of another person, or

(c) any contract for the provision of services to him by another person,

require that other person or a third party to supply him with a relevant record or to produce a relevant record to him.

(2) A person concerned with the provision (for payment or not) of goods, facilities or services to the public or a section of the public must not, as a condition of providing or offering to provide any goods, facilities or services to another person, require that other person or a third party to supply him with a relevant record or to produce a relevant record to him.

(3) Subsections (1) and (2) do not apply to a person who shows —

(a) that the imposition of the requirement was required or authorised by or under any enactment, by any rule of law or by the order of a court, or

(b) that in the particular circumstances the imposition of the requirement was justified as being in the public interest.

(4) Having regard to the provisions of Part V of the [1997 c. 50.] Police Act 1997 (certificates of criminal records etc.), the imposition of the requirement referred to in subsection (1) or (2) is not to be regarded as being justified as being in the public interest on the ground that it would assist in the prevention or detection of crime.

(5) A person who contravenes subsection (1) or (2) is guilty of an offence.

(6) In this section "a relevant record" means any record which—

(a) has been or is to be obtained by a data subject from any data controller specified in the first column of the Table below in the exercise of the right conferred by section 7, and

(b) contains information relating to any matter specified in relation to that data controller in the second column,

and includes a copy of such a record or a part of such a record.

TABLE

Data controller	Subject-matter
1. Any of the following persons— (a) a chief officer of police of a police force in England and Wales. (b) a chief constable of a police force in Scotland. (c) the Chief Constable of the Royal Ulster Constabulary. (d) the Director General of the National Criminal Intelligence Service. (e) the Director General of the National Crime Squad.	(a) Convictions. (b) Cautions.

Data controller	Subject-matter
2. The Secretary of State.	(a) Convictions.
	(b) Cautions.
	(c) His functions under section 53 of the Children and Young Persons Act 1933, section 205(2) or 208 of the Criminal Procedure (Scotland) Act 1995 or section 73 of the Children and Young Persons Act (Northern Ireland) 1968 in relation to any person sentenced to detention.
	(d) His functions under the Prison Act 1952, the Prisons (Scotland) Act 1989 or the Prison Act (Northern Ireland) 1953 in relation to any person imprisoned or detained.
	(e) His functions under the Social Security Contributions and Benefits Act 1992, the Social Security Administration Act 1992 or the Jobseekers Act 1995.
	(f) His functions under Part V of the Police Act 1997.
3. The Department of Health and Social Services for Northern Ireland.	Its functions under the Social Security Contributions and Benefits (Northern Ireland) Act 1992, the Social Security Administration (Northern Ireland) Act 1992 or the Jobseekers (Northern Ireland) Order 1995.

(7) In the Table in subsection (6) —

- "caution" means a caution given to any person in England and Wales or Northern Ireland in respect of an offence which, at the time when the caution is given, is admitted;

- "conviction" has the same meaning as in the [1974 c. 53.] Rehabilitation of Offenders Act 1974 or the [S.I. 1978/1908 (N.I.27)] Rehabilitation of Offenders (Northern Ireland) Order 1978.

(8) The Secretary of State may by order amend —

(a) the Table in subsection (6), and

(b) subsection (7).

(9) For the purposes of this section a record which states that a data controller is not processing any personal data relating to a particular matter shall be taken to be a record containing information relating to that matter.

(10) In this section "employee" means an individual who —

(a) works under a contract of employment, as defined by section 230(2) of the [1996 c. 18.] Employment Rights Act 1996, or

(b) holds any office,

whether or not he is entitled to remuneration; and "employment" shall be construed accordingly.

57. Avoidance of certain contractual terms relating to health records

(1) Any term or condition of a contract is void in so far as it purports to require an individual —

(a) to supply any other person with a record to which this section applies, or with a copy of such a record or a part of such a record, or

(b) to produce to any other person such a record, copy or part.

(2) This section applies to any record which—

(a) has been or is to be obtained by a data subject in the exercise of the right conferred by section 7, and

(b) consists of the information contained in any health record as defined by section 68(2).

Information provided to Commissioner or Tribunal

58. Disclosure of information

No enactment or rule of law prohibiting or restricting the disclosure of information shall preclude a person from furnishing the Commissioner or the Tribunal with any information necessary for the discharge of their functions under this Act.

59. Confidentiality of information

(1) No person who is or has been the Commissioner, a member of the Commissioner's staff or an agent of the Commissioner shall disclose any information which—

(a) has been obtained by, or furnished to, the Commissioner under or for the purposes of this Act,

(b) relates to an identified or identifiable individual or business, and

(c) is not at the time of the disclosure, and has not previously been, available to the public from other sources,

unless the disclosure is made with lawful authority.

(2) For the purposes of subsection (1) a disclosure of information is made with lawful authority only if, and to the extent that—

(a) the disclosure is made with the consent of the individual or of the person for the time being carrying on the business,

(b) the information was provided for the purpose of its being made available to the public (in whatever manner) under any provision of this Act,

(c) the disclosure is made for the purposes of, and is necessary for, the discharge of —

    (i) any functions under this Act, or

    (ii) any Community obligation,

(d) the disclosure is made for the purposes of any proceedings, whether criminal or civil and whether arising under, or by virtue of, this Act or otherwise, or

(e) having regard to the rights and freedoms or legitimate interests of any person, the disclosure is necessary in the public interest.

(3) Any person who knowingly or recklessly discloses information in contravention of subsection (1) is guilty of an offence.

General provisions relating to offences

60. Prosecutions and penalties

(1) No proceedings for an offence under this Act shall be instituted —

(a) in England or Wales, except by the Commissioner or by or with the consent of the Director of Public Prosecutions;

(b) in Northern Ireland, except by the Commissioner or by or with the consent of the Director of Public Prosecutions for Northern Ireland.

(2) A person guilty of an offence under any provision of this Act other than paragraph 12 of Schedule 9 is liable —

(a) on summary conviction, to a fine not exceeding the statutory maximum, or

(b) on conviction on indictment, to a fine.

(3) A person guilty of an offence under paragraph 12 of Schedule 9 is liable on summary conviction to a fine not exceeding level 5 on the standard scale.

(4) Subject to subsection (5), the court by or before which a person is convicted of —

(a) an offence under section 21(1), 22(6), 55 or 56,

(b) an offence under section 21(2) relating to processing which is assessable processing for the purposes of section 22, or

(c) an offence under section 47(1) relating to an enforcement notice,

may order any document or other material used in connection with the processing of personal data and appearing to the court to be connected with the commission of the offence to be forfeited, destroyed or erased.

(5) The court shall not make an order under subsection (4) in relation to any material where a person (other than the offender) claiming to be the owner of or otherwise interested in the material applies to be heard by the court, unless an opportunity is given to him to show cause why the order should not be made.

61. Liability of directors etc.

(1) Where an offence under this Act has been committed by a body corporate and is proved to have been committed with the consent or connivance of or to be attributable to any neglect on the part of any director, manager, secretary or similar officer of the body corporate or any person who was purporting to act in any such capacity, he as well as the body corporate shall be guilty of that offence and be liable to be proceeded against and punished accordingly.

(2) Where the affairs of a body corporate are managed by its members subsection (1) shall apply in relation to the acts and defaults of a member in connection with his functions of management as if he were a director of the body corporate.

(3) Where an offence under this Act has been committed by a Scottish partnership and the contravention in question is proved to have occurred with the consent or connivance of, or to be attributable to any neglect on the part of, a partner, he as well as the partnership shall be guilty of that offence and shall be liable to be proceeded against and punished accordingly.

62. Amendments of Consumer Credit Act, 1974

(1) In section 158 of the [1974 c. 39.] Consumer Credit Act 1974 (duty of agency to disclose filed information) —

(a) in subsection (1) —

    (i) in paragraph (a) for "individual" there is substituted "partnership or other unincorporated body of persons not consisting entirely of bodies corporate", and

    (ii) for "him" there is substituted "it",

(b) in subsection (2), for "his" there is substituted "the consumer's", and

(c) in subsection (3), for "him" there is substituted "the consumer".

(2) In section 159 of that Act (correction of wrong information) for subsection (1) there is substituted —

"(1) Any individual (the "objector") given —

(a) information under section 7 of the Data Protection Act 1998 by a credit reference agency, or

(b) information under section 158,

who considers that an entry in his file is incorrect, and that if it is not corrected he is likely to be prejudiced, may give notice to the agency requiring it either to remove the entry from the file or amend it."

(3) In subsections (2) to (6) of that section —

(a) for "consumer", wherever occurring, there is substituted "objector", and

(b) for "Director", wherever occurring, there is substituted "the relevant authority".

(4) After subsection (6) of that section there is inserted —

"(7) The Data Protection Commissioner may vary or revoke any order made by him under this section.

(8) In this section "the relevant authority" means —

(a) where the objector is a partnership or other unincorporated body of persons, the Director, and

(b) in any other case, the Data Protection Commissioner."

(5) In section 160 of that Act (alternative procedure for business consumers) —

(a) in subsection (4) —

(i) for "him" there is substituted "to the consumer", and

(ii) in paragraphs (a) and (b) for "he" there is substituted "the consumer" and for "his" there is substituted "the consumer's", and

(b) after subsection (6) there is inserted —

"(7) In this section "consumer" has the same meaning as in section 158."

General

63. Application to Crown

(1) This Act binds the Crown.

(2) For the purposes of this Act each government department shall be treated as a person separate from any other government department.

(3) Where the purposes for which and the manner in which any personal data are, or are to be, processed are determined by any person acting on behalf of the Royal Household, the Duchy of Lancaster or the Duchy of Cornwall, the data controller in respect of those data for the purposes of this Act shall be —

(a) in relation to the Royal Household, the Keeper of the Privy Purse,

(b) in relation to the Duchy of Lancaster, such person as the Chancellor of the Duchy appoints, and

(c) in relation to the Duchy of Cornwall, such person as the Duke of Cornwall, or the possessor for the time being of the Duchy of Cornwall, appoints.

(4) Different persons may be appointed under subsection (3)(b) or (c) for different purposes.

(5) Neither a government department nor a person who is a data controller by virtue of subsection (3) shall be liable to prosecution under this Act, but section 55 and paragraph 12 of Schedule 9 shall apply to a person in the service of the Crown as they apply to any other person.

64 Transmission of notices etc. by electronic or other means

(1) This section applies to —

(a) a notice or request under any provision of Part II,

(b) a notice under subsection (1) of section 24 or particulars made available under that subsection, or

(c) an application under section 41(2),

but does not apply to anything which is required to be served in accordance with rules of court.

(2) The requirement that any notice, request, particulars or application to which this section applies should be in writing is satisfied where the text of the notice, request, particulars or application —

(a) is transmitted by electronic means,

(b) is received in legible form, and

(c) is capable of being used for subsequent reference.

(3) The Secretary of State may by regulations provide that any requirement that any notice, request, particulars or application to which this section applies should be in writing is not to apply in such circumstances as may be prescribed by the regulations.

65. Service of notices by Commissioner

(1) Any notice authorised or required by this Act to be served on or given to any person by the Commissioner may —

(a)　if that person is an individual, be served on him —

　　(i)　by delivering it to him, or

　　(ii)　by sending it to him by post addressed to him at his usual or last-known place of residence or business, or

　　(iii)　by leaving it for him at that place;

(b)　if that person is a body corporate or unincorporate, be served on that body —

　　(i)　by sending it by post to the proper officer of the body at its principal office, or

　　(ii)　by addressing it to the proper officer of the body and leaving it at that office;

(c)　if that person is a partnership in Scotland, be served on that partnership —

　　(i)　by sending it by post to the principal office of the partnership, or

　　(ii)　by addressing it to that partnership and leaving it at that office.

(2) In subsection (1)(b) "principal office", in relation to a registered company, means its registered office and "proper officer", in relation to any body, means the secretary or other executive officer charged with the conduct of its general affairs.

(3) This section is without prejudice to any other lawful method of serving or giving a notice.

66. Exercise of rights in Scotland by children

(1) Where a question falls to be determined in Scotland as to the legal capacity of a person under the age of sixteen years to exercise any right

conferred by any provision of this Act, that person shall be taken to have that capacity where he has a general understanding of what it means to exercise that right.

(2) Without prejudice to the generality of subsection (1), a person of twelve years of age or more shall be presumed to be of sufficient age and maturity to have such understanding as is mentioned in that subsection.

67. Orders, regulations and rules

(1) Any power conferred by this Act on the Secretary of State to make an order, regulations or rules shall be exercisable by statutory instrument.

(2) Any order, regulations or rules made by the Secretary of State under this Act may –

(a) make different provision for different cases, and

(b) make such supplemental, incidental, consequential or transitional provision or savings as the Secretary of State considers appropriate;

and nothing in section 7(11), 19(5), 26(1) or 30(4) limits the generality of paragraph (a).

(3) Before making –

(a) an order under any provision of this Act other than section 75(3),

(b) any regulations under this Act other than notification regulations (as defined by section 16(2)),

the Secretary of State shall consult the Commissioner.

(4) A statutory instrument containing (whether alone or with other provisions) an order under –

- section 10(2)(b),

- section 12(5)(b),

- section 22(1),

- section 30,

- section 32(3),

- section 38,

- section 56(8),

- paragraph 10 of Schedule 3, or

- paragraph 4 of Schedule 7,

shall not be made unless a draft of the instrument has been laid before and approved by a resolution of each House of Parliament.

(5) A statutory instrument which contains (whether alone or with other provisions) —

(a) an order under —

- section 22(7),

- section 23,

- section 51(3),

- section 54(2), (3) or (4),

- paragraph 3, 4 or 14 of Part II of Schedule 1,

- paragraph 6 of Schedule 2,

- paragraph 2, 7 or 9 of Schedule 3,

- paragraph 4 of Schedule 4,

- paragraph 6 of Schedule 7,

(b) regulations under section 7 which —

(i)   prescribe cases for the purposes of subsection (2)(b),

(ii)   are made by virtue of subsection (7), or

(iii)   relate to the definition of "the prescribed period",

(c) regulations under section 8(1) or 9(3),

(d) regulations under section 64,

(e) notification regulations (as defined by section 16(2)), or

(f) rules under paragraph 7 of Schedule 6,

and which is not subject to the requirement in subsection (4) that a draft of the instrument be laid before and approved by a resolution of each House of Parliament, shall be subject to annulment in pursuance of a resolution of either House of Parliament.

(6) A statutory instrument which contains only —

(a) regulations prescribing fees for the purposes of any provision of this Act, or

(b) regulations under section 7 prescribing fees for the purposes of any other enactment,

shall be laid before Parliament after being made.

68. Meaning of "accessible record"

(1) In this Act "accessible record" means —

(a) a health record as defined by subsection (2),

(b) an educational record as defined by Schedule 11, or

(c) an accessible public record as defined by Schedule 12.

(2) In subsection (1)(a) "health record" means any record which —

(a) consists of information relating to the physical or mental health or condition of an individual, and

(b) has been made by or on behalf of a health professional in connection with the care of that individual.

69. Meaning of "health professional"

(1) In this Act "health professional" means any of the following —

(a) a registered medical practitioner,

(b) a registered dentist as defined by section 53(1) of the [1984 c. 24.] Dentists Act 1984,

(c) a registered optician as defined by section 36(1) of the [1989 c. 44.] Opticians Act 1989,

(d) a registered pharmaceutical chemist as defined by section 24(1) of the [1954 c. 61.] Pharmacy Act 1954 or a registered person as defined by Article 2(2) of the [S.I. 1976/1213 (N.I.22).] Pharmacy (Northern Ireland) Order 1976,

(e) a registered nurse, midwife or health visitor,

(f) a registered osteopath as defined by section 41 of the [1993 c. 21.] Osteopaths Act 1993,

(g) a registered chiropractor as defined by section 43 of the [1994 c. 17.] Chiropractors Act 1994,

(h) any person who is registered as a member of a profession to which the [1960 c. 66.] Professions Supplementary to Medicine Act 1960 for the time being extends,

(i) a clinical psychologist, child psychotherapist or speech therapist,

(j) a music therapist employed by a health service body, and

(k) a scientist employed by such a body as head of a department.

(2) In subsection (1)(a) "registered medical practitioner" includes any person who is provisionally registered under section 15 or 21 of the [1983 c. 54.] Medical Act 1983 and is engaged in such employment as is mentioned in subsection (3) of that section.

(3) In subsection (1) "health service body" means—

(a) a Health Authority established under section 8 of the [1977 c. 49.] National Health Service Act 1977,

(b) a Special Health Authority established under section 11 of that Act,

(c) a Health Board within the meaning of the [1978 c. 29.] National Health Service (Scotland) Act 1978,

(d) a Special Health Board within the meaning of that Act,

(e) the managers of a State Hospital provided under section 102 of
    that Act,

(f) a National Health Service trust first established under section 5 of
    the [1990 c. 19.] National Health Service and Community Care Act
    1990 or section 12A of the National Health Service (Scotland) Act
    1978,

(g) a Health and Social Services Board established under Article 16 of
    the [S.I. 1972/1265 (N.I.14).] Health and Personal Social Services
    (Northern Ireland) Order 1972,

(h) a special health and social services agency established under the
    [S.I. 1990/247 (N.I.3).] Health and Personal Social Services (Special
    Agencies) (Northern Ireland) Order 1990, or

(i) a Health and Social Services trust established under Article 10 of
    the [S.I. 1991/194 (N.I.1).] Health and Personal Social Services
    (Northern Ireland) Order 1991.

70. Supplementary definitions

(1) In this Act, unless the context otherwise requires—

* "business" includes any trade or profession;

* "the Commissioner" means the Data Protection Commissioner;

* "credit reference agency" has the same meaning as in the [1974 c.
  39.] Consumer Credit Act 1974;

* "the Data Protection Directive" means Directive 95/46/EC on the
  protection of individuals with regard to the processing of personal
  data and on the free movement of such data;

* "EEA State" means a State which is a contracting party to the
  Agreement on the European Economic Area signed at Oporto on
  2nd May 1992 as adjusted by the Protocol signed at Brussels on
  17th March 1993;

* "enactment" includes an enactment passed after this Act;

- "government department" includes a Northern Ireland department and any body or authority exercising statutory functions on behalf of the Crown;

- "Minister of the Crown" has the same meaning as in the Ministers of the [1975 c. 26.] Crown Act 1975;

- "public register" means any register which pursuant to a requirement imposed —

   (a) by or under any enactment, or

   (b) in pursuance of any international agreement,

is open to public inspection or open to inspection by any person having a legitimate interest;

- "pupil" —

   (a) in relation to a school in England and Wales, means a registered pupil within the meaning of the [1996 c. 56.] Education Act 1996,

   (b) in relation to a school in Scotland, means a pupil within the meaning of the [1980 c. 44.] Education (Scotland) Act 1980, and

   (c) in relation to a school in Northern Ireland, means a registered pupil within the meaning of the [S.I. 1986/594 (N.I.3).] Education and Libraries (Northern Ireland) Order 1986;

- "recipient", in relation to any personal data, means any person to whom the data are disclosed, including any person (such as an employee or agent of the data controller, a data processor or an employee or agent of a data processor) to whom they are disclosed in the course of processing the data for the data controller, but does not include any person to whom disclosure is or may be made as a result of, or with a view to, a particular inquiry by or on behalf of that person made in the exercise of any power conferred by law;

- "registered company" means a company registered under the enactments relating to companies for the time being in force in the United Kingdom;

- "school" —

  (a) in relation to England and Wales, has the same meaning as in the Education Act 1996,

  (b) in relation to Scotland, has the same meaning as in the Education (Scotland) Act 1980, and

  (c) in relation to Northern Ireland, has the same meaning as in the Education and Libraries (Northern Ireland) Order 1986;

- "teacher" includes —

  (a) in Great Britain, head teacher, and

  (b) in Northern Ireland, the principal of a school;

- "third party", in relation to personal data, means any person other than —

  (a) the data subject,

  (b) the data controller, or

  (c) any data processor or other person authorised to process data for the data controller or processor;

- "the Tribunal" means the Data Protection Tribunal.

(2) For the purposes of this Act data are inaccurate if they are incorrect or misleading as to any matter of fact.

71. Index of defined expressions

The following Table shows provisions defining or otherwise explaining expressions used in this Act (other than provisions defining or explaining an expression only used in the same section or Schedule) —

accessible record	section 68
address (in Part III)	section 16(3)
business	section 70(1)
the Commissioner	section 70(1)
credit reference agency	section 70(1)
data	section 1(1)
data controller	sections 1(1) and (4) and 63(3)
data processor	section 1(1)
the Data Protection Directive	section 70(1)
data protection principles	section 4 and Schedule 1
data subject	section 1(1)
disclosing (of personal data)	section 1(2)(b)
EEA State	section 70(1)
enactment	section 70(1)
enforcement notice	section 40(1)
fees regulations (in Part III)	section 16(2)
government department	section 70(1)
health professional	section 69
inaccurate (in relation to data)	section 70(2)
information notice	section 43(1)
Minister of the Crown	section 70(1)
the non-disclosure provisions (in Part IV)	section 27(3)
notification regulations (in Part III)	section 16(2)
obtaining (of personal data)	section 1(2)(a)
personal data	section 1(1)
prescribed (in Part III)	section 16(2)

processing (of information or data)	section 1(1) and paragraph 5 of Schedule 8
public register	section 70(1)
publish (in relation to journalistic, literary or artistic material)	section 32(6)
pupil (in relation to a school)	section 70(1)
recipient (in relation to personal data)	section 70(1)
recording (of personal data)	section 1(2)(a)
registered company	section 70(1)
registrable particulars (in Part III)	section 16(1)
relevant filing system	section 1(1)
school	section 70(1)
sensitive personal data	section 2
special information notice	section 44(1)
the special purposes	section 3
the subject information provisions (in Part IV)	section 27(2)
teacher	section 70(1)
third party (in relation to processing of personal data)	section 70(1)
the Tribunal	section 70(1)
using (of personal data)	section 1(2)(b).

72. Modifications of Act

During the period beginning with the commencement of this section and ending with 23rd October 2007, the provisions of this Act shall have effect subject to the modifications set out in Schedule 13.

73. Transitional provisions and savings

Schedule 14 (which contains transitional provisions and savings) has effect.

74. Minor and consequential amendments and repeals and revocations

(1) Schedule 15 (which contains minor and consequential amendments) has effect.

(2) The enactments and instruments specified in Schedule 16 are repealed or revoked to the extent specified.

75. Short title, commencement and extent

(1) This Act may be cited as the Data Protection Act 1998.

(2) The following provisions of this Act —

(a)   sections 1 to 3,

(b)   section 25(1) and (4),

(c)   section 26,

(d)   sections 67 to 71,

(e)   this section,

(f)   paragraph 17 of Schedule 5,

(g)   Schedule 11,

(h)   Schedule 12, and

(i)   so much of any other provision of this Act as confers any power to make subordinate legislation,

shall come into force on the day on which this Act is passed.

(3) The remaining provisions of this Act shall come into force on such day as the Secretary of State may by order appoint; and different days may be appointed for different purposes.

(4) The day appointed under subsection (3) for the coming into force of section 56 must not be earlier than the first day on which sections 112, 113 and 115 of the [1997 c. 50.] Police Act 1997 (which provide for the issue by the Secretary of State of criminal conviction certificates, criminal record certificates and enhanced criminal record certificates) are all in force.

(5) Subject to subsection (6), this Act extends to Northern Ireland.

(6) Any amendment, repeal or revocation made by Schedule 15 or 16 has the same extent as that of the enactment or instrument to which it relates

INDEX

This is an index by subject matter all references are to paragraph(s)